FORENSIC AUTOPSY

A Handbook and Atlas

FORENSIC AUTOPSY

A Handbook and Atlas

Edited by

Cristoforo Pomara
Steven B. Karch
Vittorio Fineschi

CRC Press
Taylor & Francis Group
Boca Raton   London   New York

CRC Press is an imprint of the
Taylor & Francis Group, an **informa** business

CRC Press
Taylor & Francis Group
6000 Broken Sound Parkway NW, Suite 300
Boca Raton, FL 33487-2742

© 2010 by Taylor and Francis Group, LLC
CRC Press is an imprint of Taylor & Francis Group, an Informa business

No claim to original U.S. Government works

Printed in the United States of America on acid-free paper
10 9 8 7 6 5 4 3 2 1

International Standard Book Number: 978-1-4398-0064-5 (Hardback)

Library of Congress Cataloging-in-Publication Data

Forensic autopsy : a handbook and atlas / editors, Cristoforo Pomara, Steven B. Karch, Vittorio Fineschi.
    p. ; cm.
"A CRC title."
Includes bibliographical references and index.
ISBN 978-1-4398-0064-5 (hardcover : alk. paper)
1. Autopsy. 2. Forensic pathology. I. Pomara, Cristoforo. II. Karch, Steven B. III. Fineschi, Vittorio. IV. Title.
[DNLM: 1. Autopsy--methods. 2. Forensic Medicine--methods. W 825 F7154 2010]

RA1063.4F662 2010
616.07'59--dc22   2009044677

Visit the Taylor & Francis Web site at
http://www.taylorandfrancis.com

and the CRC Press Web site at
http://www.crcpress.com

Dedication

To my son, Salvatore Giuseppe, who, with pride, carries my father's name; to my daughter, Maria Vittoria, and to her wide eyes that each day I lovingly lose myself in; to my wife, Gabriella, my light in darkness and my guide in light; to Pepo Ginestra, and to his descendents, who like him still wander our earth; to my mother. To the victims of the Mafia whose blood has marked our generation, and to the hope that they, even after death, may finally witness its end.

A mio figlio Salvatore Giuseppe, che porta con orgoglio il nome di mio padre; a mia figlia Maria Vittoria e ai suoi occhi grandi nei quali ogni giorno amo perdermi, a mia moglie Gabriella faro nella notte e guida di ogni giorno; a Pepo Ginestra e i suoi discendenti, come lui ancora in giro per il mondo; a mia madre; alle vittime della mafia che hanno marchiato le nostre generazioni che la vedranno finalmente finire.

Cristoforo Pomara

To my teacher, Professor Mauro Barni.

Vittorio Fineschi

Table of Contents

Preface

Forensic pathologists and histologists are desperately trying every other field in medicine and practice evidence-based science. Although this transition has yet to be made, we are at a critical juncture. Soon it will be possible to provide evidence-based diagnoses, not just about the cause of death, but also about the genetic changes that underlie the disease process itself.

The medicolegal autopsy must consist of more than just a final diagnosis. We are obliged to supply reasons for the diagnoses we provide, and we must be able to defend those reasons. We must be prepared to explain not only what we have done, but how we did it, and do so in sufficient detail so that someone else who reviews the same data will reach the same conclusions. Simply put: Personal experience is good, science is better.

Accurate information is required to make an accurate postmortem diagnosis and that, in turn, requires an accurate postmortem dissection examination. Reaching that goal requires an ongoing, continuous assessment of the methods used and the accuracy with which they have been applied.

Far too many forensic pathologists perform postmortem examinations that are "limited" to only the body parts that are "suspect." As a rule, this approach is to be condemned. This kind of approach inevitably causes problems. If this approach is followed, there is a serious risk that the results produced will be biased because the pathologist already believes that he or she knows the problem before performing the procedure. Even if the diagnosis that is made was expected, the results of this kind of autopsy only provides a false sense of security. A correct diagnosis can only be reached by a strict and systematic examination of the whole body.

Those with more foresight recommend a completely standardized postmortem protocol, where all dissections are performed using the same technique and take samples from approximately the same sites for histological study.

Even if standardized protocols are used and followed to the letter, this still does nothing to ensure the competence of the physician, who must actually perform the procedure and follow the protocol. Basic knowledge cannot be provided by protocol, only by knowledge, training, and experience. In short, the pathologist must be skilled.

It is impossible to ignore new imaging techniques, or that many may one day replace the autopsy with "virtopsies," which allow for qualitative–quantitative evaluations of pathological entities. This approach can lead to a reliance on "subjective" elements, dependent mainly on the investigator's own interpretation. Now, and for the foreseeable future, these techniques are only meant to supplement the pathologist's skills, not replace them.

There is, however, a middle ground, where the information gleaned from a meticulous autopsy can be a supplement with one or more of the many new techniques available. Autopsy methods and histological techniques are the tools we use to solve routine cases. Immunostaining had not yet been invented, but somehow Virchow still managed to reach the correct anatomic diagnosis, even if he did not understand the underlying molecular biology of the disease process. Like Virchow, our goal should be to provide the courts with the most accurate, up-to-date information about the process at hand.

This book has been many years in the making with years of work in dissecting rooms and constant teaching. The criticism of our peers have allowed us to develop a methodology that, when correctly applied, will lead to the correct diagnosis. This is the reason for this book: it is the only way to pass on an old methodology to a new generation of practitioners.

Acknowledgments

A warm thank you to Dr. Piccin and to his Casa Editrice Piccin Nuova Libraria in Padua, for being the first person to believe in this book. To engineer Alessandro Merola, for handling the digitized images with extreme patience and professionalism and to the photo print shop FOCUS and its owner, Giorgio Merola, for being involved with our department over the years, collaborating and supporting all our photographic activities. And warm gratitude to Professor Teresa Brentagani and Adjunct Faculty Maria Prestigiacomo Patel of the Foreign Languages Department, Southern Methodist University, Dallas, Texas, for collaborating with our authors in revising the translated text.

Contributors

F. Bucchieri
Department of Experimental Medicine
University of Palermo
Palermo, Italy

F. Cappello
Department of Experimental Medicine
University of Palermo
Palermo, Italy

S. Corrado
Department of Forensic Pathology
University of Bari
Bari, Italy

S. D'Errico
Department of Forensic Pathology
University of Foggia
Foggia, Italy

V. Fineschi
Department of Forensic Pathology
University of Foggia
Foggia, Italy

G. Guglielmi
Department of Radiology
University of Foggia
Foggia, Italy

F. Introna
Department of Forensic Pathology
University of Bari
Bari, Italy

S.B. Karch
Consulting Forensic Pathologist
Berkeley, California

M. Neri
Department of Forensic Pathology
University of Foggia
Foggia, Italy

C. Pomara
Department of Forensic Pathology
University of Foggia
Foggia, Italy

F. Rappa
Department of Experimental Medicine
University of Palermo
Palermo, Italy

I. Riezzo
Department of Forensic Pathology
University of Foggia
Foggia, Italy

A Methodological Approach to the External Examination

1

S. D'ERRICO

Contents

1.1 Introduction

Pathologists must perform a careful external examination of the cadaver prior to the actual autopsy, as the external findings may sometimes be more important than anything revealed by the internal examination. The external examination often provides significant clues and sometimes may even reveal the cause of death. External examination is especially important in forensic cases where close attention to detail is mandatory. The examination must be documented with photographs and a full written description of findings. Diagram sheets should also be used to graphically reproduce the locations of anatomical findings.

1.2 Clothing

Examination of the clothing should always be performed by the pathologist, not only in criminal cases or in cases of suspicious death, but also in traffic and industrial accidents, falls, and drownings. Each article of clothing should be carefully examined and described before and after its removal from the body. If clothes have been removed before transfer to the mortuary, the pathologist should always specifically ask for the clothes of the victim to be returned, especially when trauma is the provisional cause of death.

A record of size, type, make, and color of the clothing should always be created. In cases where trauma is thought to be the cause of death, body injuries should be matched with the damage found on the clothing, such as tears, slashes, stab wounds, and gunshot wounds. A complete photographic documentation of the clothes should be performed. The number, position, morphology, and size of lacerations should be noted. In cases of gunshot tears in the clothing, the tears should be "triangled" by measuring their distance from the upper, lower, and lateral landmarks. Gunshot residue on the clothing may provide vital evidence, revealing the range of the discharge and the type of ammunition. The Na rhodizonate technique should be used to examine bullet holes for gunshot residue.

When dealing with traffic fatalities, the clothing should be examined for tears, grease marks, road dirt, and broken lamp or windscreen (windshield) glass. Every metallic or plastic fragment related to the vehicle should be collected with the hope that it will eventually be possible to use these materials to reconstruct the event or identify the unknown vehicle in a hit-and-run. A careful inspection of pockets should also be performed. Because pockets can contain needles or other sharp objects, the examiner should always use forceps to avoid sharp injuries. All personal effects found need to be inventoried.

If possible, remove clothing in the usual way, by pulling the shirt over the head and limbs unless doing so might interfere with any injuries or cause soiling of the clothing. If rigor is intense, clothes may be cut off, taking care not to cut through preexisting damage or areas of staining already noted to be present on the garments. In cases of sudden infant death syndrome, examination of the clothing and diapers (which are often saturated with urine) is of particular importance. If a urine sample from the bladder has not been collected at the time of external examination, the diaper can be submitted for laboratory analysis as well as toxicological and metabolic screening.

Clothing examination is also very important in sex-related deaths. In these cases, the clothing of the victim could reveal the presence of bloodstains or seminal liquid, and samples should be collected for genetic testing. As with any other type of traumatic death, the clothing should be carefully examined for tears, missing buttons, dirt, gravel, grease, and leaves. Their collection might aid in later efforts at scene reconstruction.

1.3   Jewelry

Jewelry must be inventoried and a short description (e.g., a yellow metal ring was worn on the fourth finger of the left hand) included. The presence of body piercing should be recorded.

1.4   Tattoos

The shape, size, site on the body, and color of any tattoo should always be recorded. Sometimes tattoos may be found inside the mouth (particularly the mucosa of the lips). Attempts at removal of a tattoo, which usually leave a typical and unique appearing scar, should also be noted.

1.5   Sex, Race, and Age

The sex, race (white, Afro-Caribbean, Asian, and so forth) and age of the cadaver are always recorded. The color of the skin sometimes may provide clues about possible diseases (yellow discoloration of skin and mucosa in liver disease, i.e., jaundice) or suggest the mechanism of death (e.g., cherry-pink colorations of carboxyhemoglobin in carbon monoxide poisoning). The sex of

the decedent may not always be obvious; a body that is phenotypical female could be genetically male or vice versa. Estimating the age of a cadaver is generally difficult, so when stating age, the pathologist should always indicate that the margin of error is at least 3 to 5 years. Finally, the general state of cleanliness of the body should be recorded; this is of particular importance in cases where neglect is considered the possible cause of death.

1.6   Height and Weight

Once undressed, the cadaver is weighed, preferably in kilograms. The height in centimeters is also measured from heel to crown (in infants a more detailed measurement is performed). When height and weight of the cadaver are known, the body mass index can be easily calculated using the formula BMI = weight (kg)/height (cm)^2. This is important to note because a BMI above 30 may suggest the presence of certain underlying diseases, such as hypertension, coronary artery disease, or diabetes. Some comment should be made on the general state of nutrition, if it has not already been indicated in the general external examination. Note whether the decedent was obese, emaciated, edematous, dehydrated, or well nourished. These are all important observations, but they cannot always be relied upon because in today's work, addicts are increasingly likely to have a normal diet.

1.7   Time of Death Indicators

Body temperature should always be recorded, preferably at the scene. In jurisdictions where the physician does not always travel to the scene, experienced death investigators can, at least, take rectal, if not liver, temperatures. At the same time, the ambient air temperature should be recorded. Obviously, if the body is found naked in subzero weather that observation alone may help to limit the differential diagnosis. The dictated report should also note the temperature at the time of autopsy and whether the cadaver had been refrigerated. The presence or absence of rigor mortis and distribution of livor (hypostasis) should be documented at the scene and again at the time of autopsy.

1.8   General Recommendations

The cadaver should be inspected from head to foot (head, neck, chest, abdomen, pelvis), from the left to the right side, in supine and prone positions, including both the dorsal and volar surfaces of extremities (arms and legs). Bruises, abrasions, lacerations, incised wounds, burns, fractures, surgical and nonsurgical scars, medical intervention, congenital or dimorphic features, and the presence of natural diseases should all be noted, photographed, and meticulously measured, recording observations about length, breadth, orientation to the axis of the body, and position with reference to surface anatomical landmarks. When widespread burns are present, an estimate of the total area using the rule of nines should be done. A centimeter scale, along with appropriate body identifier codes and the decedent's name (if known), should always be placed near the lesion when it is photographed.

1.9 Head Examination

Record the presence or absence of head hair, as well as its color and length. If the decedent is wearing a wig, the name of the manufacturer should also be noted. A generous hair sample should always be collected and preserved, as natural hair can be used to establish race or for later toxicological analysis (e.g., drug-related death). No particular special procedures are required for the storage of hair samples (a sterile blood collection tube or even an envelope can be used) and they can be stored at room temperature for years without degradation. Although there is no particular need for hair toxicology as a routine component of every forensic examination, the retained sample may prove invaluable if the cause of death is disputed at some later date. Hair analysis may also be valuable in the diagnosis of drug-related deaths. If no drug is found in the hair root but blood drug concentrations are substantial, that would indicate the decedent had no prior exposure to the drug. On the other hand, high concentrations in the hair would indicate regular use and suggest that the decedent may have been tolerant to the drug in question.

Lacerations of the scalp can produce profuse bleeding despite their size, due to the great vascularity of the scalp. Any deformity of the skull should be carefully noted (depression or elevation). Dislocated or depressed skull fractures can be detected by firm palpation. Palpation of the cranium should be performed from the left to the right side, from the parietal region to the temporal and frontal, in this order. Palpation of the occipital region should be done when the cadaver is lying in the prone position. Small hemorrhagic cutaneous petechiae can sometimes be found behind the ears in asphyxia-related deaths or when there are temporozygomatic and orbitonasal injuries.

The color of the irises and the symmetry of the pupils should be noted. If the decedent was wearing contact lenses or glasses, these should be removed before the eye examination. The acoustic meatus and canal should be examined, using an otoscope if necessary. The nose and oral cavity should always be investigated in order to exclude the presence of blood, foam, vomit, and foreign bodies. In the case of a suspected death by poisoning, for example, foam found on the mouth and nose could be sampled for laboratory analysis. In cases of narcotic overdose, foam may be found emanating from the nostrils or the mouth. The foam is comprised of the protein rich transudate that is more often than not present in cases of narcotic overdose.

The presence of small petechiae of the eyes and conjunctivae is of particular relevance in asphyxia-related deaths, and should always be photographed. However, studies have been published demonstrating that these lesions can occur after death, so their presence should not be considered as proof of asphyxial death—they are merely consistent with it. Finally the mouth and lips, including the mandibular region, should be described. The state of dentition and the presence of dental restoration can be of very great importance when dealing with unidentified cadavers. When the body is unidentified, a detailed dental chart must be prepared. In all suspected cases of suffocation, smothering, or strangulation, bruises and abrasions of the face (e.g., fingernail marks) or oral mucosa (e.g., teeth marks) provide evidence either that the victim put up a vigorous resistance or that violent compression of the nose and mouth had been exerted.

1.10 Neck Examination

The neck should be examined from left to right, region by region (jugular vs. hyoid). Neck mobility should be examined only after rigor has resolved. This is accomplished by flexing and hyperextending the head toward the chest. Abnormal mobility should be noted. Bruises, abrasions, and lacerations should be carefully described as well as any findings suggesting ligature strangulation (i.e., hanging). In all cases of hanging, a complete description of the furrow should be provided, and it should indicate if the furrow completely encircled the neck and whether it had sharp margins. A rope will give a deep, well demarcated, and distinct furrow, often with a mirror-image impression of the twist of the rope on the skin. If a soft material was used as the ligature, the resultant groove may be poorly defined, pale, and devoid of bruises and abrasions. Should the ligature still be present, the type of material should be noted and the ligature itself submitted for further testing.

1.11 Chest Examination

External examination of the chest should be performed from the left to the right side, over all the ribs and intercostal spaces. The first thing to note is whether or not the chest is symmetric or asymmetric. Chest palpation is needed to detect the presence of rib fractures and subcutaneous emphysema, and while this examination is being performed the presence of any visible markings or lesions is noted. The cadaver must be placed in a prone position to firmly palpate the thoracic vertebrae.

1.12 Abdomen Examination

An abdomen examination of upper and lower abdominal squares should follow a careful downward inspection, from the left to the right side. Bruises, abrasions, and lacerations have to be carefully recorded.

1.13 Shoulder and Upper Extremities

Any abnormal movement of either acromioclavicular joint should be noted. External examination of the upper extremities should be performed from the shoulders downward to the hands, and any injuries of either the dorsal and ventral sides noted. When self-incised wounds have been inflicted they are usually superficial (hesitation marks), but they may be found adjacent to or overlying a fatal incised wound. When the decedent has attempted to ward off a pointed or sharp-edged weapon, defensive marks may be found on the palms of the hands, a result of attempts to grasp or ward off the knife. Defensive wounds may be found on the back (extensor surface) of the forearms and upper arms, and on the ulnar aspect of the forearms. In drug-related deaths, needle marks (recent or past) on elbows and wrists should be carefully investigated and recorded, although there is little to be gained by testing the skin for drugs, as once a drug is in the body, it circulates everywhere, including the skin. If skin around an injection site is submitted for toxicological testing, it must be accompanied by a control sample of skin taken from the other arm. Hands should also be carefully examined, as electrical marks generally are difficult to see unless the rigor of a flexed finger is overcome. Samples of the fingernails should be collected for later toxicological measurement, as questions about drug use may arise at a later date.

1.14 Lower Extremities and External Genitalia

As with the upper extremities, examination of the lower extremities is performed from the left to the right side, downward and backward. Careful palpation is needed to detect excessive joint mobility and fractures of long bones. Some drug takers inject into the interdigital spaces and these spaces must be carefully examined. Detailed perineal examination is required in cases of suspected sex-related deaths. Bruises, bites, and laceration of the perineal region can have very great investigative significance. Careful investigation for any foreign hairs mixed with the cadaver pubic hairs is required, which means that the victim's pubic hair should be combed. Sometimes, a vaginal speculum is required to complete a detailed inspection of the vagina and cervix, which should include the collection of appropriate secretions. An anal examination is often misleading because of the postmortem flaccidity of the sphincter. Therefore, the diagnosis of sexual abuse, especially in children, must not be assumed without other evidence (i.e., fresh mucosal tears or swabs positive for semen). Even if there is no suspicion of sexual assault, the presence or absence of circumcision should be noted, as it may contribute to the identification of the cadaver. The presence of semen on the external urethral meatus is a frequent finding, but one of very little significance; it is not specific to sexual activity immediately before death, nor does its presence prove asphyxial death as sometimes stated.

1.15 Dorsal and Lumbar Regions

When the external examination is concluded, the cadaver can be placed in a prone position. Dorsal and lumbar injuries should be recorded using the same methodological approach as used in the other regions, from the left to the right side and downward.

References

Di Maio VJ and Di Maio D. 2001. *Forensic pathology*, 2nd edition. Boca Raton, FL: CRC Press.

Dolinak D, Evan M, and Lew E. 2005. *Forensic pathology: Principles and practice*. Burlington, MA: Elsevier Academic Press.

Finkbeiner WE, Ursell PC, and Davis RL. 2004. *Autopsy pathology: A manual and atlas*. Philadelphia: Churchill Livingstone.

James JP, Busuttil A, and Smock W. 2003. *Forensic medicine: Clinical and pathological aspects*. San Francisco: GMM.

Ludwig J. 2002. *Autopsy practice*, 3rd edition. Totowa, NJ: Humana Press.

Pomara C and Fineschi V. 2007. *Manuale atlante di tecniche autoptiche*. Padova: Piccin.

Randall BB, Fierro MF, Froede RC, and Bennett AT. 2003. Forensic pathology. In *Autopsy performance and reporting*, 2nd edition, (eds.) Collins KA and Hutchins GM, 55–64. Northfield, IL: College of American Pathologists.

Rutty GN and Burton JL. 2001. The external examination. In *The hospital autopsy*, 2nd edition, (eds.) Burton JL and Rutty GN, 42–51. London: Oxford University Press.

Saukko P and Knight B. 2004. *Knight's forensic pathology*, 3rd edition. London: Oxford University Press.

Wagner SA. 2004. *The color atlas of autopsy*. Boca Raton, FL: CRC Press.

The Autopsy

2

C. POMARA
S.B. KARCH
V. FINESCHI

Contents

2.1 Adult Autopsy

The dissection techniques used in adult forensic autopsies, or medicolegal autopsies, do not differ significantly from those used in hospital autopsies. In both instances a regional technique is used to gather the evidence necessary to reach the correct anatomical–pathological diagnosis. However, when performing a forensic autopsy, it helps to also gather evidence that may later be of legal importance at trial. To this end, some specific requirements of the hospital autopsy may need modification to provide the answers needed by the courts. It is understood that other approaches than those described here may prove equally effective, provided they address the same basic issues outlined here.

2.1.1 General Autopsy Principles

Whatever technique is chosen, it must allow for easy access to the organs and cavities in each region of the body. It must also not take too long to do (one to three hours). The dissector must take the time to describe, in broad terms, the *in situ* appearance of the organs, which are then removed, weighed, and measured. Photographs should be taken of each body cavity showing any possible collections of liquids, the presence of clots/thrombi, tumors, and foreign bodies. Recesses of muscular, tendon, and osseous structures need only be examined if there is some particular reason to suspect an abnormality.

The extraction and resection of the single organs and tissue blocks must be done in such a way as to permit their effective study.

If a lesion extends to more than one organ, the selected technique must allow for the reconstruction of organ relationships and collection of sufficient tissue for sampling.

2.1.2 Autopsy Preliminaries

Any unique features of the cadaver must be noted and recorded, and every effort should be made to obtain detailed information about the circumstances of death. While this is being done, a technician should be preparing identification cards to be included in every autopsy photograph, otherwise the validity of the photographs might be challenged in court (Figure 2.1).

Every case is different and no one routine approach should be used to the exclusion of all others. Nonetheless, the use of x-rays and even CT (computed tomography) or MRI (magnetic resonance imaging) scanning is to be encouraged if access to these modalities is available. The interpretation of postmortem artifacts can prove a challenge, especially for less experienced radiologists and pathologists, and only people with experience in reading these scans should be asked to provide a formal opinion.

2.1.3 The Instruments

The use of forceps with rubber prongs rather than anatomic forceps, or forceps with toothed prongs, can considerably improve the quality of the specimen and the integrity of the anatomic area being studied. The examination of the vena cava in cases of suspected surgical malpractice is a good example; substantial problems can result when the injection itself can cause iatrogenic lesions. The basic instruments essential for every prosector are shown in Figure 2.2 through Figure 2.7.

2.1.4 Regulation of the Autopsy Table and Positioning of the Dissector

If right-handed, the prosector should stand on the right of the corpse, or on the left if left-handed (Figure 2.8). Once the autopsy tables has been adjusted to a height that is comfortable for examination (Figure 2.1), arrange the body in a supine position, and then place a support beneath the body's shoulders. This will ensure good extension of the neck and provide adequate exposure of the chest.

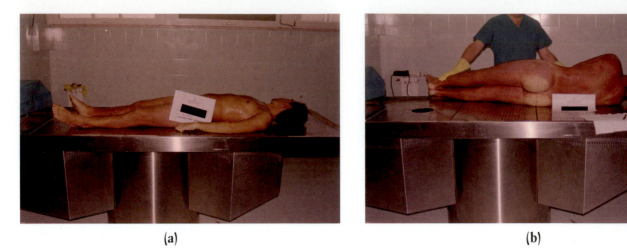

(a)   (b)

Figure 2.1 Autopsy table with adjustable height. Step by step: Positioning of the body and first collection of pictures. Identification sign in which corpse's full name, dissector's full name, date and place of autopsy, and requesting authority are specified. The first picture must be taken with the body in a supine anatomic position (Figure 2.1a); the second will be taken with the corpse in a posterior position.

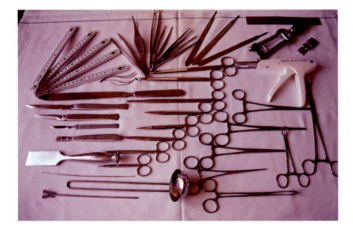

Figure 2.2 Minimum set of instruments necessary for a basic autopsy.

Figure 2.4 Blades-case sets. It is advisable to have a minimum of three of equal dimension and at least two different types (for a total of six). The figure shows three blades from case N 22 (our preferred).

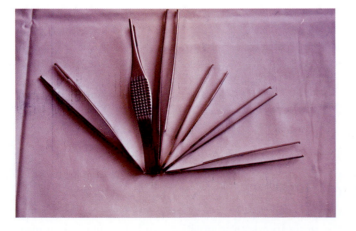

Figure 2.3 Anatomic forceps with toothed prongs. The different dimensions support the dissector's choices depending on the anatomical district operated or the organs subject to study.

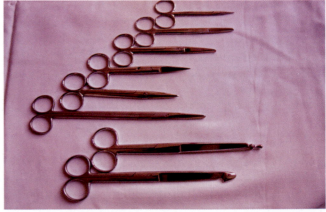

Figure 2.5 Set of scissors. It is important to have rounded blunt-tip bulbs that allow access to body cavities without the fear of parietal lesions. (Enterotomes: first two from the bottom.)

Figure 2.6 Rib shears. It is essential to the cutting of the costochondral margin. It is an instrument to use with extreme care in order to avoid injures to the lungs and heart.

2.2 Primary Incision of the Soft Tissues of the Thoracic–Abdominal Wall

The primary abdominal incision should be made before opening the skull, since extraction of the heart involves the drainage of a good part of the blood present in the cranial vault via the superior caval venous system. Removing the heart first minimizes the possibility of blood overflow within the meningeal spaces when the skull is finally opened. It is important to prevent this from occurring as it may lead to the appearance of artifactual bleeding in the neck.

Although several approaches are possible, some variation of the Y-shaped thoracic–abdominal incision is preferred (in the United States it is better known as a T-shaped incision). This first portion of the procedure involves an initial transverse incision in the upper part of the thorax, made from shoulder to shoulder (bisacromial), creating a trough that will be more or less located at the jugular bifurcation (Figure 2.9). A single midline incision is then made, passing 3 to 4 centimeters to the left of the umbilicus down to the pubic tubercle (Figures 2.10 and 2.11).

The resulting T-shaped incision is called a *calyx* because it creates a cup-like structure. At the thoracic level the blade will sink deeply into the intercostal soft tissues where they are the widest, whereas at the abdominal level this type of incision preserves the deepest

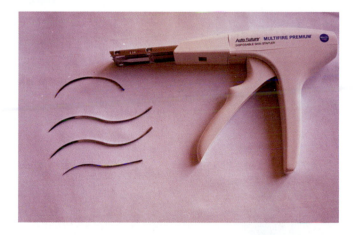

Figure 2.7 Staplers (right), particularly suitable during fetal and neonatal autopsies, and suture needles (left).

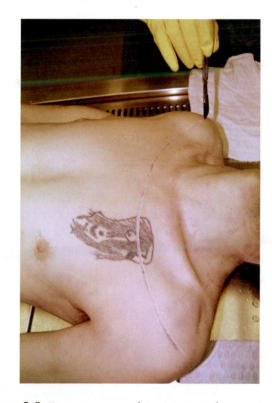

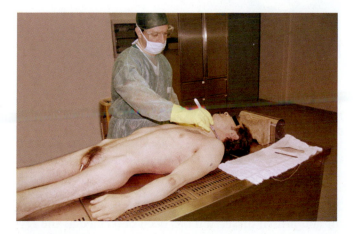

Figure 2.8 Dissector position at the autopsy table with dissection kit set.

Figure 2.9 First transversal incision with superior concavity and bisacromial extension (shoulder to shoulder).

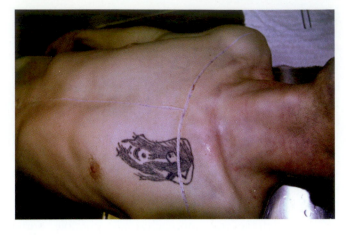

Figure 2.10 Second single midline incision passing 3 to 4 centimeters to the left of the umbilicus up to the pubic tubercle.

structure, the parietal peritoneum. This avoids opening the peritoneal cavity and the exposure of its content before intended.

2.2.1 Cutting Sequences

The sequence described here applies for all actions to be carried out on the right and left sides of the body. If possible a second prosector will stand in front on the left side of the autopsy table to help the first prosector. The second prosector follows the actions of the first and helps retract the incision.

2.2.1.1 *Handling the Scalpel*

If the prosector is right-handed, the handle of the scalpel should be held with the right hand, and vice versa. A serrated handle with forceps-like grips is the preferred instrument.

2.2.1.1.1 Thoracic Incision After the intercostals have been transacted, the following sequence or combined actions is required (Figure 2.12).* With the scalpel oriented tangentially to the plane of the ribs, dissection is facilitated by bilateral traction of the costal arches (Figures 2.13 and 2.14). Muscle and skin flaps can then be reflected to reveal the rib cage. The incision should be carried deeper at the level of the pectoralis minor muscle, always keeping the blade oriented tangentially to the rib cage. Otherwise, all costal insertions may not be detached from the chest wall. Once detached, the muscle is reflected.

---

* In women the presence of the breasts as well as in male subjects with abundant subcutaneous adipose tissue (i.e., when the tissue cannot be gripped between the prongs of toothed pliers), the dissector may use a fabric sponge on his left hand for easier grasp. With first and second finger in opposition, the dissector can cut thick, soft antecostal tissues by using lateral traction.

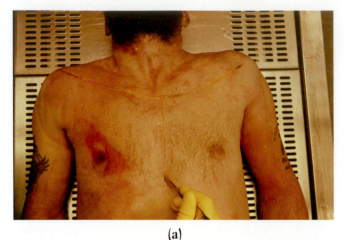

(a)

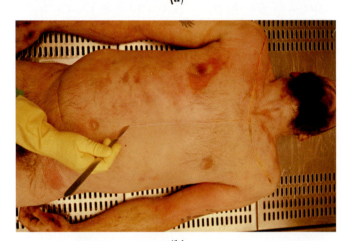

(b)

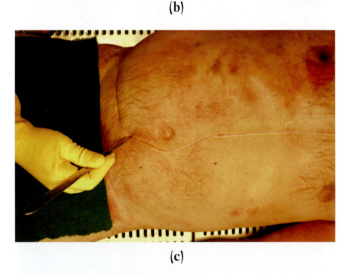

(c)

Figure 2.11 (a) The first part of the second incision of the resection at the calyx that goes down in the middle of the first (with sagittal course) along the median line of thorax and abdomen (b). The abdominal resection proceeds in the median direction, up to the proximity of the umbilical region (c).

2.2.1.1.2 Abdominal Incision Our preferred approach for abdominal dissection has been described as the *eggshell technique*. Detaching and pulling on one side of the muscle and skin flap exposes the entire peritoneum,

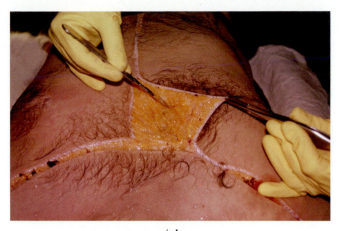

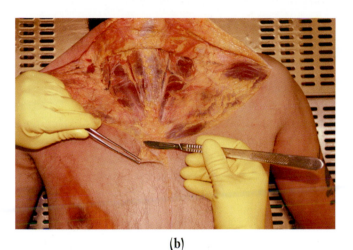

(a)

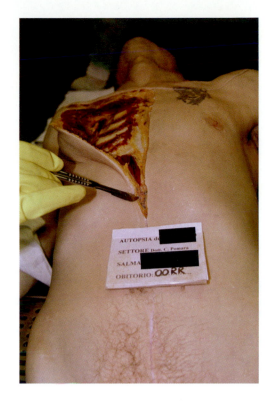

Figure 2.13 Combined pulling and cutting action. Incision phase followed by removing phase. Fully sinking the blade in the antecostal tissues, one gets a drawing action with the help of pliers. The tangentially oriented blade follows the rib cage.

(b)

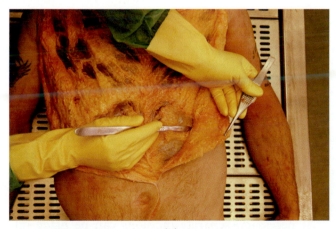

(c)

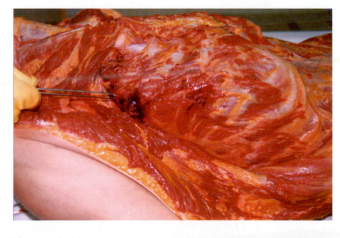

Figure 2.14 Overturning of the antecostal tissues and exposition of the rib cage. Serratus anterior muscles are very clear, as well as the pectoralis minor and major, adhered to the wall.

Figure 2.12 The resection runs 2 or 3 centimeters to the left of the umbilicus, describing a curve whose concavity will depend on the anatomic conformation of the region (fat, cutaneous ligaments, previous surgical operations). Traction of the cutaneous flaps to the origin of the secondary resection (sagittal branch of the calyx resection) (a) with combined drawing action carried out with the pliers and cutting action carry out with scalpel, duly following the margins of the incision. (b and c) Symmetrical lifting of the left and right side of the body's two antimere (left thoracic antimero section).

resulting in the appearance not unlike the diaphanous inner membrane of an eggshell (Figure 2.15).

Once the blade is inserted at the end of the xiphoid process, the incision is then carried down the linea alba to the pubis and the muscles and skin (including the rectus abdominus) are divided. Then the external and

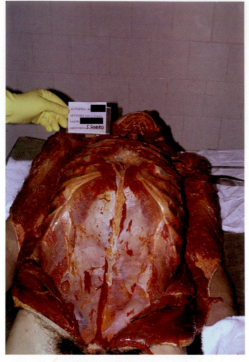

(a)

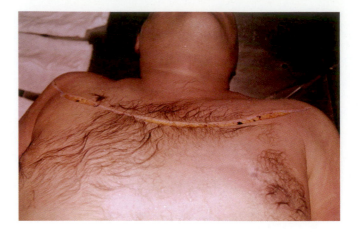

Figure 2.16 First transversal incision.

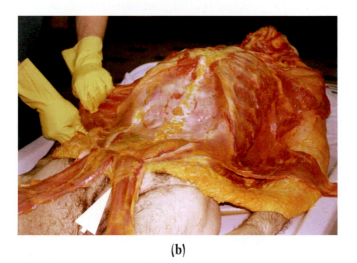

(b)

Figure 2.15 The diaphanous inner membrane of the peritoneum. (a) In evidence, the muscular insertions of the abdomen muscles. Note the symphysis of the rectum muscles (removed from the wall) and the muscular cutaneous flaps overturned (detached from the wall). (b) Recti muscles of the abdomen are indicated by the white arrow and isolated along the white line.

the internal obliques, and then the transverse abdominus are separated from the parietal peritoneum. At the same time, the preperitoneal connective tissue is dissected, and then the flaps are retracted (Figure 2.15a). Occasionally, the neck and abdomen may have to be opened separately.

2.2.2 Approaching Dissection by Single Planes: The Thoracic Wall

After producing the chest calyx incision, gently cut the skin with the point of the blade, limiting the dissection to the subcutaneous margins (Figure 2.16). Place traction on the skin using a toothed forceps held in the left hand. Each anatomical plane is cut in a row, advancing toward the midline, with the scalpel blade oriented tangentially to the planes themselves (Figure 2.17).

Incise the pectoral fascia, up to the posterior axillary line. Underlying the skin is the triangle-shaped pectoralis major muscle. At its lateral apex it attaches to the major tubercle of the humerus, located at the base of the medial sternocostal convex insertion. Sever the insertion with a continuous, half-moon–shaped movement of the scalpel, so that the incision runs vertically from above to below. Then cut the clavicular portion of the muscle from its insertion onto the clavicle. Reflect the muscle lateral to its humeral insertion (Figure 2.18).

Finally, the costal insertions of the pectoralis minor are incised, and the muscle is then severed from its bony attachments with combined traction–dissection; invert the muscle laterally on the coracoid process of the scapula, paying attention not to accidentally cut the axillary vein or any of its branches.

If necessary, separate incisions can be made into the costal insertion of the serratus anterior muscle. This allows the sternal–costal area to be easily examined for evidence of traumatic alterations (for example, hemorrhagic infiltrations, rib fracture line, and malformations) (Figures 2.19 and 2.20).

2.2.3 The Abdominal Wall

In the abdominal area, the subcutaneous edge of the incision is retracted using toothed forceps, held in the

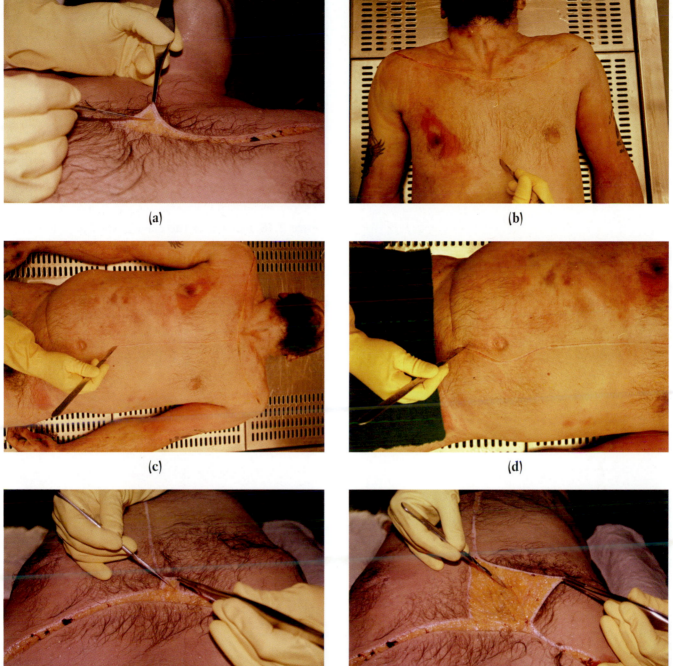

(a)

(b)

(c)

(d)

(e)

(f)

Figure 2.17 (a) The first part of the second incision of the resection at the calyx that goes down in the middle of the first (with sagittal course) along the median line of the thorax and abdomen (b and c). The abdominal resection proceeds in the median direction, up to the proximity of the umbilical region. The resection runs 2 or 3 centimeters to the left of the umbilicus, describing a curve whose concavity will depend on the anatomic conformation of the region (fat, cutaneous ligaments, previous surgical operations) (d, e, f, and g). Traction the cutaneous flaps to the origin of the secondary resection (sagittal branch of the calyx resection) (e) with a combined drawing action carried out with the pliers, and cutting action carried out with a scalpel, duly following the margins of the incision (f). Symmetrical lifting of the left and right sides of the body two antimere (left thoracic antimero section) (g and h). Well evident in the figure are the overturn of the thoracic abdominal cutaneous flaps. In particular, on the right (black arrows) is the axillary region (armpit cavity) of the costal margin at the level of the anterior middle axillary line and for the abdominal level at the level of the intersection of the oblique abdomen muscles (i).

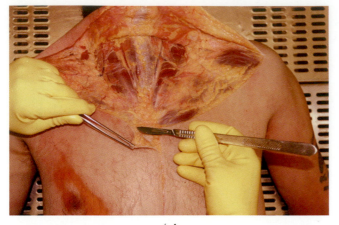

(g)

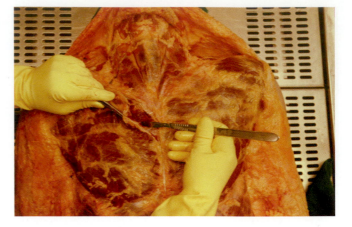

Figure 2.18 Incision of the clavicular edge of the major pectoralis muscle.

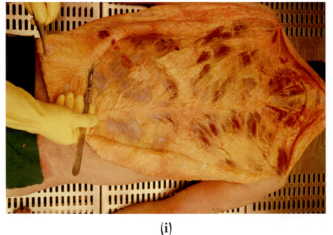

(h)

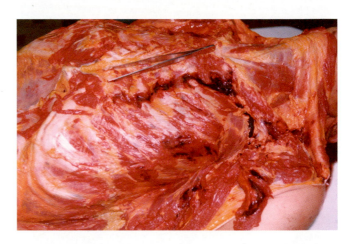

Figure 2.19 Sternocostal area revealed (note signs of deadly costal fracture lines with separated edges, diastasis).

(i)

Figure 2.17 (continued.)

left hand (use of a cloth sponge can be helpful), and the anatomic planes are dissected in succession, always proceeding toward the midline, using a scalpel oriented tangentially to the planes themselves (Figure 2.17e–i). Dissect the skin from the subcutaneous tissue beginning at the aponeurosis of the external oblique muscle (Figure 2.21 through Figure 2.23).

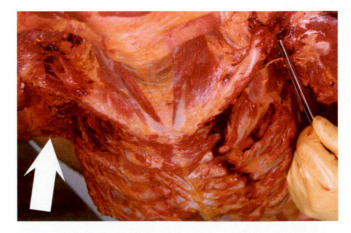

Figure 2.20 Homeral insertion in major and minor pectoralis muscles. (A clavicular fracture line with separated edges [diastasis] is indicated with white arrows on the right and pliers on the left.)

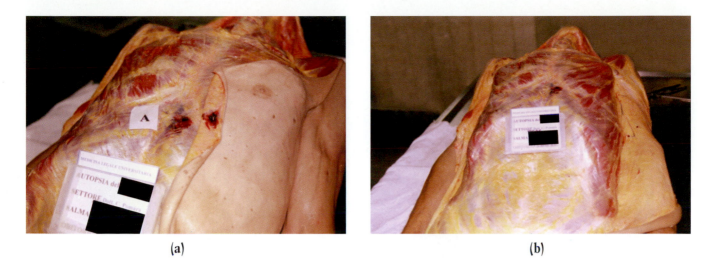

(a)   (b)

Figure 2.21 A gunshot wound with a study of the cutaneous and muscular edges. Dissection by planes in the study of injuries due to firearms. Part (a) shows the study of the macroscopic characteristics of the hole in the subcutaneous and fascial levels, strongly evocative of the entrance wound.

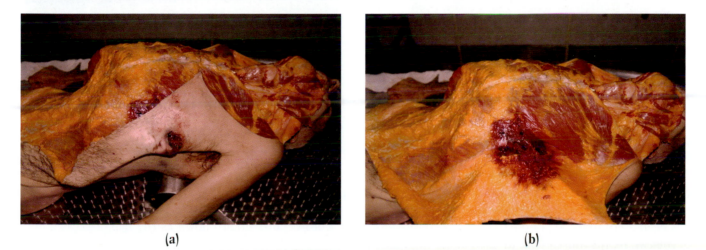

(a)   (b)

Figure 2.22 Stab wounds with a study of the cutaneous and muscular planes. Application of the dissection by anatomic planes in cases of stab wounds. Part (a) shows a comparative study in both cutaneous and muscular–fascial levels of these injuries.

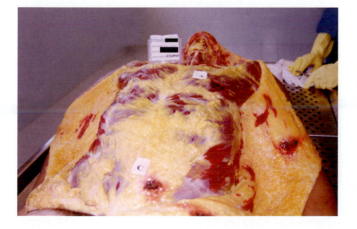

Figure 2.23 Dissection of the cutis–subcutis plane at the abdominal level.

The external oblique muscle must be detached from the posterior costal plane above. With the blade held obliquely, make a midlateral incision in the aponeurosis of the external oblique muscle, at the lateral edge of the rectus muscle, then separate the external oblique and the underlying internal oblique muscle, everting both laterally (Figure 2.24).

Divide the internal oblique muscle (sometimes called the *little oblique*), making sure that the blade continues to remain obliquely oriented toward the midline. The aponeurosis of the internal oblique blends in with the transverse muscle fibers of the abdomen. Detach the aponeurosis at the lateral margin of the rectus muscle, and then free it from the peritoneum, dissecting the

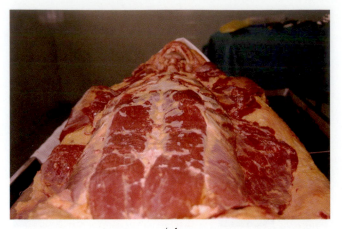

(a)

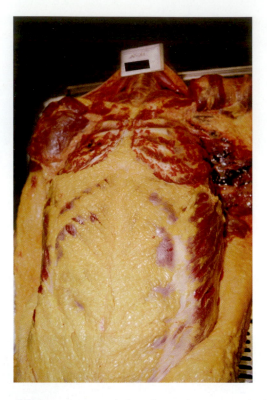

Figure 2.24 Incision and detaching the external oblique muscles.

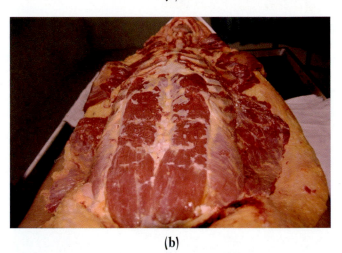

(b)

Figure 2.25 Incision and detaching the internal oblique muscles. The incision of the rectus muscles by a median cut or by a dissection known as the flap dissection (butterfly flap dissection).

preperitoneal connective tissue, reflecting it downward by traction applied laterally on one side (Figure 2.25).

At this stage, the rectus muscles of the abdomen are removed, leaving a V-shaped, upside-down incision at the severed corner of the sternal–costal area. Once that has been accomplished, all the sternal–costal insertions of the two rectus muscles are divided along their lateral margins. The muscle is then detached bilaterally, using medial to lateral traction, from the posterior laminae of the rectus sheath up to the linea alba (this technique is usually called *flap dissection* or *butterfly flap dissection*).

After creating the flaps, incise the remaining skin, detach it, then position it tangentially, oriented toward the pubis; the sheaths of the rectus muscles lying on the midline are separated from the underlying peritoneum and are simultaneously reflecting downward with their sheaths resting on the pubis (Figures 2.25a and 2.26).

Other approaches are possible. After cutting through the sternal–costal insertion of the two rectus muscles, using a perpendicularly oriented knife, incise them at the linea alba, separate them at the midline, then detach the muscle with the help of the cutter, which is placed tangentially to the peritoneal plane. This will expose the muscular fascia of the back of the peritoneum up to the pubic bone, after which it is finally reflected downward (Figures 2.25b and 2.26).

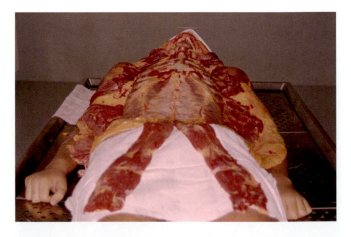

Figure 2.26 Incision and detaching of the rectus abdominis muscles. After incision and detaching the single rectus muscle, it is reflected down, leaving the distal insertion *in situ*.

2.3 Access to the Thoracic Cavity

2.3.1 Incision of the Thoracic Wall

Before exposing any individual organs, first make a keyhole incision through the intercostal muscles (external, internal, and posterior muscles) as well as the parietal pleura. This is done using the point of a blade in correspondence with the line at the second intercostal space. This is done to check for the possible presence of pneumothorax, or pleural effusion (Figure 2.27).

2.3.2 Disarticulating Clavicular Joints

The sternoclavicular joints need to be separated before the chest cavity and its contents can be inspected. A small knife with a narrow blade is used to incise the ligaments, the articular capsule, and the insertion of the sternal head into the upper sternocleidomastoid muscle on the manubrium of the sternum.

Identify the articular heads first by making an incision running through the articular line by rhythmically moving the corresponding shoulder with the left hand. Sink the point of the scalpel into the inferior or superior border of the articular line, taking care not to damage the arteries and veins of the neck that lie just below, especially the trunk of the innominate artery. The result is a half-moon–shaped incision with a lateral concavity.

2.3.3 The Chondrocostal Incision

Once the clavicles have been disconnected on each side, open the thoracic cavity by removing the sternochondrocostal surface. Each rib is severed with the rib

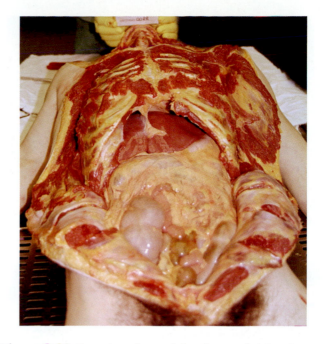

Figure 2.28 Running plane of the shears rib (chondrocostal edge).

shears (Figure 2.6) starting from below or, better still, at the costal arch of the tenth rib (an incision placed here will involve the diaphragm and its costal insertions) (Figure 2.28). The process is then carried upward to the first rib at a maximum of 1 to 2 centimeters inside the chondrocostal line.

Rib shears must be held with the right hand, perpendicularly oriented to the costal arches (Figure 2.29). Some chondral fragments will remain on the costal stump, but these will help protect the hands of the dissector (although prosectors are wearing gloves, the cartilage will protect their hands against the irregular and sharp bony surface of the costal stump).

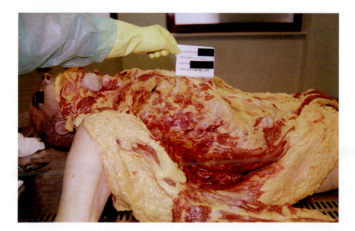

Figure 2.27 Incision and detaching of the external oblique muscles. The arrows indicate the incision plane and the parietal eyelet realized into the second intercostal space externally to the clavicular line.

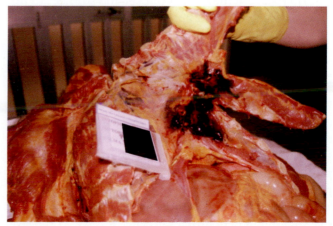

Figure 2.29 Chondrocostal edge.

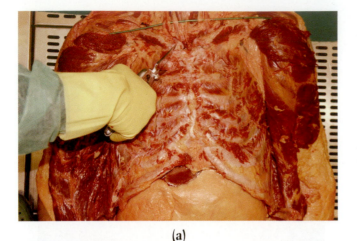

(a)

(a)

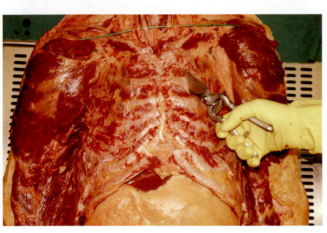

(b)

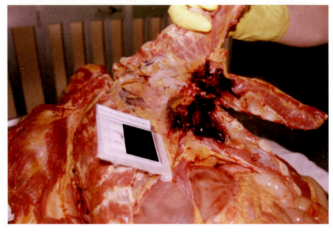

(b)

Figure 2.30 Position the rib shears (blade point bent at 30° toward the inside) for the approach to the second and first ribs.

By the time the first intercostal space is reached, position the rib shears (blade point bent at 30° toward the inside) so that they are aligned with the incision on the sternoclavicular articular surface, then resect the first rib (because the bone is thicker and stronger in this area, pressure must be applied to both ends of the rib cutter) (Figures 2.29 and 2.30).

2.3.4 Removal of the Anterior Rib Shield

Lift the right inferior corner of the sternocostal triangle with the forceps held in the left hand. At the same time use the point of a scalpel to dissect the aponeuretic sternal insertions of the parietal pleura and—from the posterior surface of the ligaments, particularly the inferior and superior sternal pericardial ligaments—proceed upward, at all times taking great care to not cut the underlying pericardial sac (Figure 2.31). At the level of manubrium sternum, the ligaments connecting with the chest plate have more strength. Be careful not to cut vessels at the base of the neck. A firmer drawing action,

Figure 2.31 (a) Manual traction of the rib shield. Hemorrhagic shedding is evident in the sternal region reflecting on the pericardial fat (sternopericardial ligaments). (b) Dissection of the aponeurotic sternal insertions of the parietal pleura with the point of a blade.

done with the left hand (Figure 2.31a), is required to the remove the rib shield, thereby opening the pleural cavities and removing the parietal pleura (Figure 2.32 through Figure 2.34).

2.3.5 Inspection of the Anterior Chest

Inspection of the internal surface of the rib shield is performed for medicolegal purposes. It is important to note possible injuries, which will usually be manifested as fractures or hemorrhagic infiltrates (Figure 2.34).

2.3.6 Inspection of the Pleural Cavities

First, explore the pleural cavities that have already been opened (Figures 2.33 and 2.34). Do this with the right hand to outline the convexity of the lung, then lower the hand downward to reach the costal–vertebral corner (Figure 2.35). Doing so will permit the detection of

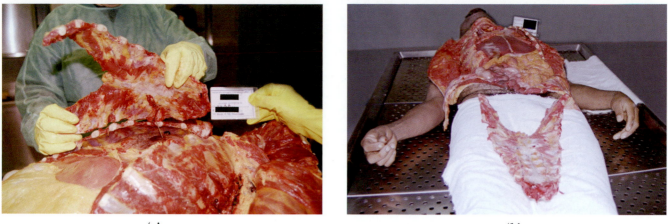

(a)   **(b)**

Figure 2.32 (a) Removal of the rib shield. The metal stylet locates a firearm shot. (b) The rib shield is removed and laid on the upper limbs. For judiciary purposes, pictures of the thoracoabdominal cavity should be taken before proceeding with a detailed examination.

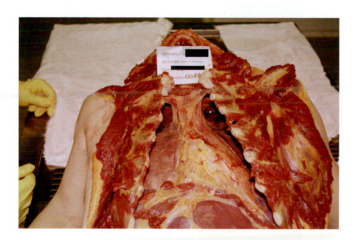

Figure 2.33 Thoracic area exposed. From bottom: cut off insertions of the diaphragm, pericardial sac, cardiophrenic ligaments, and clavicular stomps.

fibrotic adhesions that must either be trimmed or cut off with a blade. In case of very strong, extensive adhesions, as are sometimes found in the fibrothoracic chest plate, it may be necessary to cut along the endothoracic fasciae, leaving the parietal pleura adherent to the underlying lung. Pleural effusions on either side should be collected for later microscopical and toxicological analyses. Ultimately, an evaluation of the macroscopic characteristics of the lungs, pericardial sac, and the other mediastinic organs must be performed (Figure 2.36 through Figure 2.38).

2.3.7 Incision of the Pericardial Sac: The Heart Examination *In Situ*

The pericardial sac is incised by making an upside-down Y-shaped incision with rounded nose scissors

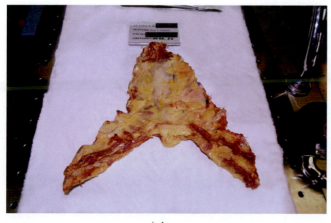

(a)

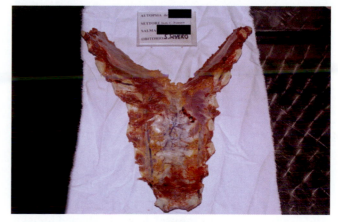

(b)

Figure 2.34 Internal surface inspection of the rib shield.

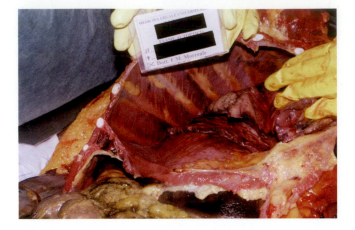

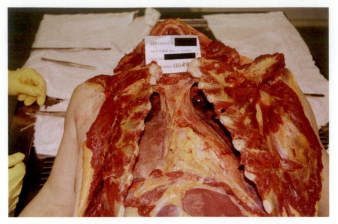

(a)

Figure 2.35 Manual examination *in situ* of the lungs. The dissector gathers the lung surface in his palm to make his way into the cavity.

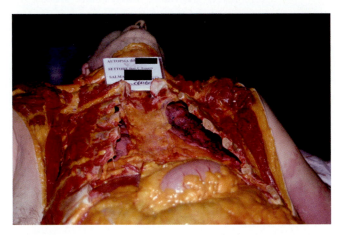

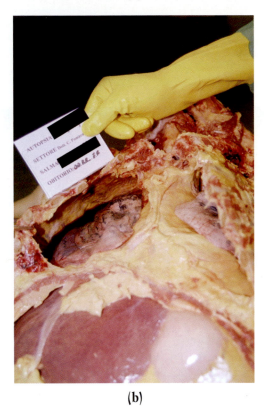

(b)

Figure 2.36 Thoracic area. Pleural and pericardial adherences cannot be trimmed off.

Figure 2.38 Inspection of the pleuric cavities. The images show the presence of abundant hemorrhagic pleural effusion, that in some of the photos (b and c) look like hemorrhagic lakes indicating the cause of the exitus in such subjects.

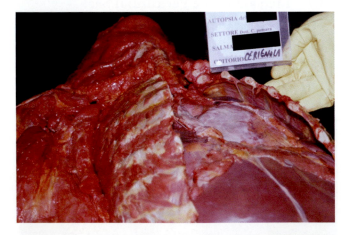

to identify the pericardial sac and to raise it from the underlying heart (Figure 2.40).[*]

Once the keyhole incision has been created, direct the prongs upward, first making a sagittal incision of the pericardial layer up to the reflection point on the heart. Then, starting again from the same keyhole incision, make two

Figure 2.37 Thoracic area. Whitish coat on the pericardial surface (pericarditis) and pleural–pericardial adherences.

(Figure 2.39). After having grasped and lifted the sternal surface of the sac, a toothed forceps, held in the left hand, is used to make a sagittal, keyhole-shaped incision 2 centimeters in length in the lower portion of the sac, just above the pericardial phrenic limit. This will help

---

[*] Sometimes there are simply too many adhesions between the epicardium and the pericardium, and the sac cannot be simply incised. The best approach in such cases, is to gently remove the adhesion using the fingers.

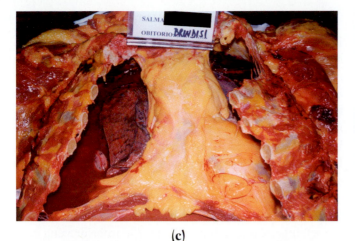

(c)

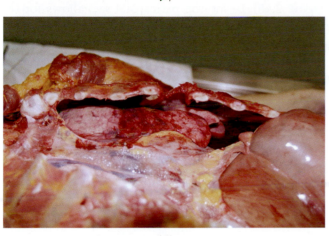

(d)

Figure 2.38 (continued.)

wide oblique incisions directed respectively to the left and right, producing oblique incisions of the pericardial layer. Then, a third oblique incision of the pericardial layer is made across the acute margin of the heart (Figure 2.39).

2.3.8 Examination of the Pericardial Cavity and Its Contents

Reflecting the pericardial flaps allows for the evaluation of its structural characteristics and also allows visualization of the inner surface of the pericardium, where adhesions may be evident (Figures 2.41 and 2.42). If a substantial pericardial effusion is present it must be collected and its physical characteristics clearly recorded, including (and particularly) the appearance of the fluid (clear, straw-colored, serosanguineous; frankly bloody or cloudy) and the volume of the infusion present should be measured in centiliters (use a graduated test tube or syringe, but never guess the volume of fluid present). If necessary, specimens should be collected for microbiological, cytologic, biochemical, and toxicological testing. For example, there is little reason to analyze a

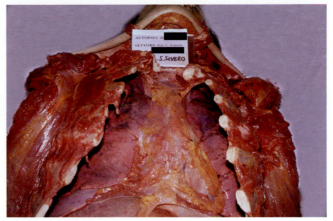

Figure 2.39 The first sagittal incision goes until the reflection point on the big vessels. Then, two obliqual incisions are performed: one runs oriented to the left toward the heart point (second oblique incision); the second, oriented to the right, runs to across the acute edge of the heart (third oblique incision).

Figure 2.40 Use of pliers with pericardial layers: round-shaped interruption of the pericardial layer.

Figure 2.41 Pericardial flaps in an upside-down, Y-shaped incision.

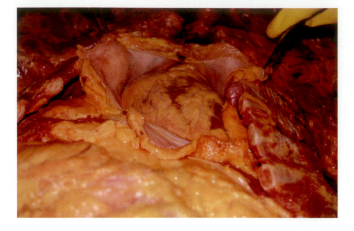

Figure 2.42 An open pericardial sac with wide open flaps.

small amount of straw-colored pericardial fluid when it is already known that the subject had congestive heart failure (Figure 2.43).

2.3.9 Cardiac Examination

Examination of the external macroscopic features of the heart and great vessels will reveal any evidence of spontaneous or traumatic damage, or preexisting malformation (Figure 2.43 through Figure 2.47). External examination of the heart also allows for examination of the shape and dimensions of the heart; these dimensions should be correlated with those made of nearby anatomic structures.

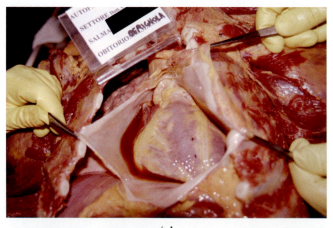

(a)

Figure 2.43 Use pliers in the pericardium sac to preserve its contents. Abundant serum-hemorrhagic effusion in pericardial cavity. Evidence of cardiovascular peduncles. Phases of inspection: Description of specimens and photographic medical report of details. Moreover, in this figure some hemorrhagic subpericardial effusions are revealed on the anterior pericardial surface of the right ventricle, pointed out by the dissector with the pliers (c) and collected for judicial purposes.

2.3.10 Collecting Blood Samples

It is well known that blood drug concentrations measured in the heart (right or left side) are inaccurate. Most of the time the results of measurements made of heart blood will suggest that more drugs were present at the time of death than was actually the case, and the measured concentrations will be much higher than if they had been measured in the periphery. On the other hand, heart blood provides an excellent medium for drug screening, simply for the purpose of detection, even if attempts at quantification provide little useful information. Venous blood should be collected with a needleless syringe. An incision through the inferior vena cava (Figure 2.48), inside the pericardial sac, allows for the passage of a syringe for blood aspiration. The blood samples must be collected in a test tube containing a preservative (usually 1% sodium fluoride), labeled with the autopsy number and the full name of the decedent, and then kept in a refrigerated environment at –2°C to 4°C until processing. If, for some reason, arterial blood is desired, samples can be taken from the descending thoracic aorta as it crosses the mediastinum. This can be an especially useful approach when there is evidence of extreme postmortem coagulation.

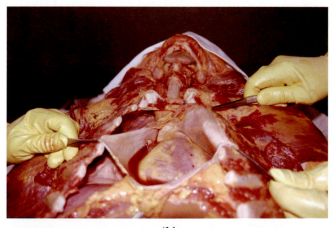

(b)

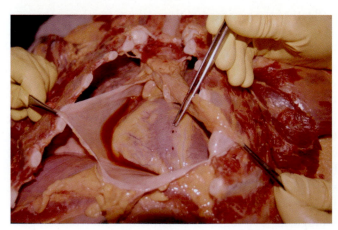

(c)

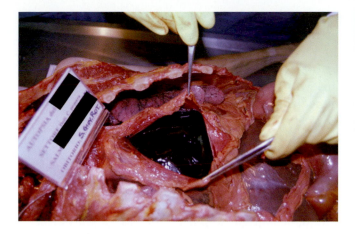

Figure 2.44 Cardiac tamponade. Large hematic intrapericardial clot surrounding the anterior pericardial surface resulting from aneurysm and aortic dissection.

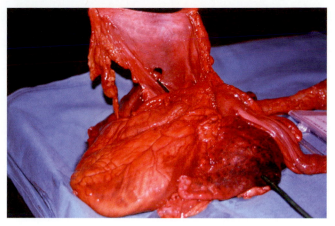

Figure 2.47 Gunshot wound running through the cardiac sac, the heart, and the left lung.

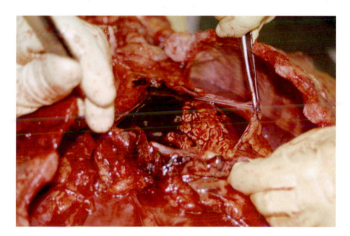

Figure 2.45 Hemopericardium.

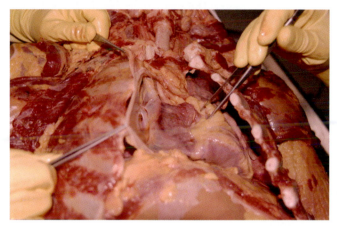

Figure 2.48 Cutting *in situ* of the pulmonary artery. The pliers put the heart in traction showing the cavity area.

2.3.11   Examination *In Situ* of the Main Pulmonary Artery

Before removing the heart, it is best to open the main pulmonary artery *in situ*. This step is mandatory when pulmonary thromboembolism is suspected. It should also be done when there is known trauma or when surgical procedures have been performed. To open the pulmonary artery *in situ*, make a keyhole incision using pointed scissors held with the right hand. At the same time, use forceps held in the other hand to pull down the heart, and draw it away from the artery; in the process the pulmonary artery will be exposed almost completely.

A sagittal incision is made at the trunk of the pulmonary artery, just above the infundibulum of the conus arteriosus, that is, the anterosuperior portion of the heart's right ventricle, at the entrance to the pulmonary trunk. If emboli are present they can be extracted using forceps. Extending the incision to the left makes it easy to explore the lumen of the left branch of the

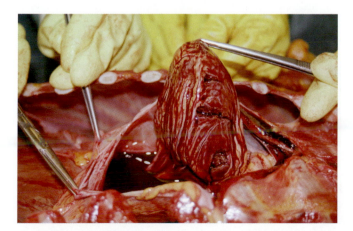

Figure 2.46 Cardiac lacerations. From the base of the heart toward the apex (top), laceration in the wall of the left atrium, and laceration with diastasis in the left ventricle wall.

pulmonary artery. However, to explore the right branch of bifurcation of the pulmonary artery, it is necessary to dissociate the main pulmonary artery from the adjacent ascending aorta artery, as they are normally juxtaposed (Figure 2.48).

2.4 Evisceration According to Virchow's Technique

The Virchow technique is used to extract the thoracic organs one by one (see Section 2.10), extracting the heart first and then both lungs.

2.4.1 Heart Extraction

To extract the heart, the examiner should hold it at its base, using the left hand in a forceps-like fashion, or even actually use forceps with rubber prongs, then lift the heart up firmly, so that the inner face of the pericardial sac can be seen, together with its cardiovascular connections. These (cardiovascular connections) are then transacted with a blade held tangentially to the serosal surface (Figure 2.49).

Cut off all the vessels, as closely as possible to the serosal surface. Then proceed clockwise, first making a half-moon–shaped cut at the superior concavity, from left to right, starting from the left, superiorly (imagine a transposed clock face set at 3 o'clock).

Cut off the two pulmonary left veins, with the incision oriented toward the inferior vena cava (at 7 o'clock). The terminal portion of the half-moon–shaped incision

will transect the two right pulmonary veins, first the inferior then the superior (at 9 o'clock).

While maintaining traction on the heart, a second incision is made parallel to the previous one, only closer. This will first cut off the pulmonary arterial trunk immediately under the pericardial point of reflection on the artery (at 1 o'clock).

Next, the half-moon–shaped resection is carried to the right to cut off the superior vena cava at its trunk (at 1 o'clock). Finally, firmly pull up the heart with the left hand and the ascending aorta, where it passes through the aortic arch, will be visible. Make a third resection running completely parallel to the others but shorter in length, thereby dividing the aorta at its internal pericardial reflection point (at 12 o'clock). All incisions must be performed firmly, with a continuous bending movement of the wrist, to avoid leaving residual elements that resemble saw cuts. It is also important to avoid any damage to the pericardium and, even more important, damage the myocardium, by carrying the incision too close to the interior pericardial sac (Figure 2.49).

2.4.2 Lung Sections and Removal

The lungs are also removed following Virchow's technique (one by one) and then extracted from the thoracic cavity, starting with the left lung and moving to the right lung. The left hand is plunged into the chest cavity from above and moving downward, keeping the hand aligned with the left costal–vertebral sinus, so that the back of the hand faces upward (Figure 2.50a,b). The fingers must be

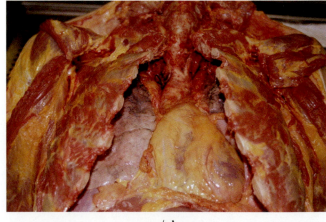

(a)

Figure 2.50 (a) Heart, superior pericardial sac, and vascular peduncle. The projection of the section planes in a sequence indicate the epiaortic vessel plane that is clearly visible after the removal of the anonymous artery on the right, the common and subclavian carotid artery on the left. (b) Scooping the lung in the hand cavity. (c) Cavalier hold and recision of the lung at the bronchial–vascular peduncle.

Figure 2.49 Vascular peduncle. Once the heart is in traction, exposing all the vascular roots, the dissector will cut clockwise the first time with a half-moon–shaped incision at the superior concavity from left to right. The blade must be tangential to the pericardial sac. Then, the second time he will make an incision parallel to the first.

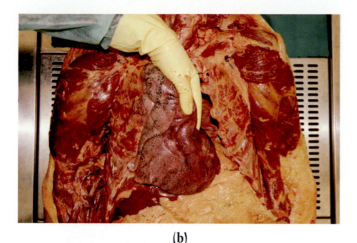

(b)

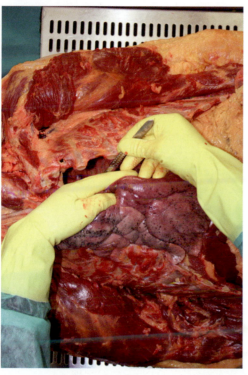

(c)

Figure 2.50 (continued.)

open like a fan, so that sliding downward the third interdigital space will be felt to correspond with the superior edge of the vascular bronchial peduncle that, in turn, will rest against the third and fourth finger in a pincerlike position. Bend all fingers simultaneously so that the lung is held in the cavity of the hand. By gently pulling, the peduncle is stretched, exposed, and transacted.

The scalpel edge must be positioned horizontally to cut the peduncle with a half-moon-shape that is concave on the right (Figure 2.50c).

We recommend using a clockwise motion to sever the connections, moving the knife from above downward, from 12 o'clock to 6 o'clock. The right lung is then

removed by repeating exactly the same set of motions, except now the incision is made with the knife moving downward, from 6 o'clock to 12 o'clock.

2.4.3 Exploration of the Anatomic Structures of the Posterior Mediastinum

After the heart and both lungs have been removed, the structures of the posterior mediastinum are then systematically explored, moving from top to bottom and from front to back. The trachea divides into two main bronchi, the aortic arch will be over the left bronchus, and a portion of the thoracic descending aorta will be seen ascending along the left anterior side of the thoracic column. Anteriorly, on the right side of the aorta, the esophagus passes through the diaphragm muscle via the esophageal (diaphragmatic) hiatus.

2.5 Access to the Neck Region

Adequate dissection of the musculocutaneous layers of the neck requires that the neck be hyperextended, elevating the shoulders if necessary. Great effort must be taken to avoid accidentally cutting the skin in this region, as it is particularly thin. If sufficient care is not taken, it may not be possible to do an adequate reconstruction of the neck. Layered dissection is the method of choice for neck dissection. If there is no reason to examine the soft tissues of the face, it is best to begin the dissection from the superior cutaneous flap produced by the primary incision. But the transversal or bisacromial incision (shoulder to shoulder), or Y-shaped incision, of the soft tissues of the thoracic–abdominal wall can be used (Figures 2.51 and 2.52).

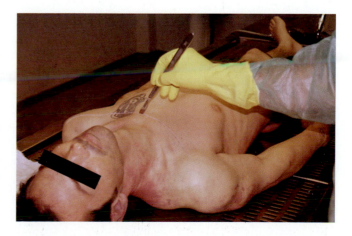

Figure 2.51 Primary incision.

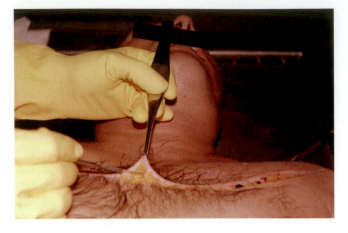

Figure 2.52 Traction and recision of the cutis and sub-cutis limited only to the neck region from an acromial extreme to the other.

Then proceed as follows:

1. Grasp the skin flap with forceps held in the left hand and pull the flap upward.*
2. Hold the scalpel so that it is oriented tangen-tially to the cervical superficial fascia. When held in this manner, the blade edge follows the cutting plane between the subcutaneous tis-sue layers and the superficial cervical fascia, which can then be detached from the other. Cut from one acromion to the other and extend the dissection cephelad to the mandibular arch (Figure 2.52). Finally, reflect the flap onto the face. This allows inspection of the anterior lat-eral region of the neck within its anatomic lim-its (the jugular–clavicular plane on the bottom, the inferior border of the mandibular arch, and a plane extending from the mastoid processes on the top to the anterior margin of the sterno-cleidomastoid muscle bilaterally) (Figure 2.53).†

---

* Alternatively the dissector can use a fabric handkerchief to seize the flap.
† The superficial cervical fascia covers the muscles in the suprahyoid region, which extend between the cranial base and the mandibular arch, and down to the hyoid bone (digastric mus-cle, stilohyoid muscle, milohyoid muscle, geniohyoid muscle), then it adheres to the hyoid bone. In the infrahyoid region, the muscle passes like a bridge over the vascular nervous bundle (vessels and nerve region) and the muscles of the superficial lay-ers of this region (symmetric and ribbon-like muscle, stretched between hyoid bone, above, and sternum and clavicle, below), wrapped by the medium cervical fasciae (sternohyoid muscle and omohyoid muscle). On the deepest surface, one can find the infrahyoid muscles (sternothyroid muscle and thyrohyoid mus-cle) wrapped by the deep cervical fasciae.

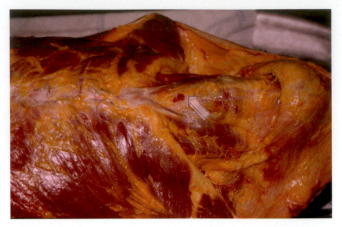

Figure 2.53 Reflection of the collar skin and exhibition of the anterior lateral region of the neck. From below upward, the jugular–clavicular plane, inferior edge of the mandibu-lar arch, and anterior edge of the trapezius muscles.

2.5.1 Removal of the Muscular Heads of the Sternocleidomastoid Muscle

An incision is made from above downward through the superficial cervical fasciae lamina, and then carried along the anterior border of the right sternocleidomas-toid muscle. Use toothed forceps to hold the muscle, which is then drawn laterally to allow for separation of the deep cervical surface (fasciae) from behind the superficial cervical fasciae. The muscle is then completely detached, including the two anterior–inferior insertions of the muscle respectively (sternal and clavicular). The muscle will be flipped upward, alongside the insertion of the mastoid (Figures 2.54 and 2.55).

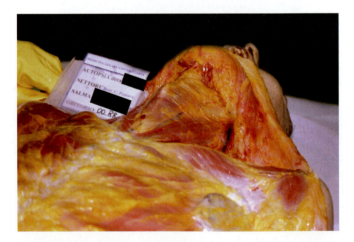

Figure 2.54 Side view of the superficial cervical band. The section edges close to the anterior margin of the ster-nocleidomastoid muscle are outlined in green.

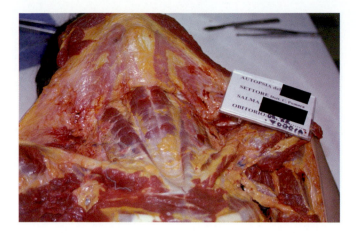

Figure 2.55 Anterior view of the superficial cervical band. Well evident are the two sternocleidomastoid muscles with their sternal insertions (heads of the sternocleidomastoid muscle) close to the jugular notch. In the median region are the two venters of the digastric muscle.

2.5.2 Removal of the Muscle of Superficial, Medium, and Deep Surface Regions

The deep fascia is divided from the middle cervical band of the muscles that comprise the superficial layer: the sternohyoid and the omohyoid, from beneath the sternothyroid and thyrohyoid muscles, taking care not to harm the nerves and vessels of the deep neck (common carotid artery, external jugular vein, and the vagus nerve [also known as cranial nerve X]) (Figure 2.56). The muscles are reflected upward over the mandibular arch, such that they resemble the segments of a fan. The sternothyroid and thyrohyoid muscles are dissected and

detached from the thyroid gland in the back and from the thyroid cartilage; these structures are also reflected upward, so that the thyroid and larynx–tracheal axes are revealed (Figure 2.57 through Figure 2.60).

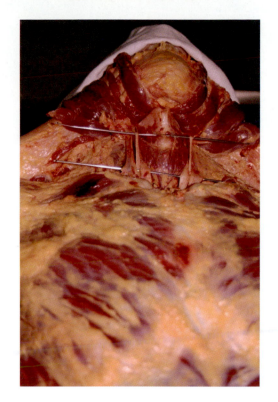

Figure 2.57 Exhibition of the thyroid gland fan-shaped muscles of the neck region overturned above the mandibular corner. The stylets draw the vascular nervous bundle of the neck. From left to right: the jugular vein, the vagus nerve, and the carotid artery.

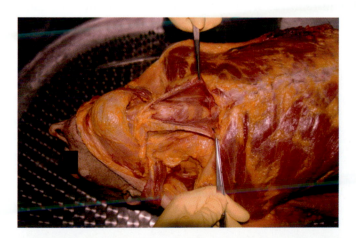

Figure 2.56 View of the middle and deep cervical band. The pliers draw the muscular venters of the omohyoid muscles (close up) offering the prosector a view of the thyroid area, the thyroid cartilage, and the cricoid cartilage.

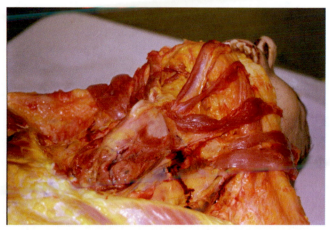

Figure 2.58 Particulars of the "fan rays" technique. It makes evident the left region of the neck. Starting from left to the right: sternohyodal and omohyoid muscle, the sternothyroid muscle, the clavicular, and the sternal head of the sternocleidomastoid muscle.

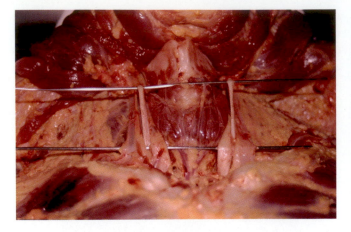

Figure 2.59 Particular of the thyroid *in situ*. The ligaments on the right and left are connected to the section planes of the gland in the larynx tracheal axe (median ligaments and lateral ligaments right and left). The stylet allows one to draw the vascular–nervous bundle of the neck separately (jugular vein, vagus nerve, carotid artery). In close-up, the stylet separates the vagus nerve.

2.5.3 Removal of the Thyroid

The thyroid is a U-shaped or horseshoe-shaped gland with a superior concavity. It is formed by two sides, or lobes, on the right and left, and connected by a median isthmus that overlays the cricoid cartilage of the larynx, extending downward to the two first tracheal rings. It is covered with an inner fibrous layer and outer perithyroid sheath, part of the superficial fascia of the neck. This fascia is particularly dense and must be removed with a scalpel. Continue the dissection superiorly until reaching the perithyroid sheath that is attached directly to the gland, along with the thyroid and cricoid laryngeal cartilage and the first tracheal rings. Continue the dissection cutting the median ligament and the right and left suspensory ligaments, which connect the glands to the thyroid and cricoid laryngeal cartilage and to the first tracheal rings (see details in Figure 2.59).

2.5.4 Inspection and Section of the Neck Vascular: Nervous Bundle

The vascular bundle must be opened *in situ*, from superior to inferior, using rounded scissors. The lumen of both the carotid artery and the jugular vein must be inspected and the condition of the vessel walls determined, even if no trauma or other abnormalities are evident.

2.6 Evisceration According to Ghon's Technique (*En Bloc*)

The preferred method for examination of the tongue, oropharynx, and hypopharynx is *en bloc extraction*,

Figure 2.60 The thyroid area, with perithyroid sheath.

taking out the larynx, trachea, and esophagus together as a block, and then continuing into the thorax, removing the tracheal bifurcation, bronchial tubes, lungs, descending aorta, inferior vena cava, and the esophagus. These are then clamped in the supradiaphragmatic area. This is the preferred technique because it facilitates the discovery of abnormalities in either the alimentary or respiratory tracts, and also allows for study of their anatomical relations with the heart and major vessels (Figure 2.66 and Figure 2.68 through Figure 2.72).

2.6.1 Direct Access to the Mouth Floor

The muscular aponeurotic structures that form the floor of the mouth are incised using a narrow blade, making a horseshoe-shaped incision, from one corner of the mandible to the other (Figure 2.61). Begin the incision just behind the internal surface of the mandibular arch and remove the posterior portion of the digastric muscle lying just behind the jaw, and the stylohyoid muscle lying in front and just above the digastric muscle. Carry

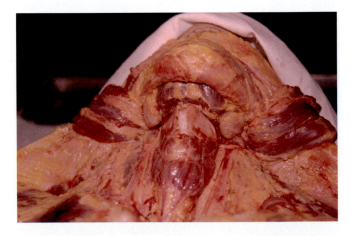

Figure 2.61 The cut section and access to the oral cavity is outlined. The close-up shows the insertion root of the anterior part of the digastric muscle surrounded by the two submandibular glands.

the incision centrally, transecting the mandibular insertions of the suprahyoid muscles of the neck, including the anterior portion of the digastric, milohyoid, geniohyoid, and genioglossus muscles.

The mucosa of the oral cavity is then incised, allowing visualization of the base of the tongue. Using a rubber pronged, toothed forceps to apply traction, expose the superior face of the tongue and the more posterior located structures, including the lingual tonsil, the three epiglottis folds delimiting the two epiglottic valleculae, epiglottis, and the two epiglottic folds (Figure 2.61).

2.6.2 The Floor of the Mouth

There are alternatives to the aforementioned method, the most effective being dissection by anatomic planes. Using a toothed forceps, first place traction on the anterior portion of the digastric muscle, then use the scalpel to cut tangentially and behind the internal border of the mandible, then sever the insertion of this muscle. Detach the muscle from the front to the back until the dissection reaches the tendinous portion of the muscle that attaches to the hyoid bone by a fibrous loop (Figure 2.62).

Proceed in the same manner with the hyoid muscle, dissecting it free from the mandibular arch, close to its insertion (Figure 2.62); the muscle is then reflected downward onto the hyoid bone. Then make a horseshoe-shaped incision behind the mandibular arch, thereby creating communication with the mouth, through which the tongue may be grasped and pulled downward, taking care to expose the superior face of the tongue, its terminal track, and the structures located at the back, such as the lingual tonsil, the three glossoepiglottis

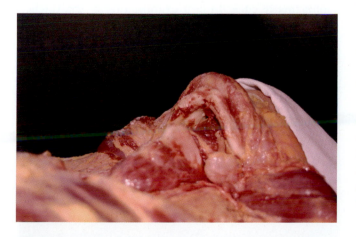

Figure 2.62 Removal of the anterior part of the digastric muscle. The mandibular edge, the hyoid bone, and the cricoid cartilage are visible. The central part of the sectioned milohyoid muscle is beneath the plane.

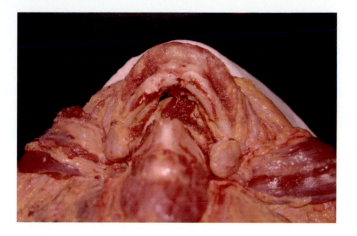

Figure 2.63 Anterior vision of the section plane of the mouth floor.

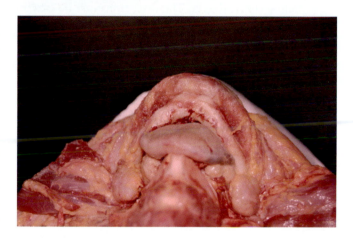

Figure 2.64 Descending of the tongue.

folds delimiting the two epiglottis valleculae, and the epiglottis (Figure 2.62 through Figure 2.64).

2.6.3 Ghon's Block

Regardless of the chosen method, the next step is to orient the scalpel blade vertically and dissect the root of the tongue, including the glossopalatal, glossopharyngeal, hyoglossus, and genioglossus muscles.

Identify the superior horn of the thyroid cartilage, then excise the overlying mucosa of the pharynx and stylopharyngeal muscles. Detach the muscles moving from proximal to distal, separate the posterior face of the hypopharynx and esophagus complex from the opposite larynx–tracheal axis, and then remove the deep cervical band at the back of the thorax.

The creation of an antivertebral cleavage plane is relatively simple. Removal of the esophageal–larynx–tracheal block requires the following combined actions: pulling the block downward with the left hand (using toothed forceps), pulling the block forward, and then

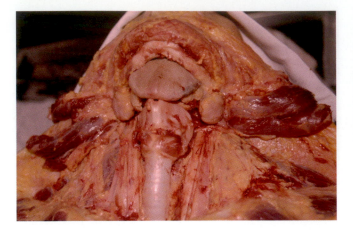

Figure 2.65 Particulars of the descended tongue. Outlined is the section plane to follow for the next of the larynx–tracheal axis. The resection plane runs very close to the rachis–cervical axis. The dissector must be careful not to injure the underlying vascular–nervous axis with the point.

cutting along the vertebral plane to isolate the tissue block from the muscular–vertebral plane at the back (Figures 2.65 and 2.66).

Once the chest is entered, the first thing to do is dissect the vessels adjacent to the aorta, the ones that supply the upper limbs, the innominate artery on the right, and the common carotid artery on the left (Figures 2.66 and 2.67). The posterior mediastinal structures are then detached from the vertebral plane at the back, beginning superiorly and proceeding inferiorly, until the area just above the diaphragmatic plane is reached. The block, so isolated, will contain neck and thoracic organs, including the heart whose pericardial cavity has been previously opened *in situ*. All of these structures are then everted downward onto the diaphragm.

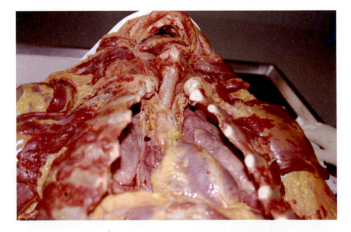

Figure 2.66 Block tongue–esophagus–trachea isolated from the vertebral–cervical segment and first thoracic tract. Still *in situ* are the epiaortic vessels. The resection plane of the epiaortic vessels is outlined. Thoracic aorta (TA): Aorta ascending trait in its intrapericardial portion with the heart sac removed and overturned.

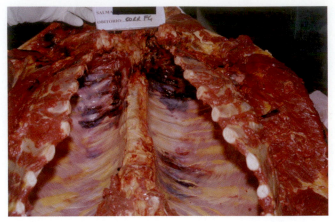

Figure 2.67 Vertebral cut plane and costal–diaphragmatic one that allows for lung recision.

To complete the cervical–thoracic evisceration, isolate the descending aorta from the esophagus lying opposite (Figures 2.68 and 2.69). Using a rubber-booted, toothed forceps, pull the aorta back so as to separate the connective tissue lying between the two structures.

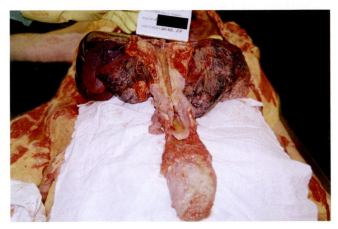

Figure 2.68 Ghon's block still *in situ* anchored to the diaphragmatic edge. *In situ* examination of the tracheal lumen with opened esophagus and aorta.

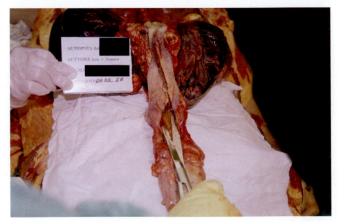

Figure 2.69 Particular of Ghon's block. The arrow indicates the cutting plane of the ascending aorta.

Figure 2.70 Ghon's block. In detail are intracorporeal trajectory of a gunshot wound.

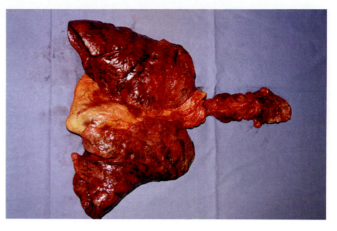

Figure 2.72 Ghon's block, anterior face.

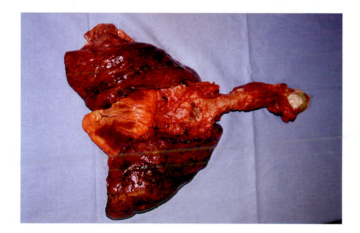

Figure 2.71 Ghon's block, posterior face.

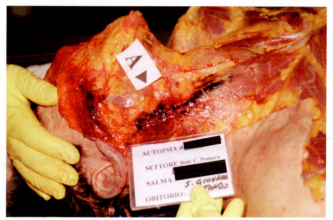

Figure 2.73 Access to the face; detaching of the over mandibular cutaneous plane.

The descending aorta is divided transversely, just below its origin, while the esophagus is incised 3 to 4 centimeters above the diaphragmatic aperture, but not before first applying an intestinal clamp. The clamp is needed to avoid an outpouring of the gastric content through the incision. Finally, raise the tissue block and cut the pericardium along the line of fusion with the tendinous center of the diaphragm. This completes the cervical–thoracic evisceration (Figure 2.66 and Figure 2.68 through Figure 2.72).

2.7 Access to the Face

In the occasional case of a gunshot wound it may be necessary to dissect the soft tissue of the face that lies in close proximity to the bony or cartilaginous framework of the head, namely, the bones of the cranium and face. When working in this area always bear in mind that the dissection should not be so radical as to preclude

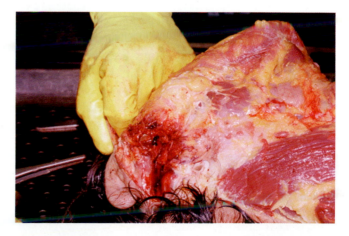

Figure 2.74 Access to the face; mandibular edge and revealing of the posterior edge of the sternocleidomastoid muscle.

adequate cosmetic reconstruction. To this end we use a slightly modified version of the Adams's incision.*

---

* Resection according to Adams: curtain resection of the neck skin plane starting from the external edge of the sternocleidomastoid muscle.

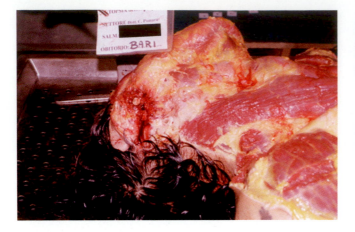

Figure 2.75 Access to the face; detaching of the soft tissues to the mastoid edge of the sternocleidomastoid muscle.

An incision is made in a plane passing behind the acromium and over the scapular edge on either side, until they join in the middle of the neck along its posterior surface. Visualize the muscles over scapular cavities, the insertions of the sternocleidomastoid muscle, and the muscular cavities of the cervical plane. Extend the incision from the front to the back edge of the mandible, allowing for direct visualization of all the facial soft tissues.

2.8   Access to the Abdominal Cavity

2.8.1   Incision of the Parietal Peritoneum

The parietal peritoneum is incised along the midline, from the xiphoid process downward to the pubis. First make a keyhole incision through the area where the prongs of the forceps are to be introduced. Hold the forceps vertically and introduce them through the keyhole, so that the scalpel blade runs between the forceps opened prongs, from the top to the bottom (Figure 2.76),

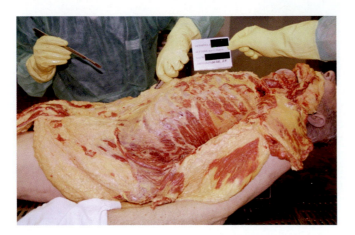

Figure 2.76 Access to the peritoneal serosa still intact.

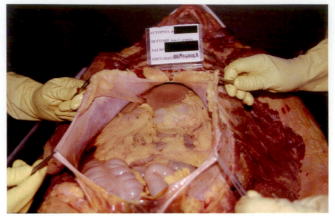

Figure 2.77 Detaching and overturning of the peritoneum. Outlined are its section planes.

tangentially to the costal arch. A midlateral oblique incision from the xiphoid process is carried up to cross the anterior axillary line with the serosal flaps being turned inferiorly and laterally. This allows the peritoneal cavity to be opened in such a way as to permit optimum visibility of the enteroperitoneal organs (Figure 2.77).

2.8.2   Abdominal Inspection

The purpose of the general abdominal inspection is to check for the presence or absence of any peritoneal effusion. If present, fluid would be of great importance. The total fluid present should be estimated, and the fluid itself should be collected in a sterile container, and then submitted for analysis. The tests to be done would include bacteriologic cultures, biochemical measurement, and microscopic examination. The presence of fibrous, visceral, and visceroparietal adhesions should also be described, as should the gross appearance of the gallbladder (Figure 2.78 through Figure 2.80).

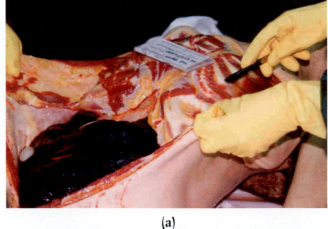

(a)

Figure 2.78 (a) Inspection of the abdominal cavity (haemoperitoneum occupying the entire cavity). (b) Hemorrhagic invasion of the renal lodge.

(b)

Figure 2.78 (continued.)

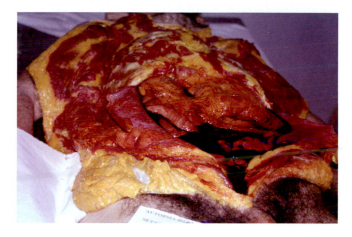

Figure 2.79 Haemoperitoneum.

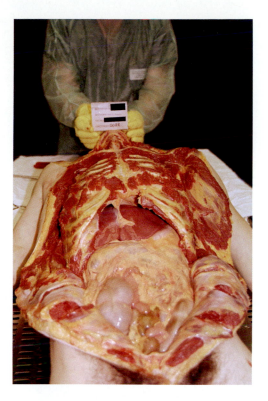

Figure 2.80 Wall opening of the abdominal cavity.

2.9 The Letulle Technique: *En Masse* Removal

The removal of the abdominal organs *en masse* is done according to the Letulle technique. This technique offers significant advantages when injuries involve or extend across the diaphragm, as, for instance, in the case of a suspected acute aortic dissection. If this is the case, proceed to the removal of the posterior surface of the organs first (Figure 2.81 through Figure 2.85). If injury is not suspected, the "organs in block removal technique" as developed by Ghon is preferred, if for no other reason than that this approach makes it convenient to preserve the abdominal vascular axis.

2.10 The Virchow Technique

When injuries are not suspected, many prefer to use the Virchow technique, with the removal of one organ at a time.

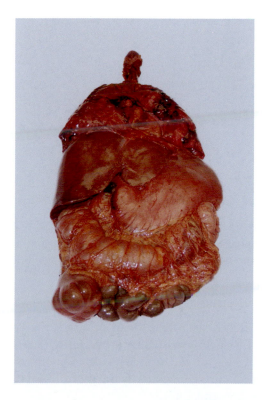

Figure 2.81 Lettule block, anterior face. The advantage of such a technique is that it allows total sight of the anatomic relations of the organs and a careful and detailed analysis (sometimes formalin fixation may be necessary for better organ inspection). The liver, transverse colon, small mesenterial, and ciecale recess.

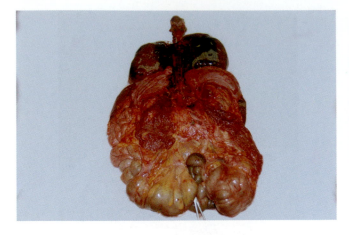

Figure 2.82 Letulle block, posterior face.

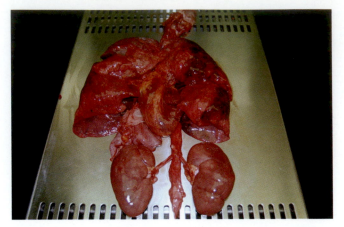

Figure 2.84 Letulle block. Serial removal of the abdominal organs in order to emphasize the tracheal–bronchial tree and the lungs, heart, thoracic–abdominal aorta, renal arteries, and kidneys *in situ*.

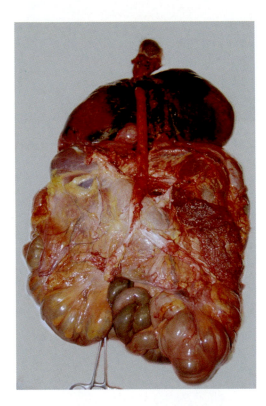

Figure 2.83 Letulle block, posterior face. Block cleaning with emphasis on the aorta in all its extension. The thoracic part, abdominal part, right iliac artery, and left iliac artery.

2.10.1 Removal of the Spleen

If the Virchow technique is to be used, the spleen is removed first. First visualize it by gently moving it to the right side of the stomach's greater curvature, to which it remains connected by the gastrolineal ligament (Figures 2.86 and 2.87).

Insert the left hand into the hypochondrium, passing along the spleen's diaphragmatic surface, until the fingertips can grasp the inferior edge of the spleen

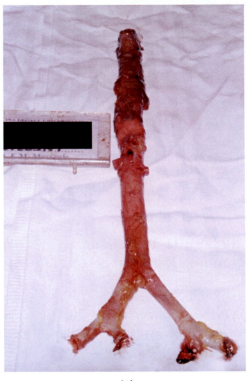

(a)

Figure 2.85 Thoracic–abdominal aorta, right and left iliac arteries, internal and external. Such a removal technique becomes protocol in the suspected or ascertained cases of aorta aneurysm, dissection, vascular operations on the aorta contingent to the autopsy (i.e., in the clinic history of the patient) and in case of injury to the aorta or its main branches. In all these cases the dissector will have to judge the possibility of fixing all the findings in formalin for a following detailed study (for instance, in the cases of aortic dissection of I and III type, according to the DeBakey classification) in order to verify origin and dissection.

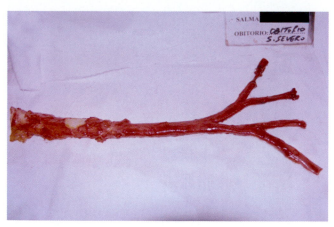

(b)

Figure 2.85 (continued.)

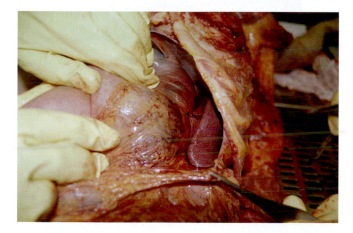

Figure 2.86 The spleen is easily visible between the vascular pole beneath the gastric–lienal ligament.

(Figure 2.88). The spleen is then everted and pulled anteriorly and to the right. This maneuver will expose both components of the spleen's posterior ligament: (1) the superior or phrenic–lienal ligament, and (2) the inferior or pancreatic–lienal ligament (Figures 2.89 and 2.90), which are then incised with a continuous, semicircular incision carried from top to bottom.

Continuing the same incision will incise the veins adjacent to the hilum, as well as the anterior gastric–lienal ligament, that fixes the spleen to the stomach body. Splenic resection must be performed quickly and gently, as the spleen is a fragile and inelastic structure.

2.10.2 Small Intestine Removal

After the spleen has been removed, proceed to the small intestine, but first examine it *in situ*. Overturn the omentum with the transverse colon and its mesocolon

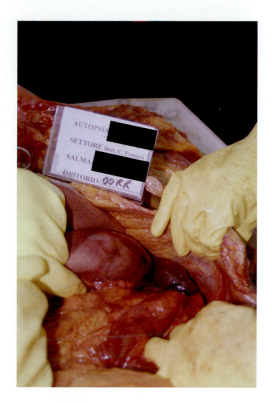

Figure 2.87 Bending of the greater curvature of the stomach.

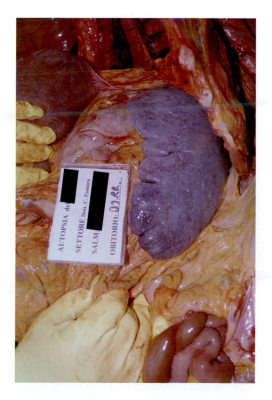

Figure 2.88 Spleen exposition. Bending of the greater curvature of the stomach, diaphragmatic face, and holding plane of the lienal organ in the dissector's left hand.

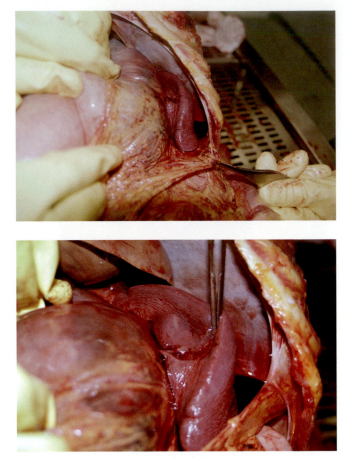

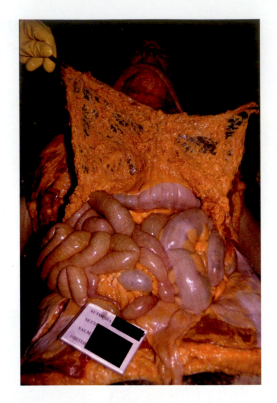

Figure 2.91 Raised caul or apron omentum, which covers the transverse colon and the small intestine.

Figure 2.89 Frenolienal ligament.

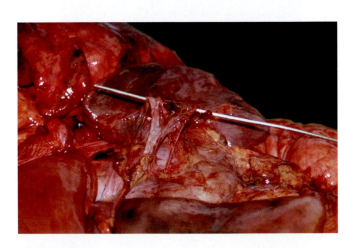

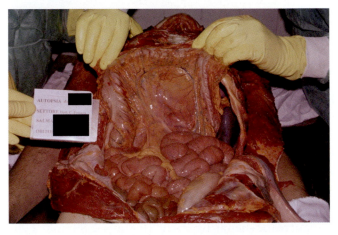

Figure 2.92 Transverse raised colon. The transverse mesocolon, colon right or epatic flexure, colon left or lienal flexure, and small intestine.

2.10.2.1 Complete Removal of the Small Intestine

Even though the small bowel can be removed as a block *in toto* (Figures 2.93 and 2.94), it is preferable to identify the first jejunal loop, where it passes between the duodenum and jejunum (the so-called *duodenal–jejunal flexure*), first. It is important to identify this first loop before attempting to remove the remainder of the intestine. The duodenal–jejunal flexure lies close to left side of the

Figure 2.90 Spleen vascular pole. Close-up of artery and lienal vein.

in order to visualize the mesentery (Figures 2.91 and 2.92). Single loops of the small intestine become visible as they are drawn through the examiner's hand. The small intestine can then be removed *in toto* by resecting the mesentery that fixes it to the posterior abdomen wall (Figure 2.93).

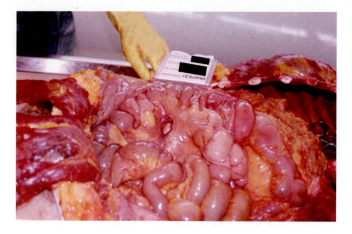

Figure 2.93 Intestinal bulk. Mesentery section edge. The duodenal–jejunal flexure.

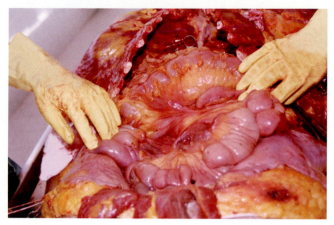

Figure 2.95 Section plane for the intestinal bulk removal passing through the first digiunal loop, high at right under the hand, and for the last loop, low at left close to the cecum.

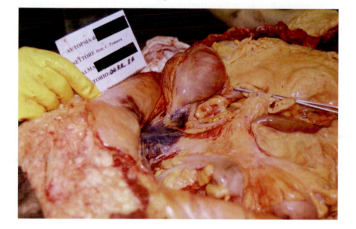

Figure 2.94 Retrocecal recess and ileocecal colon with omentum tapeworm and wormlike appendix in close-up.

2.10.2.2 Isolation of the Small Intestine through Linearization of the Single-Intestinal Loop

If one particular loop is of interest or if intestinal contents are to be collected, a slightly different approach should be used. Once the loop in question has been identified, proceed from a proximal to distal direction until reaching the ileocecal junction and release the loop from its mesentery connection (Figure 2.96). Ideally, the small intestine should be disconnected from the cecum, using the method already described in Section 2.10.2.1. Sometimes it is convenient to use forceps to dissect the wall of the small intestine axially. That will allow evaluation of both the intestinal mucosa and the endoluminal content.

2.10.3 Removal of the Large Intestine

2.10.3.1 Isolation and Removal of the Cecum

To isolate the large intestine, begin at the cecum. This first part of the large intestine is easily immobilized. Simply seize it with the left hand, pulling it forward and upward with some force (Figure 2.97).

2.10.3.2 Isolation and Removal of the Ascending Colon

The ascending colon, unlike the cecum, is a retroperitoneal structure. Free it with an incision made parallel to the posterior wall of the abdomen. Proceed from the bottom to the top and from left to right, so as to detach the colon all the way up the posterior wall, until reaching the right or hepatic flexure, situated in the right hypochondrium (Figure 2.92).

second lumbar vertebra, where the suspensory muscle of the duodenum (Treitz muscle) fixes the passage point between mesenteric and nonmesenteric intestine, anchoring it to the left middle pillar of the diaphragm (Figure 2.95).

Make another keyhole incision in the mesentery and introduce the prongs of two parallel intestinal clamps. They should be applied at a distance of 3 centimeters from each other. With the scalpel held perpendicularly to the intestinal loop, divide the wall and then proceed to the ileocecal junction at the extreme lower insertion of the mesentery, in the right iliopsoas recess. Make another small keyhole incision in the mesentery and introduce the prongs of two parallel intestinal clamps applied approximately 3 centimeters from each other, and divide the intestine with a perpendicular cut (Figure 2.95).

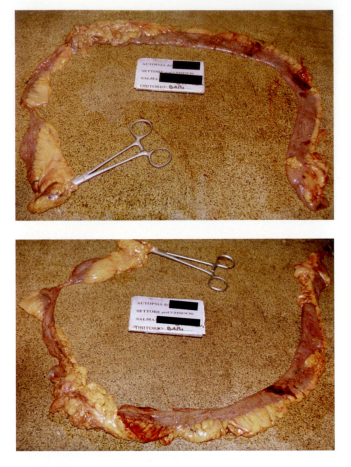

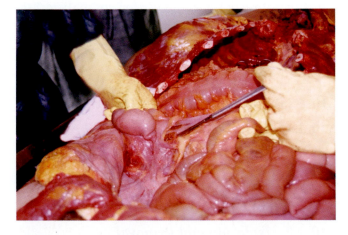

Figure 2.96 Intestinal bulk isolated by linearization of the single masses.

Figure 2.97 Left colon removal. The section line runs from the cecum to the right colon or hepatic flexure.

2.10.3.3   Isolation and Removal of the Colon Right Flexure

The colon right flexure, in addition to being intraperitoneal, is "fixed" to the overlying liver by a strong ligament known as the hepatic–colic ligament. This ligament must be incised. Hold the blade parallel to the superior

edge of the flexure. This will allow resection of the colon and, at the same time, allow for its detachment from the abdomen's posterior wall (Figure 2.92).

2.10.3.4   Isolation and Removal of the Transverse Colon

The transverse colon is interposed between the two flexures, right and left, and provided with a broad transverse mesocolon (the peritoneal process attaching the colon to the posterior abdominal wall, that is referred to either as the ascending or descending mesocolon, according to the portion of colon to which it attaches [Figure 2.92]. The mesocolon is behind the two kidneys, on the descending part of the duodenum, and on the head and body of the pancreas).*

The superior margin of the greater omentum (a large fold of the peritoneum shaped like an apron) is divided in two roots: anterior and posterior. The anterior root fits into the first portion of the duodenum and the greater curvature of the stomach. Using these two landmarks, colic and gastric colic, it is easy to locate the opposite side of the transverse colon. In fact, its posterior root fits into the transverse colon (Figure 2.91).

Using the left hand, pull the colon anteriorly. Make a broad incision from right to left. This will cut the anterior root of the omentum into its two components: the duodenum colic ligament and the gastrocolic ligament. Then, as the incision is carried more posteriorly, the posterior root is divided.

2.10.3.5   Isolation and Removal of the Colon Left Flexure

Once the transverse colon has been isolated, proceed to the colon left flexure or, as it is sometimes called, the *lineal flexure*. This is the point at which the colon becomes, again, a peritoneal organ, lying in the left hypocondrium, immediately below where the spleen was previously located, anchored to the left costal tracts of the diaphragm by a short horizontal ligament, called the *frenocolic ligament*. All of these connections are severed using sharp dissection.

2.10.3.6   Isolation and Removal of the Left, Descending, and Iliac Colon

The removal of the left colon essentially follows the same method as removal on the right (Figures 2.92, 2.95, and 2.97).

---

* The root of the meso of the transverse colon has an insertion on the colon at the posterior–superior taenia called the mesocolon. The colon's superior face delimitates the omental bag.

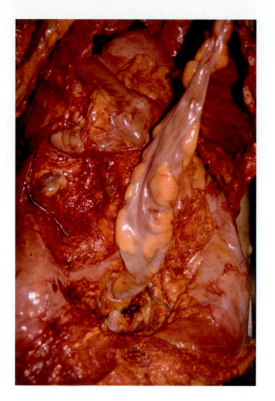

Figure 2.98 Linearization of the left pelvic colon. Top, the lineal flexure, to follow there is the left paracolic groove, then the sigmoid colon, and below the rectum.

2.10.3.7   Isolation and Removal of the Sigmoid Colon

The sigmoid portion of the colon runs a tortuous course from the medial border of the psoas muscle to the superior margin of the third sacral vertebra area, where it continues into the rectum (Figure 2.92). This part of the intestine is covered with peritoneum, actually a fold of peritoneum connecting the upper portion of the rectum, along with the sacrum. To remove the sigmoid, the peritoneum must be divided first, then the sigmoid can be pulled forward (Figure 2.98).

This technique allows for visualization of the pelvic organs and their anatomic relationships. The root of the transverse mesocolon inserts into the colon, close to the posterosuperior taenia coli, and for this reason it is called mesocolic. The superior surface of the mesocolon delimits the omental bag. At its root, it is shaped like an upside-down V, with the right sagittal and median branch lying on the bodies of the lumbar and the first three sacral vertebrae; the left branch of the medial margin of the psoas muscle ascends to converge with it on the right.

2.10.3.8   Isolation and Removal of the Rectum

The inferior half the pelvic rectum is retroperitoneal and is loosely covered with the so-called *rectal band*. Pull the

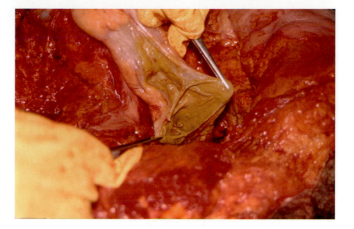

Figure 2.99 Opening of the rectum *in situ*.

rectum forward in such a way that the two pararectal recesses can be visualized. Then incise the peritoneum and the underlying rectosacral ligaments sagittally, from top to the bottom, taking care to isolate and detach the rectum from the sacral wall (Figures 2.98 and 2.99).

If the cadaver is male, locate the rectovesical cavity and pull the bladder forward. Cut the peritoneum of the rectovesical cavity, as well as the underlying connective tissue of the rectosacral ligaments, thereby isolating the rectum from the bladder. If the rectum is incised in the region of the perineum, it is possible to remove all of the large intestine merely by resecting the walls of the rectum above the external sphincter.

If the cadaver is female, first locate the rectouterine space (pouch of Douglas). With the left hand, gently pull the uterus and underlying vagina forward. Make an incision parallel to the rectum, then incise the rectouterine cavity and the underlying connective tissue, including the uterosacral ligaments. Isolate the rectum from the uterus and vagina, then remove the rectum and all of the large intestine by excising the rectum in the perineal plane area (Figures 2.98 and 2.99).

2.10.3.9   Bile Collection

The Virchow technique (removing organs one by one) requires that the liver and the biliary tract be removed together. Before removing the liver, examine the area for evidence of gallbladder inflammation or infection and, if possible, collect a bile sample. Though not absolutely necessary, in cases of poisoning, bile analysis may provide useful information about the timing and type of drug that was ingested. The simplest way to collect bile is to expose the bottom of the gallbladder and then clamp the sac midway. Using a toothed scissors make a sagittal cut across the bottom of the gallbladder. The incision should be just large enough

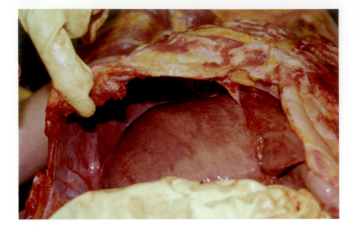

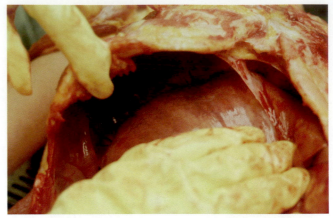

Figure 2.100 Examination of the hepatic fossa by manual traction (left) of the left costal arcade and manual lateral traction view of the liver (right).

Figure 2.101 Manual lateral traction of the liver.

to allow access of a needleless syringe for sample collection.

2.10.4 Isolation and Removal of the Liver

The liver occupies the right hypochondrium and a portion of the epigastrium. It is almost completely covered by the peritoneum and the suspensory ligaments of the liver: the falciform ligament,* the coronary ligament,† and the lesser omentum, which fix the liver in place. The inferior vena cava is also fixed to the liver's dorsal ligament‡ (Figures 2.100 and 2.101).

To remove the liver, move it laterally and medially, up and down, to free it from its suspensory ligaments (Figures 2.100 and 2.101). Then cut each of the ligaments by first placing traction on the ligament to be incised and making an incision inclined at 90° perpendicular to the

ligament and parallel to the hepatic surface curvatures. First incise the right triangular ligament, then the coronary ligament, orientating the scalpel posteriorly and parallel to the inferior surface of the liver. Take great care to preserve the right adrenal gland as it is immediately adjacent. The lesser omentum and the ileocecal folds are then divided with a crescent-shaped incision. The same procedure is followed with the triangular left ligament and the coronary ligaments. Lower one hand below the right dome of the diaphragm and stretch the fingers like a fan, thereby separating the dome itself of the liver from the diaphragm. Finally, separate the remaining ligaments and inferior vena cava, freeing the organ.

2.10.5 Examination of the Stomach, Duodenum, and Pancreas

The stomach is normally opened *in situ* so that the characteristics of the wall and the stomach contents, if any, can be observed. The physical characteristics of any fluid present should be described and the quantity measured. The best way to collect stomach contents is to lift up the greater curvature with toothed forceps in one hand and scissors in the other. Make a keyhole incision roughly 5 centimeters from the pylorus. Then, use the scissors to cut along the greater curvature of stomach, beginning at the pylorus and cutting toward the cardia (Figures 2.102 and 2.103).

A ladle is used to collect the stomach contents, which are then measured. Samples for toxicological testing can then be prepared if necessary. Microscopic examination of the gastric contents is to be encouraged, as microscopic pill fragments, even if not visible to the naked eye, may have important evidentiary value. When the stomach has been emptied, complete the initial incision to obtain an optimum view of the stomach wall. If the decision is made to remove the stomach together with its contents, two ligatures must be applied: one close to

---

* Except for where it lies in contact with the diaphragm, the liver is entirely covered by peritoneum. The peritoneum folds back on itself to form the falciform ligament and the right and left triangular ligaments. These "ligaments" are not true anatomic ligaments, like those found in joints, and they have essentially no functional importance; but they are easily recognizable surface landmarks. The round ligament (in Latin called the *ligamentum teres*) represents the remnant of the fetal umbilical vein and is a degenerative string of tissue located in the free edge of the falciform ligament of the liver.

† The convex diaphragmatic surface of the liver (anterior, superior, and a little posterior) is connected to the concavity of the inferior surface of the diaphragm.

‡ The lesser omentum is extremely thin and is continuous with the two layers of peritoneum that cover, respectively, the antero-superior and posteroinferior surfaces of the stomach and first part of the duodenum. On the left of the posterior the fold is attached to the bottom of the fossa for the ductus venosus, then continues on to the diaphragm, where the two layers separate to embrace the end of the esophagus. At the right border of the lesser omentum the two layers are continuous and form a free margin that constitutes the anterior boundary of the epiploic foramen. Enlarged lymph nodes are often found in this area and are usually a sign of chronic intravenous drug abuse.

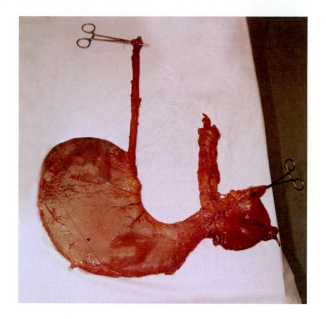

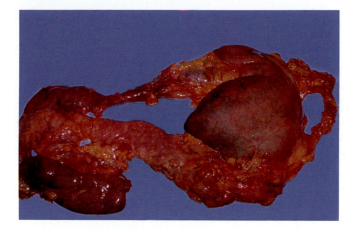

Figure 2.104 Stomach–duodenum–pancreas block. The head, body, and end.

Figure 2.102 Esophagus, stomach, and duodenum resected. The great curvature, esophagus, little curvature, duodenum, and first loop.

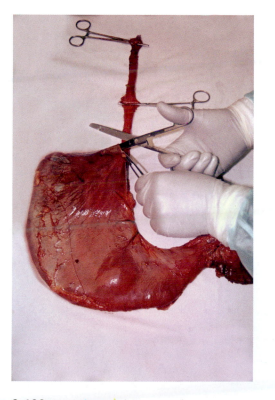

Figure 2.103 Opening of the stomach.

the cardia, the other close to the pylorus, after which the stomach is incised (Figure 2.102).

The duodenum is also normally opened *in situ* along with the stomach, so that the walls and the papilla of Vater can be inspected. The best way to do this is to make the incision with scissors, cutting along the anterior wall of the duodenum, extending from the pylorus to the ligament of Treitz (Figure 2.102).

Because of the close anatomic and functional links between the duodenum and pancreas, it is best to remove these organs *en bloc*, together with the esophagus and stomach. To remove the esophagus–stomach–duodenum–pancreas block, first slide the esophagus (previously transacted close to the pharynx–esophageal opening) through the hiatus of the diaphragm (medial pillar of the diaphragmatic muscle), by resecting its connections, then moving the block to a subdiaphragmatic location (Figure 2.104).*

The stomach is then isolated and removed, except for the connection with the duodenum, close to the pylorus. The duodenum, which is the initial part of the small intestine, located between the stomach and jejunum, is a retroperitoneal structure. The C-shaped duodenum contains the head of the pancreas, which secretes into the duodenal lumen as does the liver; the ducts of these two glands, whether isolated at the origin or fused at their insertion, drain into the superior portion of the papilla of Vater. This structure is easily recognizable in the descending duodenum segment (Figure 2.102).†

The pancreas stretches transversally in the retroperitoneal space and it is attached to the abdomen's posterior wall, at approximately the same height of the L1–L2 vertebral bodies.

---

* The stomach is kept *in situ* from the peritoneum. It presents ligaments in certain points: anteriorly, the lesser omentum with its components (hepatic–gastric ligament and hepatic–duodenal ligament); posteriorly, the reflection folds on the diaphragm holding the gastric–phrenic ligament and, inferiorly, the gastric lienal and the gastric–colic ligaments.
† The peritoneum covers the duodenum only on its anterior surface; it is fixed to the hepatic ileum by the hepatic duodenal ligament containing the lesser omentum, which receives in its interior bile duct, portal vein, and hepatic artery (from right to left). Inferiorly, it is attached to the medial left pillar of the diaphragm by the ligament of Treitz at some point near the duodenal–jejunal junction.

The head of the pancreas is the largest part of that organ that becomes progressively thinner in its midportion (body) and thinner still in the tail located on the left (Figure 2.104).[*] After removing the liver along with the right side of the lesser omentum, including the hepatic–duodenal ligament, incise the parietal peritoneum along the C-shaped duodenal convexity, then completely remove the tissue block.

Starting at the pylorus, detach the duodenum and pancreas from the structures behind them, following the cleavage plane of the retropancreatic sphincter of Oddi (this structure is also called the hepatopancreatic sphincter or Glisson's sphincter). The sphincter of Oddi controls the flow of secretions passing from the liver, pancreas, and gallbladder into the duodenum of the small intestine. It is actually composed of muscle located at the surface of the duodenum. It is located slightly distal to the point where the common bile duct and pancreatic duct join as they enter the descending duodenum to form the ampulla of Vater. The opening is on the inside of the descending duodenum, the sphincter of Oddi, is a muscular valve that controls the flow of digestive juices (bile and pancreatic juice) through the ampulla of Vater into the second part of the duodenum.

2.10.6 Removal of Kidneys and Suprarenal Glands

The kidneys are symmetric in appearance and retroperitonal in position. They are located at roughly the height of the eleventh and twelfth vertebra.[†] To remove the kidney, first locate it by palpation. Once it is identified, wrap your hand around it and pull it medially and upward.

2.10.6.1 Access to the Renal Cavity and Excision In Situ

To gain access to the kidney cavity, make an incision in the parietal peritoneum and the underlying kidney fascia, hold the scalpel sagittally to the organ, and make an incision from the top to the bottom. The edges of the incision can then be widened by inserting the fingers of the left hand to reveal the top part of the suprarenal gland. The suprarenal gland is extremely delicate and must be removed very carefully.

2.10.6.2 Excision of the Renal Cavity and Ureter In Situ

Alternatively, the parietal peritoneum can be detached from the posterior structures of the renal cavity using a pointed scalpel. The scalpel is moved from superior to inferior to resect the hilar structures. Then, taking great care not to damage the urethra, follow it and separate it from the underlying structure continuing on up to the pelvic recess behind the posterior wall of the bladder, and then resect it (Figure 2.105). Once the kidney has been removed, peal off the renal fascia and capsule by first making a sagittal incision. In the absence of chronic renal disease, the capsule will strip easily. In the presence of chronic disease the surface will appear granular.

2.10.6.3 Inspection and Resection of the Ureters

If the links to the ureters are kept attached during the process of kidney removal, their endoluminal surfaces can be examined. Using scissors with rounded blades, create a keyhole incision, insert the scissors, and then open the ureter from top to bottom to reveal the ureteral mucosa.

[*] The anterior surface of the head of the pancreas is covered by omentum. At its inferior margin the mesocolon crosses its root. Posteriorly, it is linked to the bile duct, the portal vein, the inferior cava vein, and to the right kidney vein with the interposition of Told's retropancreatic band. The head and body of the pancreas are covered anteriorly by the peritoneum of the omentum sac, and it is linked to the stomach and to the lesser omentum. The posterior surface is located at the L1 level, and it is covered with a ligament linking the lower mesenteric vein and the aorta, as well as the celiac and superior mesenteric vessels, the left medial pillar of the diaphragm, the renal vein, the left kidney, and the suprarenal gland.

[†] The right kidney is generally 3 centimeters lower than the left kidney because of the overhanging liver. Each kidney, together with its suprarenal gland, is contained in a separate cavity called the renal cavity. The cavity is created by the splitting of the renal band and the thickening of the peritoneal subserosa into two layers: the anterior (prerenal) and the posterior (postrenal). Inside such a cavity, a wall of connective tissue divides the kidney from the overlying suprarenal gland. Between the two layers of the renal band and the kidney capsule can be found some more adipose connective tissue located adjacent to the kidney.

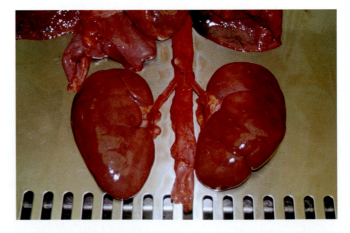

Figure 2.105 Particular of the kidneys and their vascular connections. The ideal resection plan is outlined. In red, opening of the capsule and kidney removal; in blue, removal of the capsule and of the ureter; close-up, the renal arteries.

2.10.7 Examination and Removal of the Bladder

2.10.7.1 Drawing Urine

Unless the presence of a tumor is suspected, the main reason to examine the bladder is to obtain a urine specimen. Use a toothed forceps and scalpel to detach the soft structures of the prevesical space, then grasp the bladder with a forceps, and cut a keyhole incision sufficiently large as to allow access with a needleless syringe and withdraw a urine specimen. Unfortunately, urine is present in the bladder only about one-third of the time, though it may still be possible to collect a sample for the kidney calyx.

2.10.7.2 Bladder Removal

If the bladder is to be removed it is important to remember that it is a retroperitoneal organ. It is located in the front part of the pelvic fundus, behind the pubis, where it is attached by the pubic–vesical ligaments. In males the bladder is located in front of the rectum. In females this ligament is located in front of the uterus and vagina.[*]

To remove the bladder, grasp it with a toothed forceps and pull it superiorly and posteriorly while incising the peritoneum. Begin first at the bladder's posterior concavity and the peritoneum where it extends from the anterior abdomen wall to cover the superior and lateral face of the bladder, then incise the middle and lateral umbilical ligaments. Holding the blade turned parallel to the bladder surface, enter the prevesical space of Retzius (the extraperiteneal space between the pubic symphysis and urinary bladder) and incise the two pubic–vesical ligaments, which constitute the floor of this space. Stop the incision once the trigone is reached, as the trigone should be preserved intact. Finally, make bilateral incisions in the paravesical space, with the incision running parallel to the Levator ani, onward to the trigon. Resection of the peritoneum depends on the sex of the cadaver.

In males the peritoneum reflects itself from the bladder to the rectum located behind it in the area known as the vesical–rectal cavity. This cavity is surrounded on both sides by the two vesical–rectal folds, and by the homonymous ligaments that must also be divided (if this has not already been done), together with the terminal portion of the ureters. The vesical fascia lies beneath the ureter and must be detached from the rectum posteriorly (Figure 2.106 through Figure 2.108).

In women the peritoneum reflects onto the uterus behind the vesical–uterine area. It should be detached from the wall of the bladder and from the attached vagina with an incision along the vesical–vaginal region.

2.10.8 Removal of the Uterus and Adnexae

The uterus is midline and partly retroperitoneal. It is located behind the bladder and in front of the rectum. The pelvic peritoneum only partially covers the uterus, so that while most of the uterus is preperitoneal (body and posterior face of the supravaginal part of the cervix), the remaining part lies deep in the connective tissue of the subperitoneal pelvic space.[†]

Remove the uterus and adnexae with toothed forceps while placing tension on the peritoneum that covers the pelvic organs, pulling the peritoneum toward the

---

[*] The bladder is normally held firmly in place by its ties with the urethra and the ureters, by the adherence to the underlying tissues in males, and to the vagina in females. The peritoneum that covers its superoposterior and lateral faces of the bladder also fixes it in place. Specifically, the peritoneum extends from the bladder to the abdominal wall anteriorly and it is elevated by the umbilical medium (uraco obliteratus) and lateral (umbilical artery obliterata) to the right and to the left, respectively. The bladder has three ligaments: the middle and two lateral umbilical folds. When the bladder is full, the peritoneum descends along the anterior wall of the bladder before continuing on to the abdominal wall. The peritoneum in males reflects itself onto the rectum behind, creating the vesical–lateral cavity, surrounded on both sides by the two vesical–rectal folds, composed by the homonymous ligaments. In women, the peritoneum is reflected onto the uterus behind, creating the vesical–uterine cavity. The tela subserosa (sometimes just referred to as the subserosa, a layer of tissue between the muscularis and serosa) lies just under the peritoneum. It forms the so-called vesical fascia. In males, this fascia merges with the rectal band making the rectovesical band (fascia) posterior and deep. In women, this fascia adheres to the connective tissue that surrounds the vagina, creating the vesicovaginal fascia. The bladder also has a so-called prevesical fascia, located anteriorly, where it is partially joined to the vesical fascia.

[†] Anteriorly the peritoneum sinks between the bladder and uterus creating the vesical–uterine cavity. The cavity formed by the peritoneum is even more evident where it is surrounded by the two rectouterine folds. The peritoneum then is reflected from the posterior surface of the uterus and the rectum behind it, which form the rectouterine cavity or pouch of Douglas. The peritoneum covers the whole uterus and then stretches out bilaterally to form a large fold that extends to the wall of the pelvic cavity, at which point it spreads out as the parietal peritoneum; these are two large ligaments. Each ligament adapts to the formations that install themselves close to the tubaric corner of the uterus, that is, the uterus–ovarian ligament, or proper ovarian ligament, to which it supplies a meso and round ligament. At a deeper level, the subperitoneal portion of the uterus is surrounded by connective tissue, the so-called parametrium, which contains substantial amounts of fibrous tissue. Uterine suspensor ligaments link to nearby organs and to the pelvic walls. The transverse and lateral uterine ligaments, or cardinal ligaments of Mackenroth, are joined to the pubic sacral ligaments near the uterine cervix in midline and laterally (these ligaments go from front to back and are inserted in the pelvic wall). The back or uterine rectal ligaments are inserted in the two homonymous folds, and linked to the rectum and to the sacral bone behind it; the anterior or vesical–uterine ligaments attach to the bladder and to the pubis anteriorly.

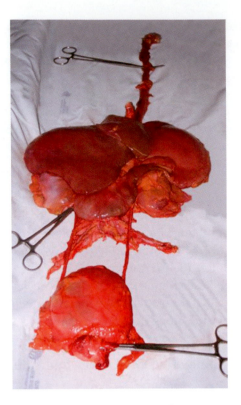

Figure 2.106 Abdominal viscera and urinary system, removed *en bloc*.

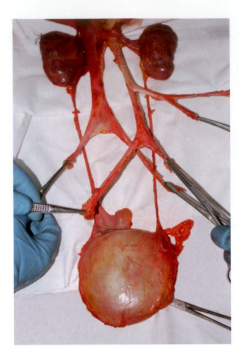

Figure 2.108 Urinary apparatus. Removal of the kidney–urether–bladder is performed by sparing the aorta and inferior vena cava.

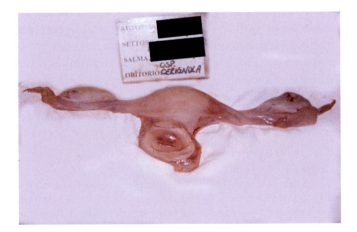

Figure 2.109 Uterus and annexes removed *en bloc*. Tubes, ovaries, and the uterus dissected to the uterine cervix are shown clearly.

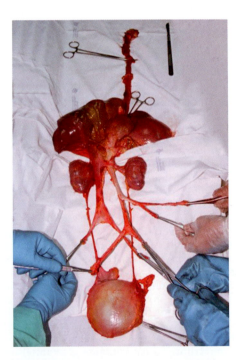

Figure 2.107 Anatomic study of the main abdominal arteries and veins. The hepatic portal vein is shown.

midline, just medial to the hilar veins. Dissect along the anatomic borders of the organ (Figure 2.109), then incise the peritoneum forming the broad ligament (the wide fold of peritoneum that connects the sides of the uterus to the walls and floor of the pelvis), cutting from back to front. Finally incise the infundibular ligament and round ligaments.

Then make a second, deeper incision, and divide the transverse cervical ligament (ligament of Mackenroth), thereby isolating the uterus from its lateral suspensory structures. Once the round ligament has been divided, continue on and divide the peritoneum of the vesical–uterine cavity located in front of the uterus and behind the bladder. At deeper levels, use sharp dissection to detach the bladder wall from the contiguous vagina,

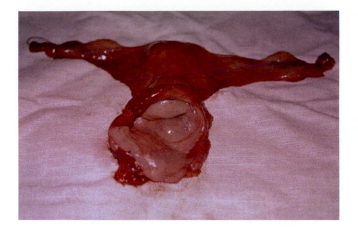

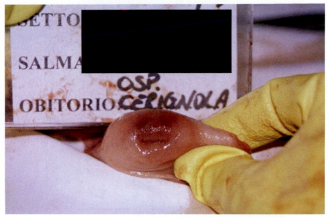

Figure 2.110 Close-up of trait of the vaginal canal, part of the vault of the vagina, and external vagina.

Figure 2.112 Examination of the uterus external orifice.

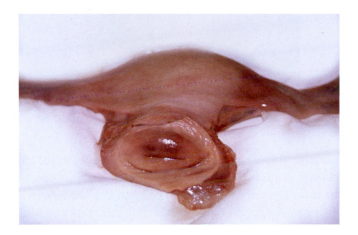

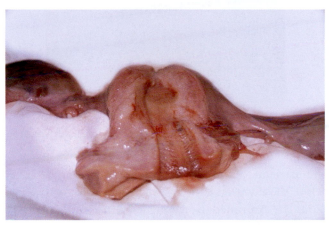

Figure 2.111 Uterus. Side view of the cervix.

Figure 2.113 Opening of the cervix and the uterus body. The cervical duct (CD) and the palmed folds are clearly shown.

cutting along the vesical–uterine septum. After separating the uterus from the nearby structures, both in front of it and on its side, it is necessary to detach it from behind the rectum.

Pull the peritoneum back using toothed forceps while cutting the peritoneum close to the uterine–rectal fold and the pouch of Douglas. Once the pouch of Douglas has been excised, use forceps to grip the rectum and move the blade forward to excise the back wall of the vagina, and then the vaginal vault, moving from the back to the front and from top to bottom. This will allow for the extraction of the uterus together with the vaginal vault (Figure 2.109 through Figure 2.114).

2.10.9 Examination and Removal of the Large Arterial–Venous Retroperitoneal Pelvic Veins

A complete autopsy examination of the abdominal-pelvic region cannot be performed without the examination of the large retroperitoneal vessels, such as:

Figure 2.114 Wide opening of the uterus (piece subjected to formolic hardening).

the abdominal aorta, with its two branches, the left and right iliac arteries; and,

the inferior vena cava with the two vessels that form it, the right and left iliac veins.

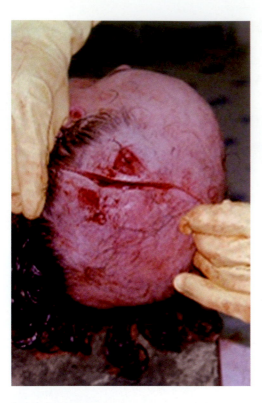

Figure 2.115 Bimastoideum resection, left side. Positioning of head on metal support.

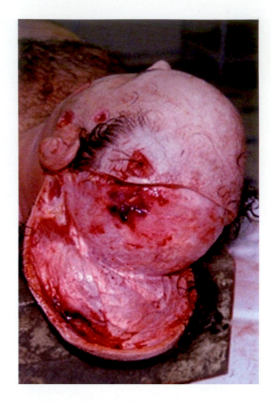

Figure 2.116 Detaching of back half of the scalp to the occiput.

The parietal peritoneum must be cut and detached before these vessels can be seen. The whole aortic trunk should be examined (i.e., along its entire length from the arch to the abdominal and thoracic aorta) and finally both internal and external iliac arteries can be removed (Figure 2.85).*

2.11 Dissection of the Head

2.11.1 Preparation of the Dissection Field

The head must be slightly raised with appropriate supports. There is no one correct device; each autopsy surgeon prefers his or her own method (Figure 2.115 through Figure 2.125). The hair is divided with a comb along an imaginary coronal plane that runs across the cranial convexity connecting the two mastoids. A No. 22 blade on a long scalpel holder should be used

---

* The aorta is the body's main arterial vessel. It emerges from the heart's left ventricle and, as the ascending aorta first heads superiorly, forward, and slightly to the right. It then turns toward posteriorly and to the left, passing over the left bronchus. It then descends as the thoracic aorta within the posterior mediastinum. It crosses the aortic diaphragmatic tract, then descends as the abdominal aorta, at which point it is a retroperitoneal structure. Finally, at the level of the IV lumbar vertebra, it splits in the two common iliac arteries and terminates in the thin sacral median artery.

to incise the whole scalp from the outside. Before the incision is made, a generous sample of hair should be cut from the vertex and preserved, should toxicological testing prove necessary at a later date (an empty red-top tube or even a glassine envelope can serve as a container). Once deposited in hair, drugs do not degrade, and can be detected and even quantified years or decades later.

2.11.2 The Bimastoid Resection

Begin the incision on the right side of the head, as low as possible just behind the earlobe, but without going below it. Then extend the incision to the same point at the opposite side of the head. This is the so-called *bimastoid resection*. When the incision is made in this fashion, it facilitates overturning the scalp. A big enough strip of tissue behind the auricle must be saved to allow for suturing the scalp back in place (Figure 2.115 through Figure 2.118). After enough of the scalp has been incised to allow the prosector to grasp the two edges with the hands, the front and back halves of the scalp are overturned, anteriorly and posteriorly, respectively (Figures 2.117 and 2.118).

Using a strip of cloth placed on the free edges of the scalp simplifies the procedure. If considerable resistance is encountered, slide the scalpel along the edge being retracted, with the blade inclined at 15° to the edge. With

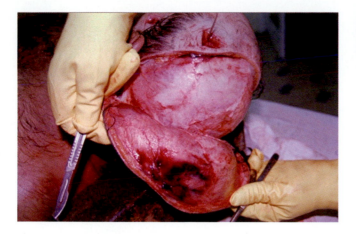

Figure 2.117 Scalp and galea capitis inspection (hemorrhagic area in the front parietal side of the scalp, not reflecting on the galea capitis.

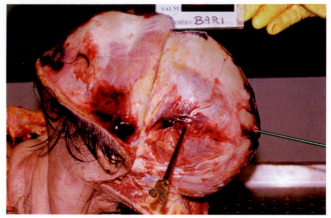

Figure 2.119 Inspection of temporal muscles and resection plan.

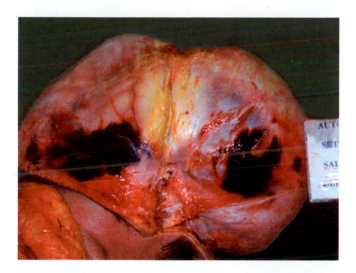

Figure 2.118 Front and back scalp overturning. Clearly shown is the root of the bimastoideum resection, slightly below the external acoustic meatus, 1 to 2 centimeters behind the auricle.

the other hand, continue to stretch the scalp. The scalpel blade must be pointed toward the bony outer table of the skull, not toward the scalp (Figure 2.117).

The front strip of scalp must be turned back 1 to 2 centimeters above the supraorbital edge, while the back strip should be pulled just slightly over the occipital swelling. The only exception would be if the examiner thought there was a need to visualize the orbital cavities (Figure 2.118 through Figure 2.120).

2.11.3 Inspection and Resection of the Temporal Muscles

After overturning the scalp strips, while the top of the skull is still intact, examine and describe the scalp thoroughly before it is dissected. Hemorrhagic infiltrations or gunshot

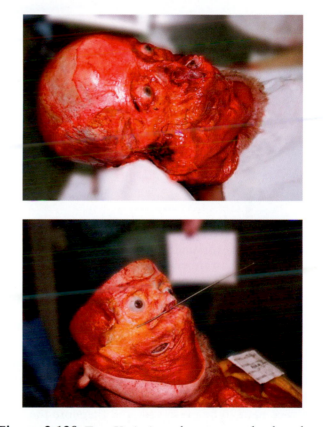

Figure 2.120 Top: Variation of access to the face from an extended bimastoid resection. Bottom: Access to the skull and face in a case of suspected rhinoplasty surgery malpractice.

fragments should be removed and submitted for microscopic examination, and evidence of bruising noted.

2.11.4 Removal of the Skullcap

The skull is generally opened using an electrical saw, usually referred to as a Stryker saw after the name of the most common brand (Figure 2.123). Alternative

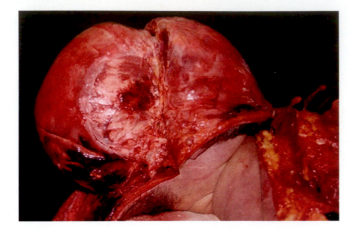

Figure 2.121 Insertion of temporal muscle (outlined).

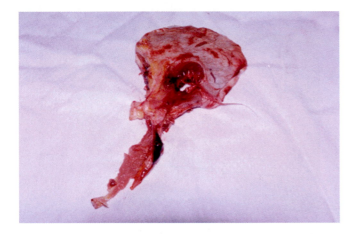

Figure 2.123 Electric portable swinging saw sample.

Figure 2.122 Dissected temporal muscle. Continuous solution of a roughly round shape (entrance hole of a bullet fired with a shotgun armed with single ammunition).

methods to this extremely common practice can be used when a particular surgical intervention on the skull is required. A less bloody and more conservative approach (such as sawing by metallic wire or hacksaw) may be more appropriate. For example, in cases of massive head trauma and occasionally when examining skeleton remains, findings of historic archaeological relevance need to be preserved, and therefore the least destructive approach is preferred (Figure 2.126 through Figure 2.128). The bony dust dispersion produced by the use of the Stryker saw constitutes a health hazard, so the procedure must be carried out with appropriate means of protection. Collecting the dust inside a plastic protective bag or, alternatively, by wearing protective suits should minimize dispersion of potentially infectious bone dust. Whatever the method, the Stryker saw should always be equipped with a vacuum aspirator.

The shape of the cut through the skull should be designed so that it reduces the slipping of the cranial vault during the reconstruction of the head. Ideally, the cut through the outer table of the skull should not go

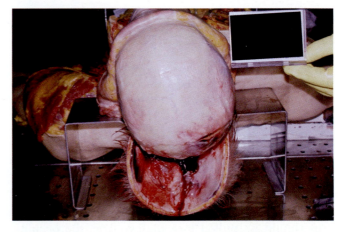

Figure 2.124 Posterior view of a bare skullcap with the ideal resection line and the orientation of the swinging saw. Note the primary plunging zone where the resection has to start.

beyond the internal face of the skull, since the latter can be easily removed with a scalpel. The goal is to leave the dura mater and the underlying arachnoid untouched, thus allowing the visualization of the brain and the surrounding cerebrospinal fluid (Figure 2.128 through Figure 2.130).

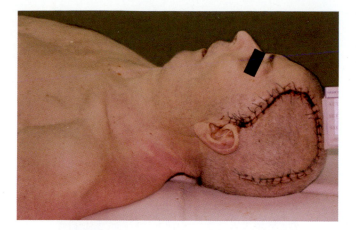

Figure 2.125 Surgical suture of scalp, following the neurosurgical operation.

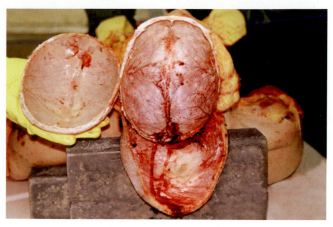

Figure 2.128 Conservative incision of the skullcap with preservation of the dural cover, which appears intact.

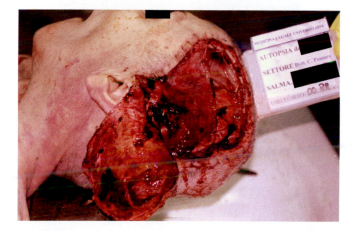

Figure 2.126 Access to the skullcap through detaching of surgical sutures. The cranial breach and the dura with bent edges by suture are clearly shown.

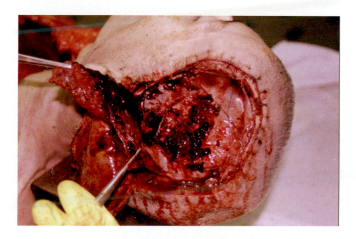

Figure 2.127 Dura mater removal and visualization of the encephalon portion seat of the operation in the depleting of subdural acute hematoma.

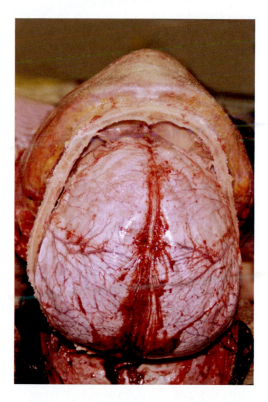

Figure 2.129 Left access to the dura. Top, close to the left frontal lobe, detaching of the dura mater made with a scalpel. It is imperative in this phase to describe the macroscopic characteristics of the dura carefully, in particular with reference to its translucency, to the blood injection of dural veins. It is also important to palpate the part to evaluate its consistency.

After the cranial vault has been removed, the dura must be incised along the resection line of the saw and then everted. To protect the brain, the forefinger of the hand holding the saw has to measure the penetration level of the blade. The Stryker blade must be moved from one side to the other to avoid excessive penetration. Many saws are equipped with a safety system that features a mechanical depth mechanic block designed to prevent excessive penetration (Figure 2.123).

Actual removal of the brain begins in the thinner parietal region. This allows for better assessment of the

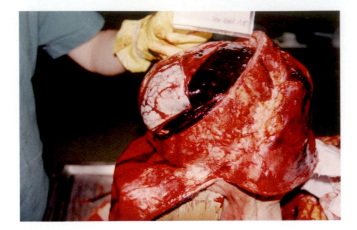

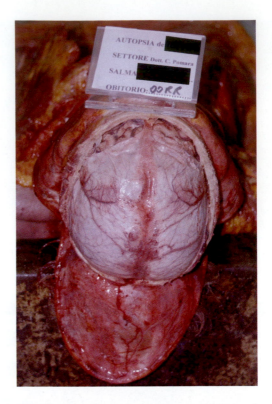

Figure 2.130 Subdural acute hematoma, starting from the left side, and dura still *in situ* and raised as a strip. The correct application of this technique will allow the dissector to obtain the correct documentation of the hematoma expansion seat, the measuring he will make *in situ* (extension in centimeters), the taking *in toto,* and its weight (in grams), as well as the taking of samples for possible immunohistochemical surveys, which, together with all the other surveys, will allow a timing of the event.

resection depth and visibility of the curving line that links the superorbitary, biparietal, and occipital structures (Figure 2.124). The incision must begin approximately 2 fingers' width above the supraorbital lobes. The goal should be to preserve as much of the dura mater as possible. When the dura is left intact, the cranial vault can be easily removed. Once the dura has been opened, the fingers can easily enter inside the cranium, making it possible to pull the skullcap off with minimal trauma to the skull (Figure 2.128).

With a scalpel, incise the dura along the line produced by the Stryker saw and the anterior connection of the falx cerebri to the skull, where the dura passes between the frontal lobes (Figure 2.129 through Figure 2.131). The posterior portion of the falx can be incised from the inside skull once the cranial vault has been overturned, and the dura removed from the vault. The inferior sagittal sinus can be then be opened with forceps. Remaining dural strips on either side can be easily removed from the brain using the bridge veins for traction (Figure 2.131 through Figure 2.136).

2.12   Removal of the Brain

2.12.1   Examination *In Situ* of the Lateral Ventricles

Before removing the brain, an *in situ* assessment of the lateral ventricles should be performed. Gently divide the cerebral hemispheres by placing the fingers on the cingulate gyrus (Figure 2.137a). Then, with the scalpel

Figure 2.131 Symmetric incision and bilateral of the dura in the frontal lobes area. This first cut emphasizes the dural sinus, median, that will be macroscopically described *in situ.*

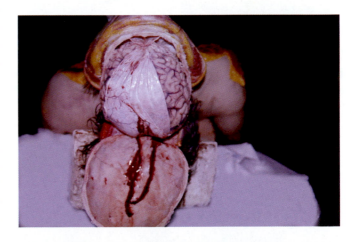

Figure 2.132 Incision and detaching "as a book," along the parietal–occipital line at right and the parietal at the left.

blade inclined at about 45° to the cingulated gyrus, make a semicircular incision in the inferior concavity, with the blade inserted to a depth of about 0.8 centimeters. The incision will expose the lateral ventricles; describe their appearance and take samples if necessary (Figure 2.137).

2.12.2   Brain Cutting

After examining the ventricles, gently lift the frontal lobes (Figure 2.138), and the mammillary bodies along

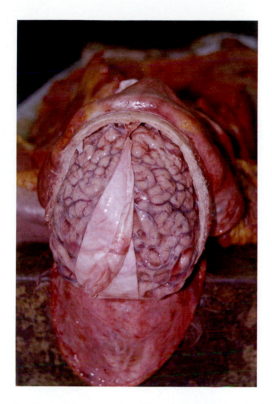

Figure 2.133 Incision and median overturning of the dura mater and front parietal–occipital resection at the right.

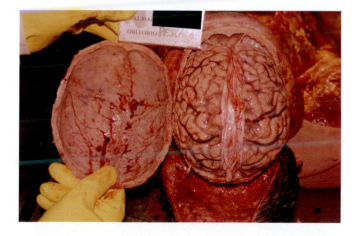

Figure 2.134 Dura mater resected and overturned still *in situ*. The abscised skullcap portion must always be documented by photos to prove by autoptic documents the substantial anatomic integrity (granted the integration of eidologic datum if necessary).

with the optic tract lying on the cribriform plate. The optic nerves are stretched and easily visible when the frontal lobes are retracted. Divide them, preferably at their entrance in the optic foramina (Figure 2.139a). The brain will then fall, under its own weight, from the anterior recess of the brainpan into the prosector's hands. The hands should be placed as closely as possible to the brain as it falls forward (Figure 2.138).

The pituitary stalk is then transected, followed by the internal carotid arteries at their entrance in the cranial

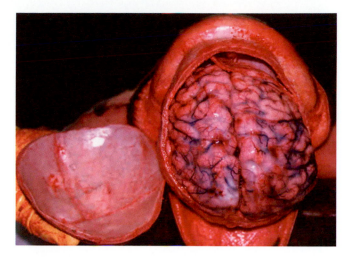

Figure 2.135 Encephalon exhibition with the dura mater incised and resected.

Figure 2.136 Incised dura mater. Inspection of the dura.

cavity. Cranial nerves II, IV, V, and VI must be cut as near as possible to the base of the skull (Figure 2.139a). Then the attachment of the falx tentorium to the petrosal bone is divided bilaterally (Figure 2.139b). The falx must be cut with the scalpel blade held parallel and close to the bony edge of the greater wings of the sphenoid. At this stage be very careful not to allow stretching of the cerebral peduncles. Removal of the brain is facilitated with the neck in hyperflexion, so rest the head on a firm, elevated support.

Cranial nerves VII, VIII, IX, XI, and XII are the next structures to be divided, but prior to their isolation describe their position and course *in situ*. The vertebral arteries are described and divided in the same fashion (Figure 2.139b). Last, the cervical portion of the spinal cord is transacted. It is easier to insert the scalpel blade if the brainstem is slightly stretched (Figure 2.139c). If a critical lesion is identified, a section should be taken, then cut transversely across the area.

The cerebral peduncles are exposed by gentle force, pushing the brain backward with the hands. They

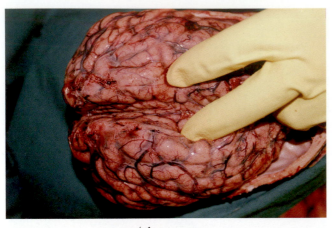

(a)

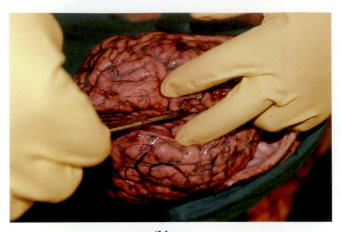

(b)

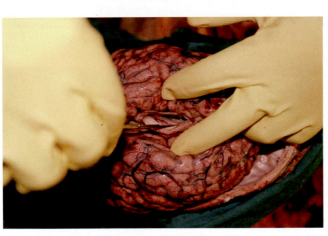

(c)

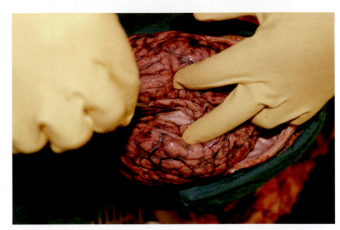

(d)

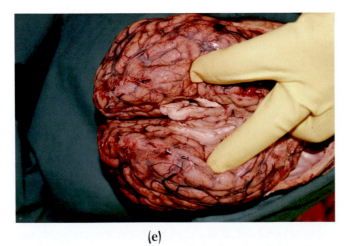

(e)

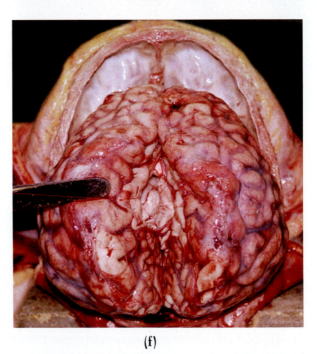

(f)

Figure 2.137 (a) Divaricating of telencephalic hemispheres in the girus cingoli area. (b) Incision and semicircular resection of lateral ventricles. (c) Opening of left lateral ventricle. (d) Opening of left lateral ventricle. (e and f) Lateral ventricles opened and shown. After exposing the ventricular cavities, they will be described in detail and a photograph will be taken, to support the description record.

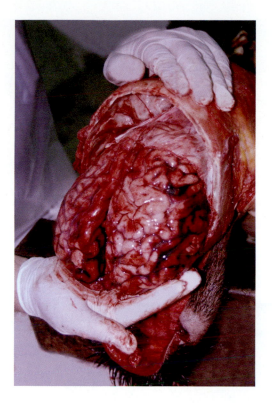

Figure 2.138 Extraction of encephalon. Frontal lobes raised and encephalon received in the forensic surgeon's left palm.

are then extracted from the cranial vault, along with the brainstem. Care should be taken to avoid excessive stretching of the upper portions of the cervical cord. The lateral portions of the tentorium are incised close to the petrosal bone freeing the brain, which can then be lifted out. A detailed examination of the cranial skull-cap, of the cranial cavities, and a proper photographic record follows (Figures 2.140 and 2.141).

2.13 Vertebral Resection and Cord Removal

The spinal cord can be removed relatively quickly and easily using a Stryker saw (removal should add no more than 15 to 20 minutes to the process), and should always be performed, unless there is insufficient time.

2.13.1 Posterior Approach

There are many different approaches and entrances to the dorsal spine, though these are seldom used unless there is trauma, especially from a gunshot wound or prior surgery (Figure 2.142 through Figure 2.145).

In fact, though seldom performed, the entire autopsy can be accomplished using a posterior approach to access

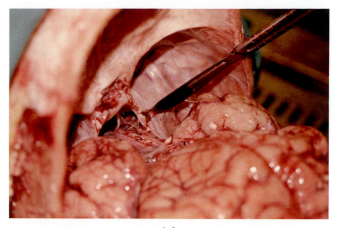

(a)

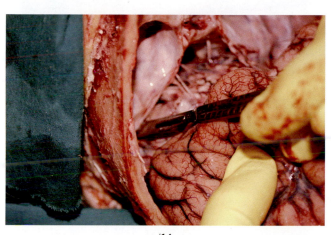

(b)

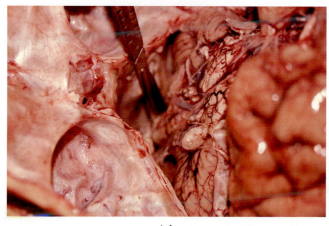

(c)

Figure 2.139 (a) Cut of optical nerves and hypophysis peduncle. In the figure, the scalpel point hits the tentorium base on the petrosal bone. (b) Resection of the tentorium of the petrosal bone and access to the posterior cranial cavity. Note how the scalpel proceeds with the blade oriented near the bony edge of the petrosal bone along the great wings of the sphenoid. (c) Dissection of stretched portion of the intraforaminal marrow. Note the orientation of the scalpel blade, orthogonal to the marrow plane.

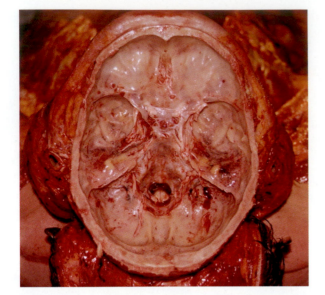

Figure 2.140 View of the anterior, medial, and posterior cranial cavities, and resected encephalon.

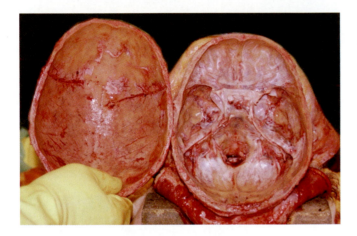

Figure 2.141 Examination of the skullcap and cranial cavity, and photographic record.

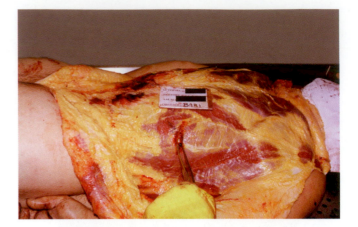

Figure 2.142 Posterior access by bisacromial resection.

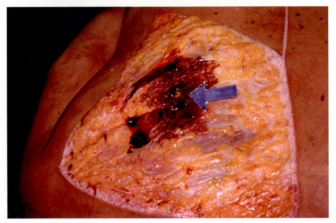

Figure 2.143 Posterior partial access: Right scapular region. Note the subcutaneous retention of spitted ammunition.

2.13.2 Anterior Approach

The anterior approach is the fastest and simplest way to remove the cord because the cadaver does not have to be turned. The peripheral nerves can be followed after removal of the cord. Detailed examination of the vertebral bodies is also possible. Removal of only a part of the cord is another option with this approach, but it is generally better to take the entire cord. The lumbar–sacral muscles are easily removed from the spine by the saw. Depending on the technique used (Letulle, for instance), the cord can often be removed whole, free from any muscular connections.

Freeing the cauda equina from the sacral bone requires some time, as it is difficult to use the saw inside the pelvic cavity. In rare cases it will be necessary to remove a bone wedge near the midline and then remove the remaining side of the sacrum with a rongeur. This

the thoracic and abdominal cavities using a semicircular bisacromial incision or a median perpendicular/sagittal incision (Figure 2.142 and Figure 2.146). The latter allows for the inspection and isolation of the arches of the posterior neck muscles, paravertebral muscles, ligaments, vertebrae (spinal and transverse processes as well as vertebral bodies), and vertebral arteries (Figure 2.142 and Figure 2.146).

Once the spinal cord has been exposed, make an incision with a scalpel blade inclined at 30° to either vertebral body. This method provides easy exposure of the superior part of the cervical trunk, permits direct visualization of the cranial–cervical joint, and, of course, allows for complete resection and isolation of the cord (Figure 2.147). This is the preferred method in cases when death occurs as a consequence of surgery.

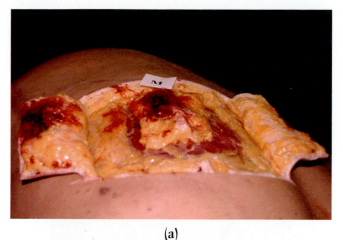

(a)

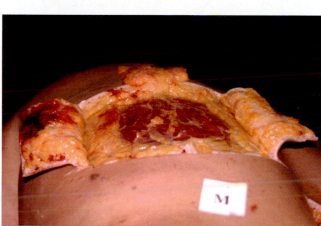

(b)

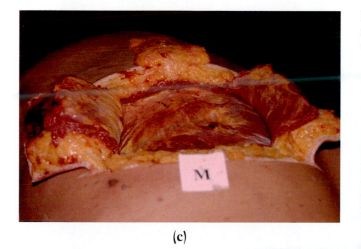

(c)

Figure 2.144 Posterior partial access: (a) thoracic rachis, (b) subcutaneous plane, and (c) superficial muscular plane. The hole left by a single round of ammunition is clearly shown.

is the best way to avoid damaging nerve roots as they traverse the vertebral foramen. The causa equina is covered by the dura mater, and it should be lifted out of the spinal canal with as many spinal ganglions as possible (Figures 2.147 and 2.148).

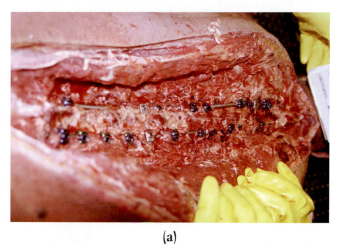

(a)

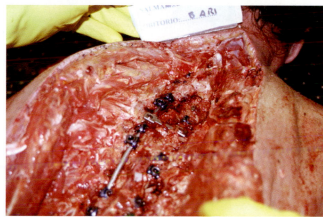

(b)

Figure 2.145 Rachis exposition by posterior access, as per median resection. (a) The rachis–thoracic–lumbar axis. (b) Close-up of rachis–cervical axis (spinal surgery).

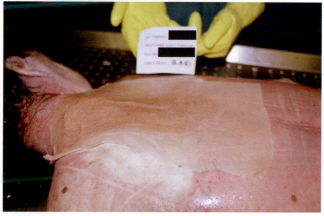

Figure 2.146 Pronation position. Note the bisacromial plane and median.

2.14 Arm Dissection

The arms at autopsy must first be x-rayed. Once the x-rays have been performed, make a bisacromial incision along

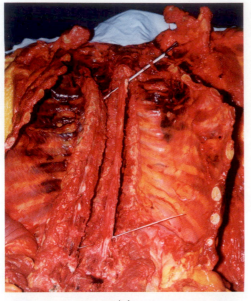

(a)

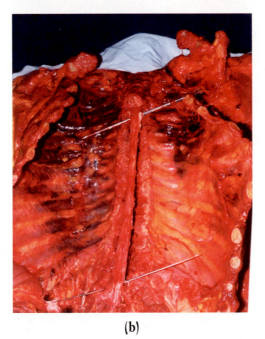

(b)

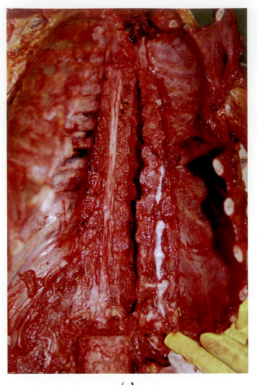

(c)

Figure 2.147 (a) Anterior access: resected rachis. Wide opening (*a libro*) of the right resecting border. (b) The probes subtend the spinal marrow, leaving visible the vertebral canal (medullar bed). (c) Wide opening (*a libro*). Close-up to the right, the anterior side of the rachis canal (medullar roof).

the volar surfaces of the arm and forearm, stopping at the wrist. Then continue with a layered dissection, taking pains to expose all aponeurotic bands and muscle tendons. Ideally, the dissection should be extended up to the axilla and the posterior axillary line; then continue the incision back to the thoracic–abdominal wall.

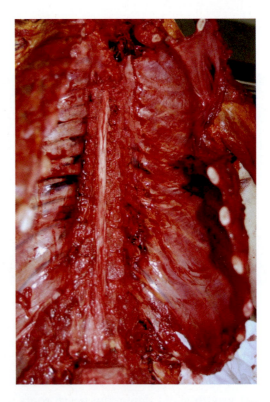

Figure 2.148 Medullar resection carried out from the extreme clavicular to the extreme lumbar. Resections at complete borders and vertebral removal.

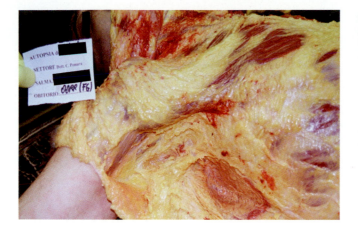

Figure 2.149 Right armpit cavity.

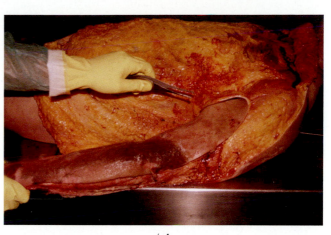

(a)

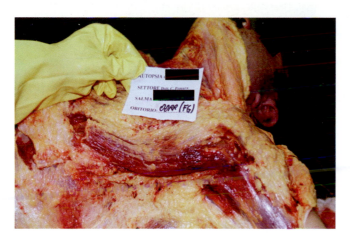

Figure 2.150 Left armpit cavity.

This approach allows visibility of the muscular tendons and the vascular and nerve bundles of the axilla (Figures 2.149 and 2.150). Last, isolate and incise the individual muscle heads until reaching the acromio-clavicular capsule and the humeral diaphysis (Figure 2.151 through Figure 2.153).

2.15 Leg Dissection

As with the arms, radiological evaluation of the legs must be completed before beginning the dissection. Make the initial incision in the femoral triangle, at the medial third of the inguinal fold, and continue it along the medial border of the thigh–knee and, if necessary, the leg, until reaching the medial malleolus (Figure 2.154). The first structures to be encountered will be the femoral nerve, artery, and vein. Once they have been individually isolated, they should be followed along their entire course (Figure 2.155 through Figure 2.158). Dissect by

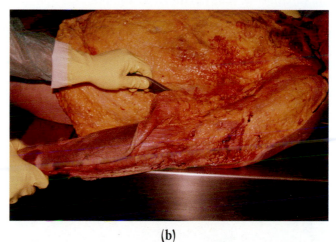

(b)

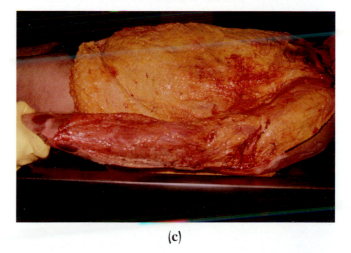

(c)

Figure 2.151 Sequence of stratum opening of the superior limb; clearly shown is the extension of the bisacromial resection at calyx (pointed out from the forceps). (a) The resection is extended until the median face of the wrist. (b) Overturning of cutaneous planes of the arm–forearm. (c) Stripping of left superior limb, limited to the cutaneous and subcutaneous planes only.

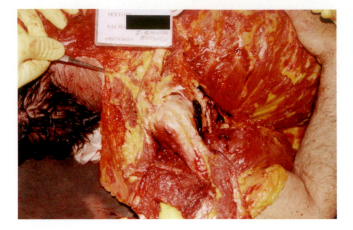

Figure 2.152 Glenohumeral cavity with humerus (head) and vascular–nervous bundle in a close-up.

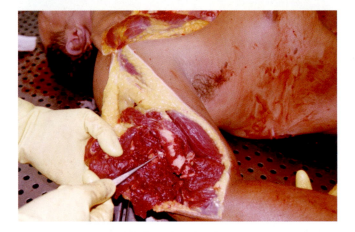

Figure 2.153 Arm resection carried out along the border of the descending cut. In the detail, the fracture of the third distal from the humeral diaphysis with retention of gunshot bullet.

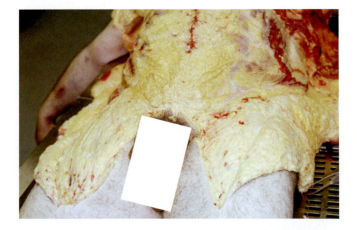

Figure 2.154 Resection of inferior limbs bilaterally. Cutaneous plane.

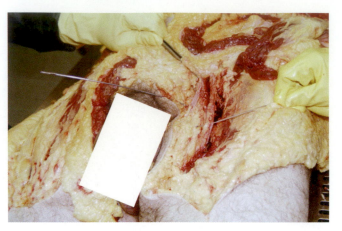

Figure 2.155 View of nerve, artery, and femoral vein.

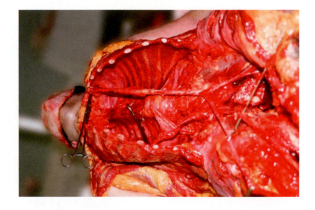

Figure 2.156 Anatomic study of the thoracic and abdominal aortas.

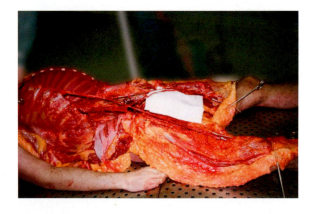

Figure 2.157 A view of the lower limb artery and vein.

anatomic planes, always preserving the underlying muscular structures. Make sure to expose all muscles and their insertions, including that of the sartorious muscle.

The dissection must be tailored to the individual case, and any method chosen will have to take into account the specific features of the case. Whatever method is chosen, always pay special attention to the isolation and the examination of the vascular

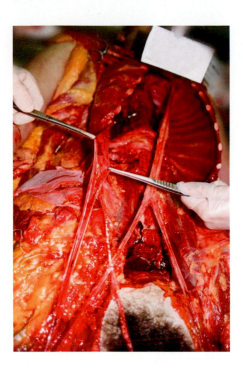

Figure 2.158 A compared study of the left leg vascular system. The thrombus on exploration of the femoral vein.

structures. The muscles should be removed one by one to allow for the visibility of bone segments and articular structures.

2.16   Macroscopic Examination and Resection of the Resected Organs

2.16.1   Brain

Prior to brain dissection, photographs should be taken. If there are suspicions about vascular integrity, photographs of the circle of Willis (also called the Willis polygon) should be taken before it is incised and removed as one block (Figures 2.159 through Figure 2.166).

2.16.1.1   *The Ludwig Scheme*

Many methods have been proposed for examination of the infant brain. The Ludwig method seems the most attractive, as it combines the best features of classic anatomopathologic methods and the classical method of Virchow. An adequate basic examination can be performed no matter whether the brain is fixed, though it is possible to observe a good deal more detail if the brain is fixed for 2 weeks prior to dissection; in either case, the brain is cut into coronal sections.

Initially the hindbrain must be severed from the cerebral hemispheres. The best way is to use a long-handled scalpel with a No. 22 blade to incise both of the cerebral peduncles. Hold the blade at a right angle to

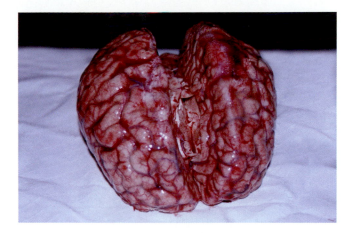

Figure 2.159 Telencephalon hemispheres: frontal view.

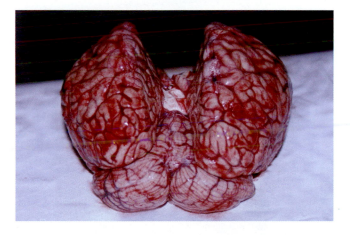

Figure 2.160 Telencephalon hemispheres: occipital view and cerebellum.

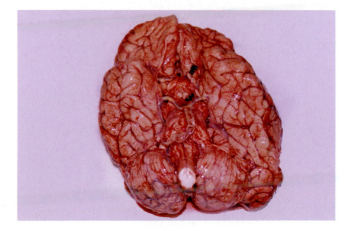

Figure 2.161 Telencephalon hemispheres: inferior surface. Clearly shown is the Willis polygon.

the brain for as long as possible. Once the incisions are made, the brain can be removed and placed on a cloth or large sheets of absorbing paper. Position the brain so that the hemispheres rest on the cloth and the inferior

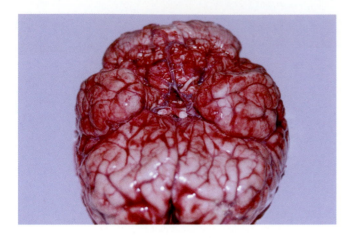

Figure 2.162 Close-up of the Willis polygon.

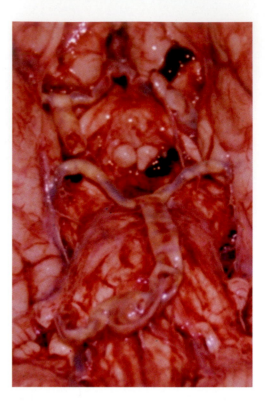

Figure 2.163 (continued.)

2.16.1.2 *Classic Variations*

Classic variations are based on sagittal and coronal cuts, made 2 to 3 centimeters from one another, producing symmetric slices, and bilateral cuts made at 45° into the two hemispheres, beginning with the lateral ventricles (Figure 2.167).

2.16.1.3 *Blood Samples*

The origin of blood samples must always be specified. This is especially true when a subdural hematoma is present; the origin of the blood must be described in great detail (origin, extension of the hematoma, estimated volume). The brain should also be inspected for areas of possible dural coagulation anterior to, and contiguous with, the margins of any hemorrhagic zone. If a subdural hematoma is present, it provides an ideal matrix for toxicological testing, as centrally acting drugs persist for much longer in the hematoma than in peripheral blood.

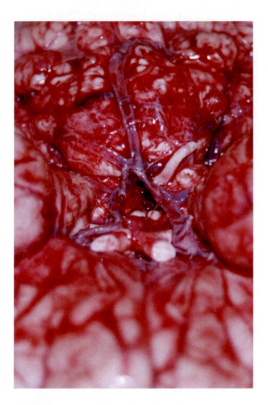

Figure 2.163 Particulars of the Willis polygon. Evident parietal calcified plates.

surface of the brain faces upward, with the frontal horns oriented anteriorly.

The first incision is made approximately 1 to 2 centimeters anterior to the mammillary bodies, separating the hemispheres. If the brain has not been preserved, it will only be possible to make two more coronal cuts. If the brain has been fixed, it will be possible to cut each slice with a thickness of approximately 1 centimeter, allowing a much more detailed view of the cerebral parenchyma. An analogous procedure is used for the corpus callosum and the cerebellum, which are incised at right angles at 2 to 3 centimeters.

2.16.2 Heart

There are several ways to examine the heart of the infant and each has adherents. No matter which method is chosen, the external description of the heart is very important. Cardiac enlargement may indicate the presence of hypertrophic cardiomyopathy, hypertension, or even maternal drug abuse. Hypertrophic cardiomyopathy occurs as a consequence of many different polymorphisms, some of which do not produce obvious changes

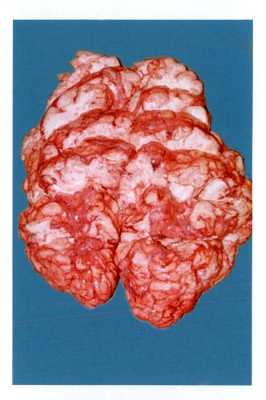

Figure 2.164 Isolated Willis polygon after formalin hardening.

that are macroscopically obvious, whereas others, such as the LAMP2 cardiomyopathy (lysosomal-associated membrane protein 2), manifest anatomic changes that are diagnostic. When suspicion of heritable cardiomyopathy is strong, DNA testing must be requested, if for no other reason than to determine whether the rest of the family must be screened.

The normal heart is vaguely cone shaped. If its shape is globular or irregular, as in the case of ventricular aneurysm, then extensive sampling for subsequent histological examination is necessary. If the subepicardium has a grayish tinge, this suggests congenital heart disease. In the case of preexisting heart failure and chronic anemia, the myocardium may appear pale, or spotted, or even hemorrhagic when there is acute heart failure or heart rupture. The consistency of the left ventricular can be hard (suggesting hypertrophy, fibrosis, amyloidosis, calcification, or rigor mortis) or soft (due to acute myocardial infarct, myocarditis, dilated cardiopathy, or decomposition).

Most of the old methods of dissection are really not practical for routine diagnostic purposes, which is why only the inflow–outflow and the "short-axis" methods have survived. The last technique is useful in virtually every form of cardiac dysfunction. A number of recent methods have been developed that are very useful for teaching purposes, as they allow for easier comparisons and easier demonstration of the normal heart structures.

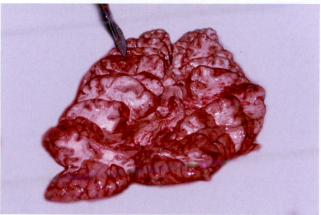

Figure 2.165 Anatomic cut according to coronal resections made on a "fresh" encephalon.

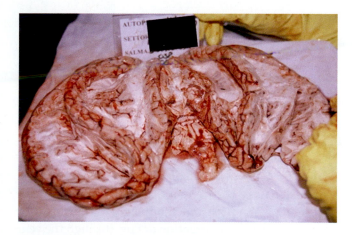

Figure 2.166 Virchow resection.

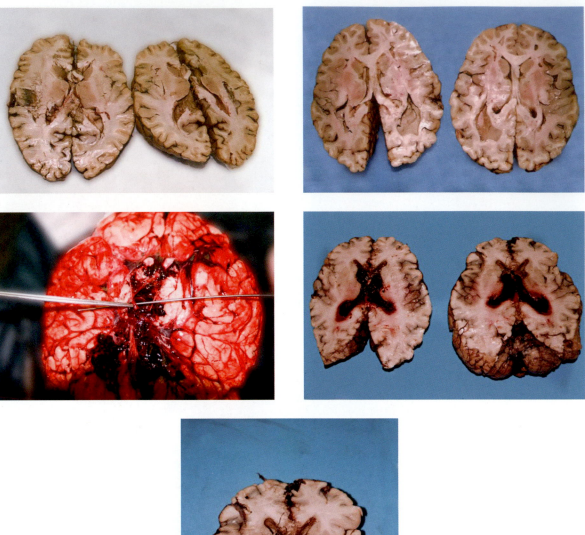

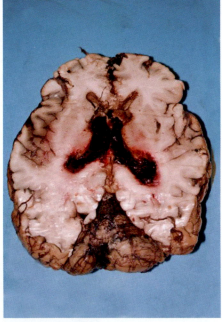

Figure 2.167 Dissection of the brain. A first sagittal cut is perfomed by passing the corresponding geniculate bodies.

2.16.2.1 *Inflow–Outflow Method in the Cardiac Dissection (Fineschi and Baroldi Variation)*

The most widely used technique is the one originally proposed by Virchow and modified by Prausniz. The heart is opened in the direction of flow through the vena cava, adjacent to the right heart border, up to the conus

and the pulmonary artery. On the left, the chambers of the atria are opened by cutting the pulmonary vessels, then continuing the incision to the infundibulum and aorta (Figure 2.168).

Recently, it has become common practice to open the coronary arteries along their course, and then remove them before complete dissection. The problem

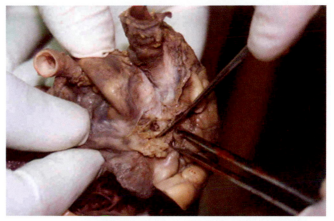

Figure 2.168 Outlined are the access ways of the resection according to the blood flow. The resection follows, for example, the venae cavae flow to the right border of the heart, at the cone and pulmonary artery. To the left, it opens the atrial diaphragm by resection of the pulmonary vessels, and then it continues with the left border dissection of the infundibulum and the aorta.

Figure 2.169 Method of Fineschi and Baroldi. After disconnecting the aorta from the pulmonary artery, the forensic surgeon locates the origin of the left coronary (common trunk) and with a scalpel starts the resection following the artery course.

with this approach is that it becomes impossible to precisely estimate the lumenal diameter, remove clots, and still do an adequate examination of the myocardium itself. For those reasons, most now prefer to make transverse scalpel cuts *in situ*, at intervals of 3 mm (Figures 2.169 and 2.170).[*]

Once the heart is removed from the pericardial sac, the chambers must be carefully washed, the heart weighed, and only then externally inspected.[†] Regrettably, many forensic pathologists forgo the next step, but the heart should then be suspended in a large container filled with neutral 10% formalin solution, for 24 hours. Even though a period of only 24 hours does

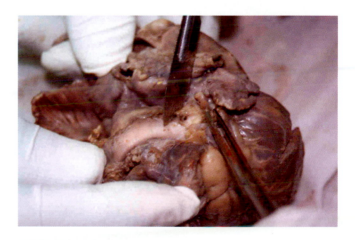

Figure 2.170 Scalpel placed at the base of the open common trunk.

not allow for complete fixation, it will harden the tissue, allowing myocardial dissection without any damage to the tissue itself. Transverse incisions through the semi-fixed heart are made at intervals of 3 millimeters, along the course of the extramural arterial branches, and each segment is then removed (Figure 2.172).

Once these measures have been undertaken it becomes possible to section the whole heart with a mechanical slicer, producing slices that are each about 1 centimeter thick, cutting from apex to base, parallel to the atrioventricular sulcus. The final slice is made at the apex of the papillary muscles (Figure 2.173). The heart slices, atria and valves, and the coronary segments are then placed in anatomic sequence and photographed in color, using a camera equipped with a metric scale (Figure 2.174a,b and Figure 2.179). This affords the option of calculating macroscopic data (walls width, cavity volume, etc.) and the ability to estimate the

---

[*] Many methods have been used to examine coronary arteries. Chalk injection was first introduced by Bianchi in 1904; injection of radiopaque materials, sometimes colored, into intact hearts (Gross, 1921); diaphanization as introduced by Spalteholz in 1924; opened and spread out heart (Schlesinger, 1938); injection of plastic substances while at the same time dissolving myocardium (James, 1961); and tissue abscission for a histological examination before myocardial dissolution (Baroldi et al., 1967). If the goal is to make comparisons with echocardiographic images, specific dissection planes must be created. Each method has its advantages and disadvantages, depending on the intended purpose of the examination. Nevertheless, a method that allows the study of population groups (Baroldi et al., 1974) has been adopted, allowing a quantitative and morphologic-functional valuation of the parameters to be correlated with the clinical history. It is a modification of Baroldi's method and can be adopted without an excessive waste of time or material (Fineschi et al., 2005).

[†] When hearts are surgically excised prior to transplantation, most of the atria remain in the pericardial cavity. To allow comparison with autopsy hearts, the weight of the first has been reported as the total weight of the heart, adding the theoretic weight according to the following formula: weight of the heart without atria × 100/75 (Reiner, 1968).

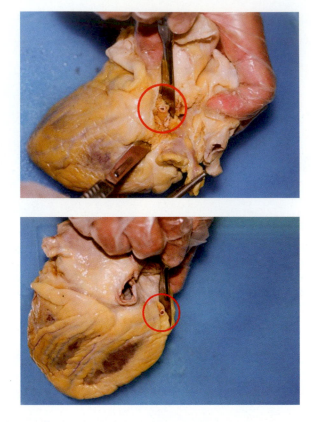

Figure 2.171 Coronary study according to Fineschi and Baroldi method. Into the red circle, cross section of the left and the right (bottom) coronary arteries.

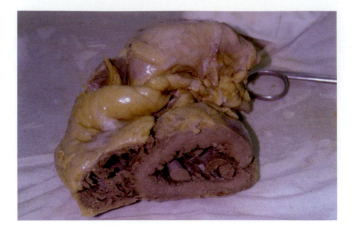

Figure 2.173 Base of the heart.

border of the right ventricle, the obtuse border of the left ventricle, and the interventricular septum. The incision must extend through the mitral valve, the tricuspid, and the atria (Figure 2.180). When this type of incision is used, it is possible to split the heart in two, allowing for easy comparison of all four chambers of the heart. The superior half will be opened along both ventricular outflow paths, following the "flow-down" flow method (Figure 2.181).

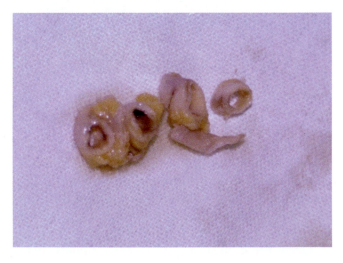

Figure 2.172 Descending coronary artery isolated and cut.

extension of a lesion as a percentage of the total heart mass. Finally, atria, valves, and any other structure are easily examined by whichever technique seems appropriate (Figures 2.177 and 2.178).

2.16.2.2 *Dissection by Chamber*

Using a long-handled scalpel, make an incision at the apex of the heart, and extend the incision past the acute

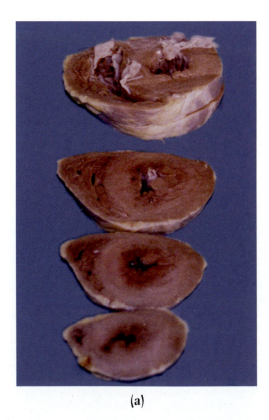

(a)

Figure 2.174 A manual heart section in slices, carried out from the apex to the base until the apex of the papillary muscles (a and b) and in particular (c).

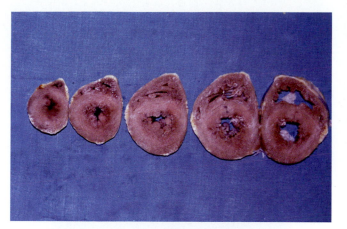

(b)

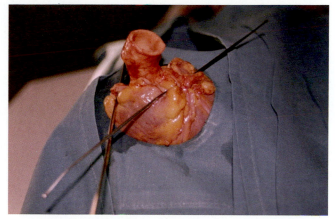

(a)

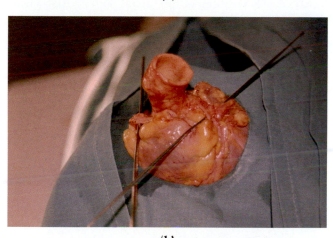

(b)

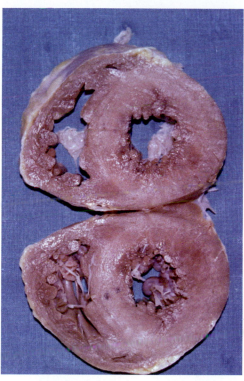

(c)

Figure 2.174 (continued.)

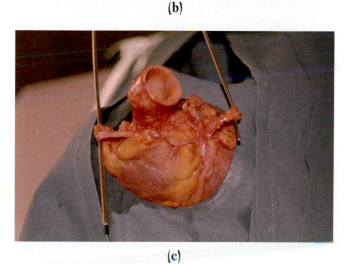

(c)

Figure 2.175 Coronaries with stylets placed in traction. The isolation and the use of the stylets are essential in cases in which the forensic surgeon wants to prepare the heart for the resection, according to the method of the heart base.

2.16.2.3 Dissection of the Heart Base

Using the dissection of the heart base method preserves all four valves, and it is also very helpful in demonstrating the anatomic relations between the valves themselves, adjacent coronary arteries, and the atrioventricular conduction system. This technique is more suitable for hearts with major valve disease. It is also useful in individuals who have received prosthetic valves. The right coronary artery, left main, and left anterior descending coronary arteries must be examined individually, and should be isolated prior to sectioning the base of the heart (Figure 2.175).

The ventricles are incised so that coronary flow to the papillary muscles can be traced. One incision allows for the removal of the atria. It is made through the atrial free wall, taking care not to tear the adjacent coronary artery, which should be supported and held under traction. In

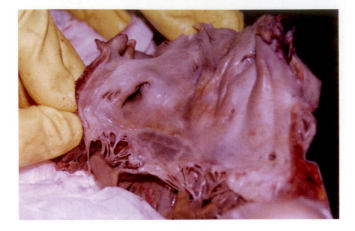

Figure 2.176 Opening of the "atrial dome." Also visible are the infundibulus and valvular flaps, with the tendinous chords and the papillar muscles.

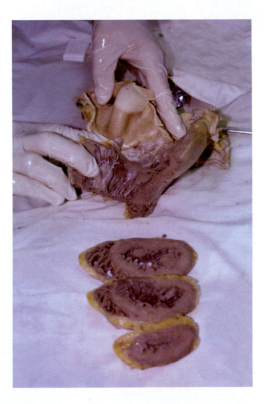

Figure 2.177 Heart section following the blood flow; previous manual reduction into slices of the apex at the heart base.

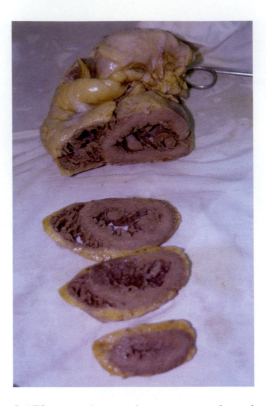

Figure 2.178 Heart base and section into slices from the apex to the base.

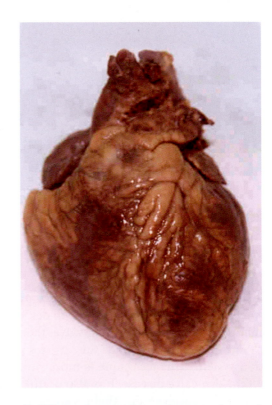

Figure 2.179 Resection plane. Starting from the heart apex, extend the resection through the acute edge of the right ventricle, the obtuse edge of the left ventricle, and the interventricular septum. The resection must be extended at last through the mitral valve, the tricuspid, and the atria.

the left atrium, the ostium of the coronary sinus is held next to the inferior vena cava, and then incised posteriorly, along the external wall of the coronary sinus up to the ventricular atrium. The incision should extend from the inferior edge of the interatrial septum as far as the level of the left atrial appendage.

Next, extend the incision below the mitral annulus valve, including the left atrial wall that lies opposite the ascending aorta. At the top edge of the interatrial septum, the left atrial incision should meet with the incision

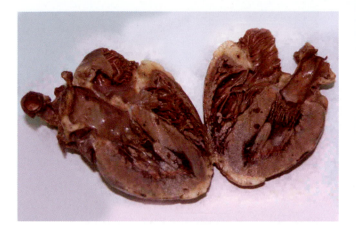

Figure 2.180 Four chambers. The right atrium, interatrial septum, interventricular sectum, apex, and left ventricle.

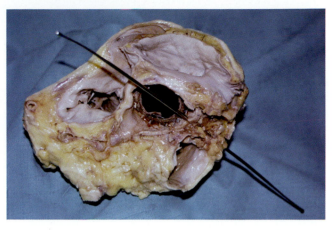

Figure 2.183 Base of the heart method. Shown are the aortic ostio (with mechanical, valvular prosthesis), the ostio of the pulmonary, and the two atrial floors.

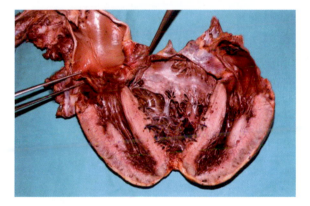

Figure 2.181 Heart examination according to the "Four Chambers" method.

have been removed, the arterial sinus may be removed as well, using only forceps. This allows for better vision of the pulmonary valves. The circumflex artery should not be dissected until after the first part the dissection has been photographed (Figure 2.183).

More sophisticated and time-consuming methods of study can be used for heart examination. Furthermore, by comparing clinical imaging, for example, echocardiographic imaging, different plane dissections can be adopted. Each method has its advantages and disadvantages, and not one of these may actually evaluate all the needed variables. Positioning the heart on the front surface, the first cut begins 2 cm up to the atrioventricular right sulco and continues in a circular way as a short axis modification, passing through the upper right atrioventricular valve, the pulmonary semilunar valves, and through the interventricular septum. The cut is completed, finally, passing through the upper left atrioventricular valve and the aortic semilunar valves (Figures 2.184 and 2.185).

Now, the sufficiency of the atrioventricular valves of the pulmonary and aortic semilunar valves can be investigated. Put some water into it, taking care not to

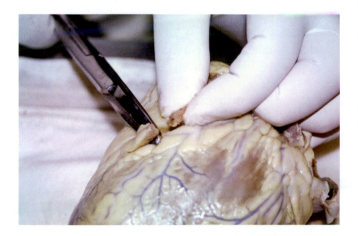

Figure 2.182 Coronary cutting in a cross section.

on the right. Cut through the interatrial septum, from the superior to the inferior edge, and then remove the two atria. A transverse incision is made of the two great arteries along their sinotubular junction, up to the valves. After the ascending aorta and the pulmonary artery

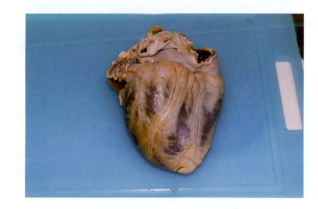

Figure 2.184 Posterior side view of the heart.

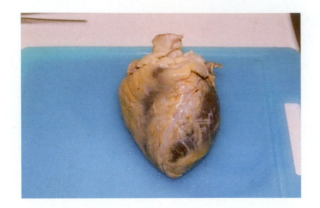

Figure 2.185 Anterior side view of the heart.

Figure 2.188 A heart examination according to the base method. A circular cut is performed 2 cm up to the atrioventricular sulco.

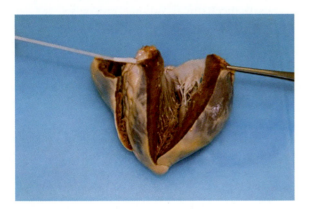

Figure 2.186 Base of the heart method. Exploring the left atrioventricular valve, papilla muscles, and ventricular endocardium.

Figure 2.189 Base of the heart method. Examination of the valve sufficiency.

let any coagulum of blood to form, because it can pass through the left ventricle up into the aorta, and prevent the semilunar valves from flattening under the water pressure; this can feign the insufficiency of valves of the aorta (Figure 2.187 through Figure 2.189).

Then, the origin of the big arteries has to be cut in order to explore the intima and the valves as well as the atrium and ventricular valves to explore the atrioventricular valves, their papilla muscles, and the state of the ventricular endocardium (Figure 2.186).

2.16.2.4 Recommended Cardiac Samples

Certain specimens should be taken as a matter of routine:

1. The major coronary arteries and their main extramural branches should be sampled. Any segment where macroscopic lesions are evident should be removed as well, although they may need decalcification prior to fixation.
2. Sections of epicardium and myocardium should be collected in every case.
3. A 2-centimeter, full thickness block should be taken from the wall of each ventricle. Sections should be taken from the front, side, and back of each ventricle as well.

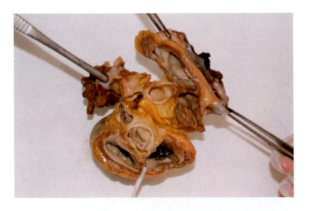

Figure 2.187 The base of the heart method (top view). In evidence, atrioventricular valves and aortic and pulmonary semilunar valves.

4. The anterior and posterior interventricular septum must also be sampled, as well as any areas where abnormalities are apparent on visual inspection.

5. If a more complete survey is required, both the inferior and superior portion of each ventricle should be sampled. The remaining tissue should be completely fixed, then preserved in hermetically sealed plastic bags for possible further examinations.

2.16.3 Upper Respiratory Tract

2.16.3.1 *Examination of the Larynx and Pharynx*

A single block should include not only the trachea, but also the larynx, cervical esophagus, the floor of the mouth, the tongue, the soft palate, and the tonsils (Figure 2.190). As a rule, the larynx and pharynx are opened with forceps following the posterior median line; the sides are stretched outward to study the mucosa (Figure 2.191). In adults, this operation could require disruption of the bony laryngeal cartilage. If the cartilage is not totally ossified, the larynx may easily be incised transversely, yielding good specimens for subsequent histological examination.

During the dissection, look for any alterations of the mucosa and cricoarytenoid joint. This joint lies just below the vocal chords, at both sides of the median posterior line of the larynx.

In cases of suspected strangulation, the hyoid must be carefully isolated and studied, both *in situ* and after its removal to detect possible fracture and hemorrhage.

2.16.4 Trachea and Principal Bronchi

Three separate incisions are required to open the trachea and the main bronchial tubes along their posterior membranous walls (Figure 2.194); one for each segment of the trachea and the bronchial tubes (Figures 2.192 and 2.193). In case of suspected drowning and aspiration, or when medical misadventure following bronchoscopy is a concern, use an anterior incision made *in situ*. If a tracheal–esophageal fistula is suspected, it is better seen through an incision made in the anterior midline or, alternatively, by completely removing the anterior portion of the trachea.

2.16.5 Lungs

2.16.5.1 *Lung Resection*

For this procedure the classic method was, and still is, to begin dissection in the hilum with dissection

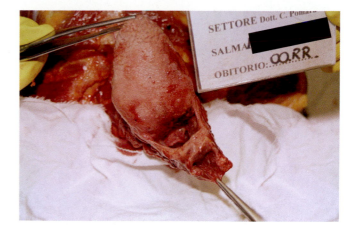

Figure 2.190 Soft palate, tongue, trachea, larynx, and esophagus.

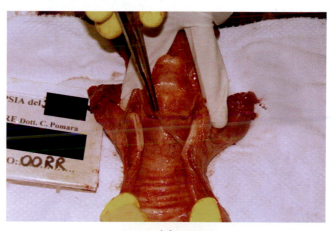

(a)

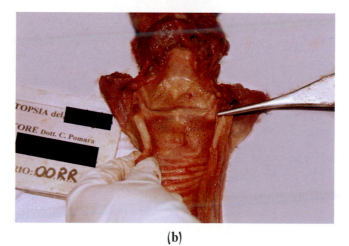

(b)

Figure 2.191 Larynx–pharynx examination.

progressing outward. First locate the hilar pulmonary structures, and then observe the macroscopic characteristics (caliber, width, content). The pulmonary arteries and the bronchi are opened from the hilum, with the incision extending outward to the distal portion of the mediastinal pulmonary margin. The lungs are then

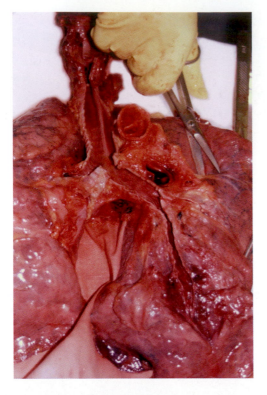

Figure 2.192 Tracheobronchial tree.

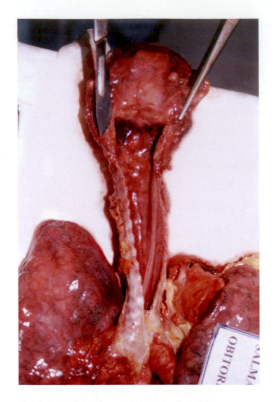

Figure 2.194 Inspection of the tracheal lumen.

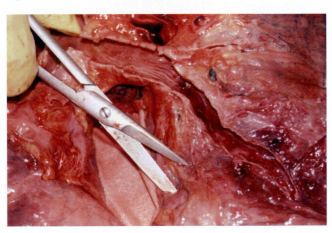

Figure 2.193 View of the tracheobronchial lumen.

incised with a series of sagittal cuts made in parallel to the mediastinal surface. This allows for the study of multiple transverse sections of both lung parenchyma and vessels. The limitation of this process is its destructive nature. If a lesion is found, it may become difficult to identify its original location.

2.16.5.2 Lateral Lung Resection

With this approach, an incision is made from the apex to the base of the lungs, with the incision running along the major lateral axis of the lungs. When this approach is used, the hilum is preserved. Using this method allows the reconstruction of the lung with the hilum intact (Figure 2.196a,b).

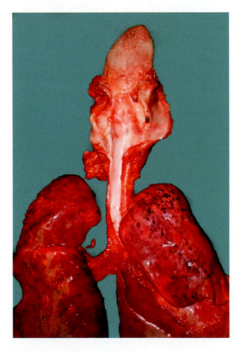

Figure 2.195 Tracheobronchial tree. Opened trachea along its posterior membraneous wall.

2.16.5.3 Sampling

Tissue samples from pulmonary lacerations, ecchymotic areas, and contusions should always be collected. A thorough basic examination should include samples taken from each lobe and the hilum (to study the vascular–bronchial component of each). In forensic

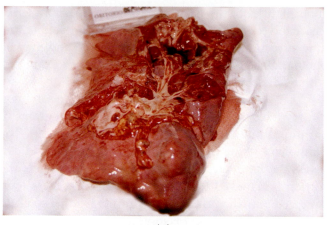

(a)

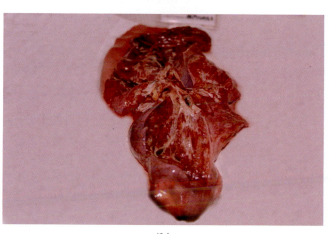

(b)

Figure 2.196 Lungs resection starting from the hilum. The pulmonary arteries and the bronchial tubes are opened from the hilum toward the distal portion of the mediastinum pulmonary border or, according to a more complex method, from the resection planes obtained with the introduction of buttoned forceps inside the vascular–bronchial hilum tree. This last method leads to a resection, so to say "umbrellalike," and it is certainly more conservative then the previous one, since it allows the reconstruction of the lung with unharmed hilum region.

cases it is always appropriate to mark the site where the sample was obtained in order to provide more accurate topographic and histopathologic information. Under no circumstances should sampling of the pleural serosa be omitted. Rapid fixation will be required if examination with an electronic microscope is to be performed.

2.16.5.3.1 Special Procedures for Pulmonary Tissue

Lungs should be fixed in formalin, using a perfusion device that forces preservative fluid through the lungs. This allows for the collection of well-preserved samples, making histological examination easier and more accurate.

A somewhat more cautious approach involves the perforation of one lung, and the dissection of the other, when it is still "fresh." This will allow for the collection and study of samples that can be used for subsequent microbiologic studies or staining, as in cases of infection thought to be caused by *Pneumocystis carinii*. Using this method also allows for better evaluation of edema and pulmonary embolism, all conditions better appreciated when examining an unfixed lung. If a perfusion machine is not available, the lungs can be inflated with a 10% formalin solution, injected through the main bronchus. Nearly 2 liters of fluid will be required to inject an adult lung. Infusion can be performed using a large bore syringe or, even better, with a bottle suspended 30 to 40 centimeters above the lungs so that the fluid drains by gravity. After all the fluid has been infused, the main bronchus is closed, and the lung is immersed in a formalin bath. The lungs will swell slightly during the process.

2.16.5.3.1.1 Lung Removal and Preparation Prior to Wet Fixation With most of the specialty studies performed on isolated lungs, measures must be taken to preserve the lung intact during the evisceration process. We normally induce a pneumothorax through a small parasternal incision. In many cases, the thoracic chest plate can be removed with minimal, if any, damage to the lungs. To protect the lungs even more, incise the anterior connections of the diaphragm up to the chest, so that the hand of an assistant can be introduced and the lung gently removed at the same time of the chest plate.

The resected rib ends should be covered with thin, absorbent paper or plastic, as the bones could tear the pleura or injure the prosector. Before removing the lungs, connections to the parietal pleura must be carefully severed. This is particularly difficult to do when the posterior base of an inferior lobe is diseased, because adhesions are likely to be present. If the adhesions are extensive, try to remove the lungs together with the parietal pleura, which must be separated from the muscular and bony regions of the thoracic wall.

Any small pleural lacerations that occur during the removal process should be repaired with a fixative spray. Connection of the lung to the perfusion apparatus is much easier if the extra pulmonary, bronchoarterial rami are left connected to the lung. Note that the bronchial arteries are typically enlarged and tortuous in chronic pulmonary thromboembolic hypertension. It is also possible to leave the lungs attached to the trachea to be able to examine them both at the same time. Pulmonary angiography can also be performed by leaving the lungs connected to the main pulmonary artery. Both procedures may be executed *in situ*. Prior to beginning the perfusion, aspirate any mucous or pus from the bronchial tubes. If all of the obstructing material cannot be cleared completely, the lungs should be perfused through the pulmonary vessels.

Fixation time. Normally 3 days are required to completely perfuse and fix the lungs, but hardened or fibrous lungs could require more time, and filling of the bronchial tubes can be delayed by the expansion caused by fixation. If that is the case, portions of the damaged lungs will not inflate.

Pressure fixation. If a pressure fixation machine is available, the normal pressure range of 15 to 95 centimeters of water may be too high for routine purposes, and alternative methods should be considered. This same device can also be used to perfuse livers or other organs, such as hearts or kidneys, at autopsy and for surgical pathology. With pressure fixation, fixation fluid enters through valves that have been connected to the main bronchus or to the trachea. An electric pump allows the fixative to circulate; modified Kaiserling solution is the preferred fixative but formalin can also be used. If angiography is to be performed, introduce a 10% formalin solution into the lungs first. After three days of pressure perfusion, the lungs are incised with a very long knife.

Dry lung preservation. Many obsolete techniques that allow perfusion fixation without pressure have been attempted; fixation with formaldehyde gas or with formalin vapor has been used with the expectation that it will help "dry the lungs." After drying, the macroscopic characteristics of the lungs are well preserved, but tissue samples for histological study are generally unsatisfactory.

2.16.5.3.1.2 Resection of Fixed Lungs A special knife and a resection table should be used for resection of fixed lungs. Resection tables are made of cork set on a metallic support, where drained formalin solution is collected. The knife should be 78 centimeters long to allow the cuts through the entire lung with a single movement. This ensures that the cut surface will be intact and free of artifacts. The same type of knife is also useful for sectioning the liver and spleen. The lung is usually cut on a frontal or sagittal plane, in thin slices of about 1.5 centimeters thick. For incisions along the frontal plane, the lung is positioned in such way that the hilum is turned upward, allowing the first incision to be placed adjacent to the hilum. If the resection is located along the axis of a bronchus, guide the knife with previously inserted probes. For the preparation of very thin but large sections, gel infiltrations are required.

Barium sulfate saturation. This method of preparation opacifies the pulmonary tissue, making abnormalities of the parenchyma, such as emphysema, easier to see. After saturation with barium sulfate, the lung is sectioned, immersed in the water, and may be photographed, studied with a naked eye, or examined with by dissection microscopy.

The "listening" method. Place a section of lung, already fixed, in a barium nitrate solution (75 grams of barium nitrate dissolved in 1 liter of warm water). The pulmonary tissue is slowly pressed so the solution can penetrate the tissue. After approximately 1 minute, the section is removed from the solution and excess fluid squeezed out. Then the tissue is immersed in a solution containing 100 grams of sodium sulfate dissolved in 1 liter of warm water. The pulmonary tissue is squeezed again, withdrawn from the solution, drained, and placed in a bath of barium nitrate. Repeat this operation as many times as needed until the air bubbles have been completely eliminated from the tissue and the barium sulfate precipitate has made the pulmonary tissue opaque with a white-grayish color.

Storage. "Fresh" lungs may be kept refrigerated for a few days provided the temperature is kept below zero. Fresh lungs may remain frozen for months, but better histological results are obtained if the samples are collected earlier rather than later. Lungs that have already been fixed are best cut and stored in plastic bags, warmed, and then sealed in a 5% to 20% formalin solution. Several sections may be stacked on top of one another without damaging the pulmonary tissue.

Paper mounting. For teaching demonstrations, cut 2-centimeter thick sections of formalin-fixed lung, wash them, and then immerse them in a gel mixture containing a disinfectant. After the gel mixture has penetrated the tissue, the sections to be examined are frozen, and cut into 400-millimeter thick sections, then refixed again in the gel solution, and finally mounted on paper. This same technique may be applied to other organs, such as the liver.

2.16.6 Liver

After positioning the organ convex face down, and with the diaphragmatic convex surface turned toward upward, it will be possible to decide if some cuts at full width are required. If so, cut coronal sections, each to 3 to 4 centimeters thick.

2.16.7 Spleen

Place the spleen with its anterior facing downward and make a series of parallel coronal sections.

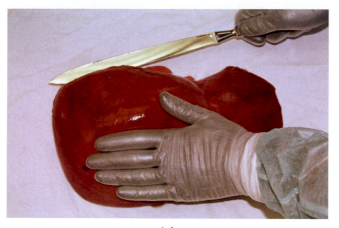

(a)

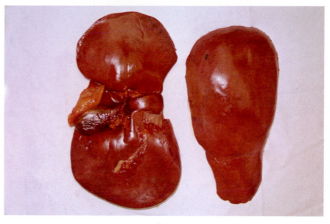

(c)

Figure 2.197 (continued.)

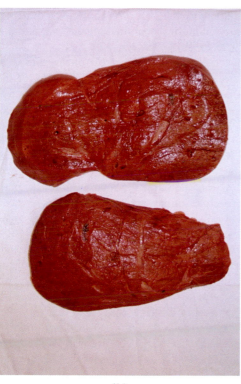

(b)

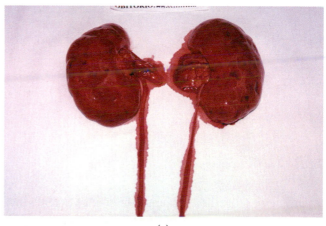

(a)

Figure 2.197 Liver. Full width resections performed by resections parallel to the support plane in a front-to-back direction.

2.16.7.1 Sample Collection

Obvious lesions are always sampled, but it is appropriate to collect some samples, even from tissue that appears normal. For a standard examination, three samples are more than sufficient.

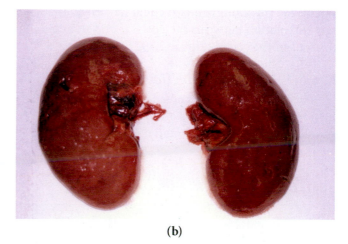

(b)

Figure 2.198 After placing the kidneys in anatomic position, perform a transverse resection with a sole cut, on the convex border of the organ, from the superior pole to the inferior.

2.16.8   The Kidneys

Place the kidneys in their anatomic position, make a small incision in the capsule, and then strip off the

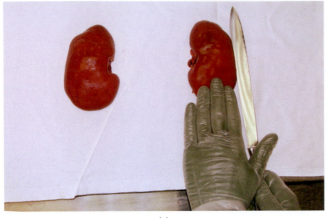

(c)

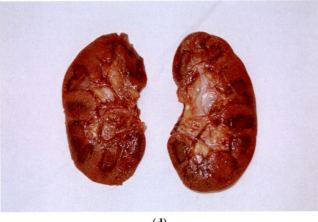

(d)

Figure 2.198 (continued.)

capsule with a toothed forceps. Make a transverse incision through the convex border of the organ, from the superior pole to the inferior, ending at the hilum. This will divide the kidney in two equal halves, allowing for easy distinction between the cortical and the medullar portions of the organ (Figure 2.197a–c).

2.16.8.1 Sample Collection

Samples must include the capsule, cortex, and medullary portions of the kidney. It is always a good idea to take a sample from the hilum, though it is not mandatory.

References

Adams, JH, and Murray, MF. 1982. *Atlas of Postmortem Techniques in Neuropathology.* New York: Cambridge University Press.

Adams, JR, and Mader, RD. 1976. *Autopsy.* Chicago: Year Book Medical Publishers.

Adams, VI. 1991. Autopsy technique for neck examination II. Vertebral column and posterior compartment. *Pathol Annu* 26: 211–226.

Anderson, RE, Fox, RC, and Rolla, BH. 1991. Medical uncertainty and the autopsy: Occult benefits for students. *Hum Pathol* 21: 128–135.

Anderson, RE, Rolla, BH, and Gorstein, F. 1990. A model for the autopsy-based quality assessment of medical diagnostics. *Hum Pathol* 21: 174–181.

Baker, PB, and Saladino, AJ. 1993. *Autopsy Contributions to Quality Assurance: Data Analysis and Critique.* Northfield, IL: College of American Pathologists.

Brinkman, B. 1999. Harmonization of medico-legal autopsy rules. *Int J Legal Med* 113: 1–14.

Collins, KA, and Hutchins, GM. 2003. *Autopsy Performance & Reporting.* 2nd edition. Northfield, IL: College of American Pathologists.

Collins, KA, Bennett, AT, and Hanzlick, R. 1999. The autopsy and the living. *Arch Intern Med* 159: 2391–2392.

Culora, GA, and Roche, WR. 1996. Simple method of necropsy dissection of the abdominal organs after abdominal surgery. *J Clin Pathol* 49: 776–779.

Devers, KJ. 1990. The changing role of the autopsy: A social environmental perspective. *Hum Pathol* 21: 145–153.

Ernst, MF. 2003. Medicolegal death investigation and forensic procedures. In: *Handbook of Forensic Pathology.* ed. Froede, RC. Northfield, IL: College of American Pathologists.

Fineschi, V, Baroldi, G, and Silver, MD. 2006. *Pathology of the Heart and Sudden Death in Forensic Medicine.* Boca Raton: CRC Press.

Fineschi, V, and Pomara, C. 2004. A forensic pathological approach to sudden cardiac death. In: *Forensic Pathology Reviews,* Vol. 1, ed. M. Tsokos. Totowa, NJ: Humana Press, 139–168.

Froede, RC. 2003. *Handbook of Forensic Pathology.* 2nd Edition. Northfield, IL: College of American Pathologists.

Hill, RB, and Anderson, RE. 1998. Contributions of autopsy to society. In: *The Autopsy: Medical Practice and Public Policy.* Boston: Butterworths, 123–145.

Hutchins, GM. 1990. *Autopsy: Performance and Technique.* Northfield, IL: College of American Pathologists.

Hutchins, GM. 1994. Practice guidelines for autopsy pathology, autopsy performance. Autopsy Committee of the College of American Pathologists. *Arch Pathol Lab Med* 118: 19–25.

Ludwig, J. 2002. *Handbook of Autopsy Practice.* 3rd Edition. Totowa, NJ: Humana Press.

McCulloch, TA, and Rutty, GN. 1998. Postmortem examination of the lungs: A preservation technique for opening the bronchi and pulmonary arteries individually without transection problems. *J Clin Pathos* 51: 163–164.

Okasaki, H. 1979. Nervous system. In: *Current Methods of Autopsy Practice,* ed. Ludwing, J. Philadelphia: W.B. Saunders, 96–129.

Powers, JM. 1995. Practice guidelines for autopsy pathology. Autopsy procedures for brain, spinal cord and neuromuscolar system. Autopsy Committee of the College of American Pathologists. *Arch Pathol Lab Med.* 119: 777–783.

Riboli, E, and Delendi, MA. 1991. Autopsy in epidemiology and medical research. IARC Scientific Publications n. 112. New York: Oxford University Press.

Rolla, BH, and Anderson, RE. 1991. Pathologists and the autopsy. *Am J Clin Pathol* 95: S42–S49.

Sarode, VR, Datta, BN, Banerjee, AK, Banerjee, CK, Joshi, K, Bjusnurmath, B, Radotra, BD. 1993. Autopsy findings and clinical diagnoses: a review of 1000 cases. *Hum Pathol* 24: 194–198.

Silver, MM, and Silver, MD. 2001. Examination of the heart and of cardiovascular specimens in surgical pathology. In: *Cardiovascular Pathology*, eds. Silver, MD, Gotlieb, AI, Schoen, FJ. New York: Churchill Livingstone, 1–29.

Spitz, WU, and Platt, MS. 1993. *Medicolegal Investigation of Death*. Springfield, IL: Charles C. Thomas, 716–722.

Turillazzi, E, and Pomara, C. 2006. Cardiovascular traumatic injuries. In: *Pathology of the Heart and Sudden Death in Forensic Investigation*, eds. Fineschi, V, Baroldi, G, and Silver, MD. Boca Raton, FL: CRC Press, 303–326.

Veress, B, and Alafuzoff, I. 1994. A retrospective analysis of clinical diagnoses and autopsy findings in 3,042 cases during two different time periods. *Hum Pathol* 25: 140145.

Wilson, JP. 1966. Post-mortem preservation of the small intestine. *J Pathol* 92: 229–230.

Pediatric and Fetal Autopsies

3

I. RIEZZO

Contents

There are important differences in the techniques used for perinatal and pediatric autopsies than those used for adults. Only experienced physicians should perform these autopsies. The dissection should be performed by a forensic pathologist and the histological examination by someone with experience in perinatal histology.

The case history should be thoroughly reviewed before entering the autopsy suite. If no information is available, the parents must be interviewed, even if this requires the approval of the police or a judge. The examination of an abandoned newborn or fetus must be undertaken with greater caution, if such a thing is possible. If the forensic pathologist omits any part of the examination, he or she will be quickly reminded by the courts.

3.1 The External Examination

The external examination of the fetus or newborn should focus on the search for malformations (Figures 3.1 and 3.2). Some of these may be obvious, as in the case of a cleft palate, congenital coronal atresia or stenosis, or anal and vaginal atresian. Examination of the oral cavity begins with digital palpation of the palate, followed by direct observation of the gums (Figures 3.3 and 3.4). The face, ears, and hands may display characteristic signs, for instance, in Down's syndrome and renal agenesis (always suspect this diagnosis when there is anhydramnios [from 17 weeks] and an empty fetal bladder [from as early as 14 weeks]) (Figures 3.5 and 3.6). The main measurements of the body regions should also be recorded (Table 3.1).

The cadaver is always measured and weighed first (Figures 3.7 and 3.8). Certain measurements, such as the crown–rump, the crown–heel, and the rump–heel length are absolutely required and must be measured with a centimeter ruler. The head, chest, and abdominal circumferences are measured with a flexible measuring tape (calibrated in centimeters) (Figure 3.9 through Figure 3.16). The chest circumference is measured at the level of the nipples, while the abdominal circumference is measured at the level of the umbilicus (see Table 3.1). The fontanels must be measured, as should the landmarks of the face. The interpupillary distance, the distance between inner and outer canthal folds, the interalar distance, the length of the lips, upper and lower lip thickness, and the intercommisural distance should all be measured and compared with what is considered normal for an infant at the same stage of development. In addition, the color of the sclera, iris, and conjunctiva should also be recorded, as should the configuration of the ears. The genitalia must be inspected and the scrotal contents assessed.

A whole body radiograph is done routinely in stillborns and newborns. In cases of stillbirth, the degree of skin slippage, bleb formation, maceration, as well as the laxity of the joints, and the presence of overlapping cranial bones should be recorded as they may give some indication of the time of death *in utero*. In some facilities, CT scanning is available and should be utilized.

3.2 Removal of the Brain

Removal of the newborn brain is performed in exactly the same way as in adults (Figures 3.17 and 3.18). If ossification is not totally complete, make a transverse incision, starting from the fontanel and ending at the occipital–parieto–parietal apex, and then manually

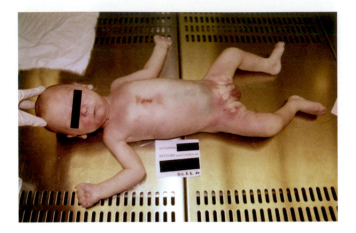

Figure 3.1 Supine position of the cadaver.

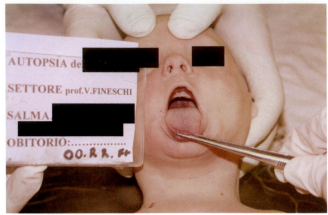

Figure 3.4 Inspection of the tongue.

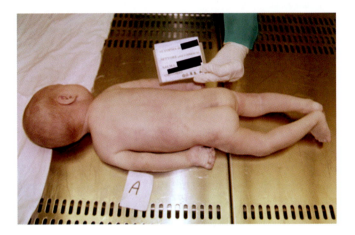

Figure 3.2 Prone position, recommended for measurements.

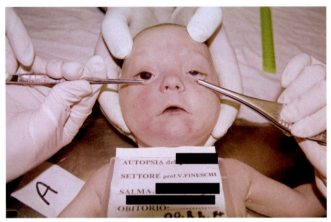

Figure 3.5 Inspection of lids and nasal openings.

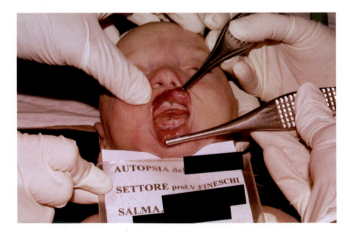

Figure 3.3 Inspection of oral cavity, lips, gums, and mouth roof.

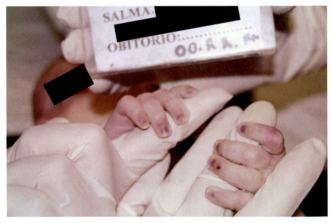

Figure 3.6 Examination of the fingers.

spread the four segments that have been created to facilitate removal of the brain.

In the fetus or if the sutures have not yet fused, and the theca is still soft enough to cut with a handheld scalpel, then open the cranium using the Benecke technique. The scalp is reflected, as in adults, by a mastoid incision. Beginning at the lateral portion of the frontal fontanel, the skull and the dura are incised at the same time, using a scalpel with a rounded point (unlike adults, at this age it is difficult to separate the

Table 3.1   Anatomical Fetal Measurements

Crown–heel length
Crown–rump length
Femur length
Foot length
Head circumference (measured above the eyebrows
    and ears and around the back of the head)
Biparietal diameter
Thoracic circumference (nipples)
Abdominal circumference (umbilical)
Weight

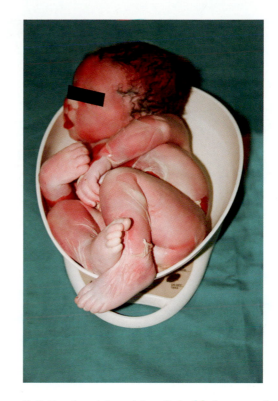

Figure 3.8 Fetal weight with a digital balance scale.

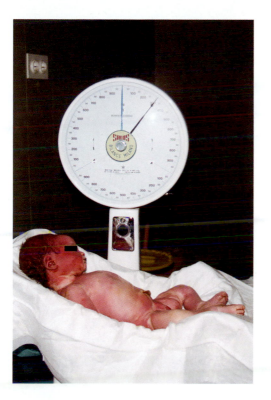

Figure 3.7 Fetal weight with a mechanical balance scale.

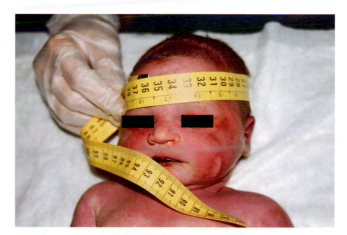

Figure 3.9 Head circumference.

dura from the skull). This incision leaves an opening about one centimeter wide along the midline. Through the opening the superior sagittal sinus and the falx cerebri can be seen, as well as an intact area along the occipital squamae on both sides. Visible suture lines can be followed by cutting along the posterior base of the frontal bone on both sides. The falx is then incised just as it is in adults.

Several different methods have been suggested for minimizing damage during removal of the brain. In most European countries the tendency is to inject a fixative solution (10% formalin in 70% of alcohol) through the arteries of the neck. Partial fixation will make the brain much firmer, which, in turn, makes removal easier. Alternatively, the fixative solution may be injected through the skin directly into the lateral ventricles and also through the lateral edge of the anterior fontanels.

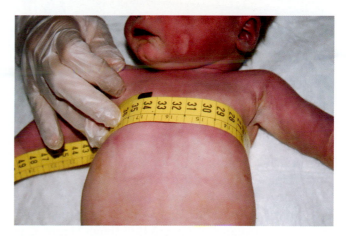

Figure 3.10 Chest circumference.

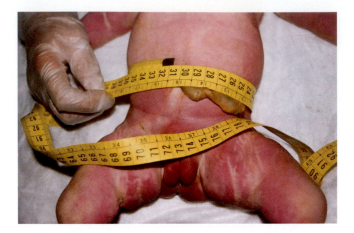

Figure 3.11 Abdominal circumference.

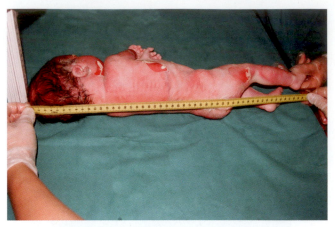

Figure 3.14 Crown–heel length with tailor's tape.

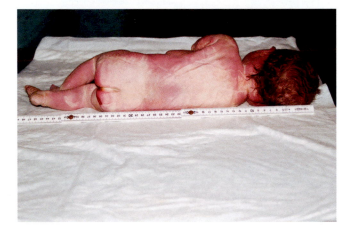

Figure 3.12 Crown–heel length with a tape measure.

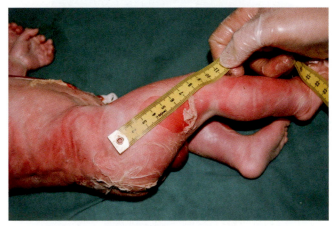

Figure 3.15 Femur length.

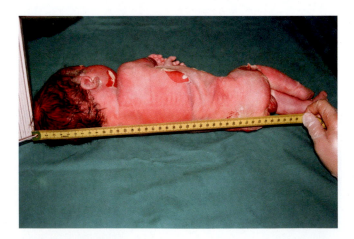

Figure 3.13 Crown–rump length with tailor's tape.

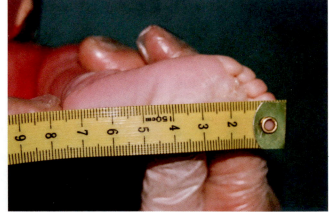

Figure 3.16 Foot length.

Unfortunately, none of these access methods are suitable if microbiologic studies are to be performed.

In one variant of the Benecke method, known as the butterfly variant, the skull is incised along the cranial structures and the fontanels (Figure 3.19 through Figure 3.21). This approach access to the cranial cavities is achieved by manually detaching the underlying structures with a scalpel and then freeing the brain from the underlying dura by hand. The bony flaps are manually luxated by the forensic surgeon and then a little cut at the base of each single bone is carried out. The dura (falx) must be cut from its bony attachments as close as possible to the skull.

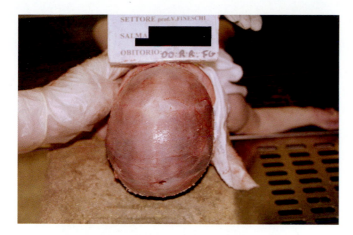

Figure 3.17 Skull cut scheme for circular cut.

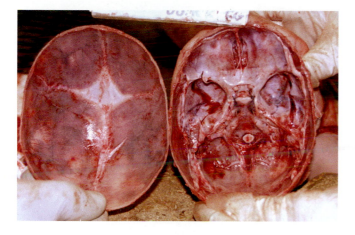

Figure 3.18 Inspection of skull and base.

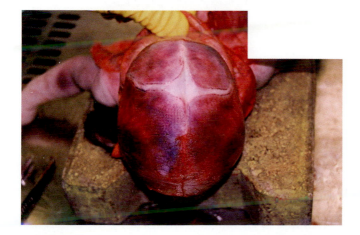

Figure 3.19 Fetal skull with ossification not totally complete.

According to Ludwig, damage to the brain may be further minimized if the scalp and the skullcap are opened and the falx is incised while an assistant keeps the head stationary. The tentorium and the great vein of Galen are transversally divided with the head held in this

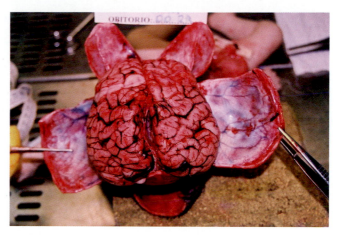

Figure 3.20 Butterfly variant: the skull is incised along the cranial structures and the fontanels.

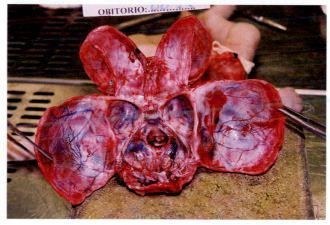

Figure 3.21 Butterfly variant: inspection of base.

position, gently detaching the parietal–occipital lobes. After the tentorium has been incised, an assistant must immobilize the cadaver, and the brain is held in place by the prosector. The brain is then lifted from the base of the skull. The brain must not be directly touched during this procedure, and when the connections are cut, we may let it fall, preferably in a container full of water and not on a hard surface. The Benecke method to leave the tentorium and remove the cerebral hemispheres from the encephalon trunk and from the cerebellum is rather controversial. The butterfly variant offers the forensic surgeon the huge advantage of being able to proceed to the removal of the encephalon with the theca still *in situ* (since it offers resistance and steadiness to the forensic surgeon operativeness), by the luxation of the theca bones and the obtainment of a large action spot in all the inspection phases and during the evisceration procedure. Therefore, as for the adult and for the newborn fetus, it is preferred to opt for the opening *in situ* of the lateral ventricles (Figures 3.22 and 3.23).

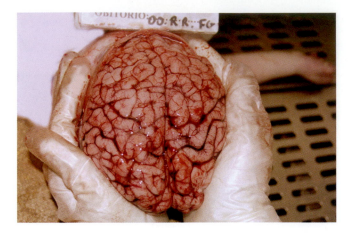

Figure 3.22 Examination *in situ of* encephalon without dura mater.

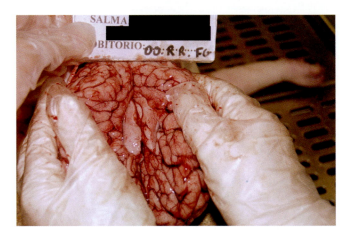

Figure 3.23 Opening *in situ* of lateral ventricles.

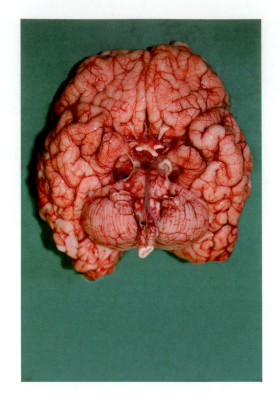

Figure 3.24 Examination of a fresh brain.

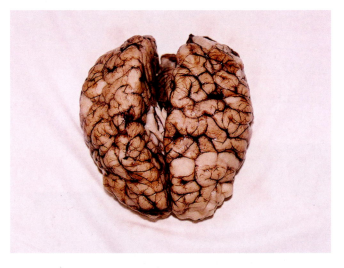

Figure 3.25 Gross examination of a fixed brain.

Before actually cutting the brain, it should be weighed and measured. Note its dimensions, shape, consistence, cerebral hemisphere symmetry, and apparent stage of development (Figure 3.24). The brain should then be fixed for 1 to 2 weeks and cut into coronal sections approximately 1 centimeter thick using a long sharp knife (Figures 3.25 and 3.26). Once the brain has been cut into sections, collect multiple samples for histological examination (midfrontal gyrus, mild corpus callosum, basal ganglia, parietal cortex, splenium, thalamus, caudate, hippocampi, etc.). The removal of the spinal cord is performed the same way as described for adults.

3.3   Access to the Chest

Some texts recommend submerging the fetus/newborn under water to rule out the presence of pneumothorax. However, this method actually yields a fairly high rate of false-negative results. The submersion technique certainly should be attempted if CT scanner is not available, but the latter is preferred. With one exception, the chest is opened in the same way as in adults: The jugular–pelvic resection must be 1.5 cm to the left of the median line to allow, when divaricating the abdominal parietal strips, the visualization of the umbilical artery. However, when the section is made by single planes (by an expert forensic surgeon) and the thin skin and the subcutis are raised, it is possible to analyze the correct vessel insertion and its relationship with abdominal wall structures (Figure 3.27 through Figure 3.43).

The same cuts are valid for thoracic structures removal, but the forensic surgeon will use only forceps

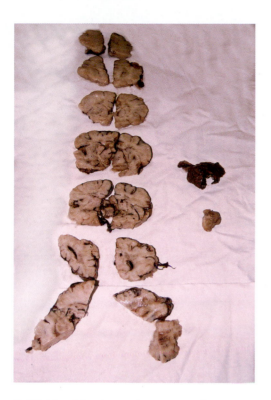

Figure 3.26 Fixed brain cut into coronal sections.

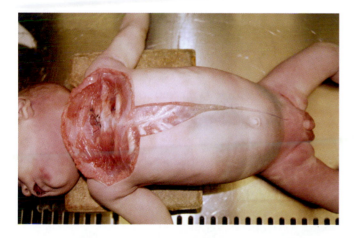

Figure 3.27 "Calix cut" and opening by single planes.

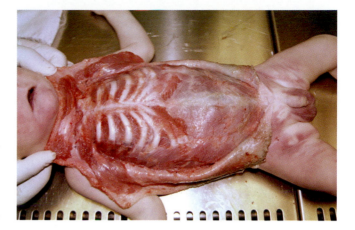

Figure 3.28 Showing of the thorax–abdominal area performed by opening single planes and overturning of skin obtained by peritoneum *in situ.*

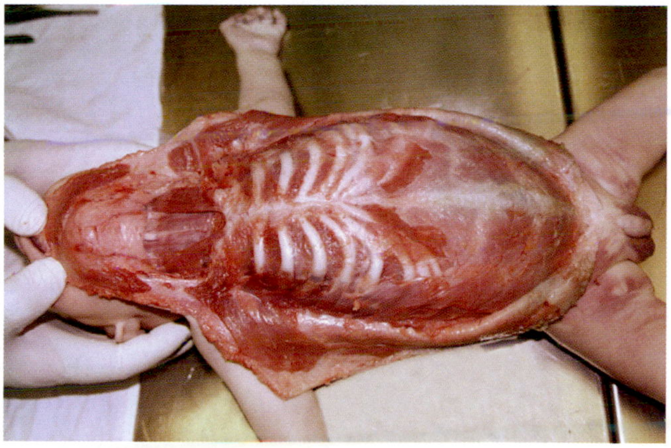

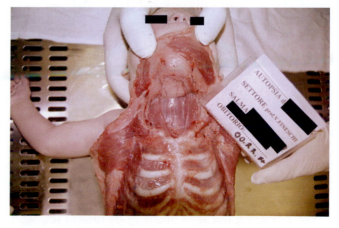

Figure 3.29 Extension of the section plane to the neck, with the front part of the neck showing.

and scalpels to assault the cartilaginous structures of the thoracic walls.

Age cannot be evaluated simply by looking at the cadaver. The body must be x-rayed and the apparent age confirmed with the appropriate histopathology and immunohistochemical methods. After the chest and abdomen have been opened, anatomical relationships can be studied *in situ*. The umbilical arteries, coursing along either side of the bladder, must be identified (Figures 3.44 and 3.45). The fluid contents of the pleural and abdominal cavities should be collected, measured, and submitted for bacterial culture and microscopic examination. Then, before actual evisceration, the thymus must be dissected

Figure 3.30 Neck skin flap turnover, performed at mandibular height. Exposure of the front part of the neck.

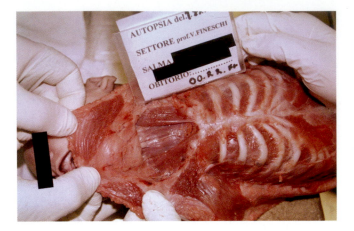

Figure 3.31 Inspection of the platysma muscle.

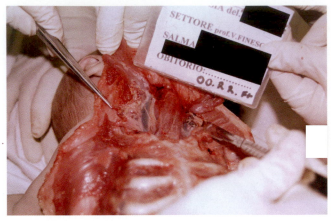

Figure 3.34 Isolation of the right sternocleidomastoid muscle and visualization of the vascular–nervous tract.

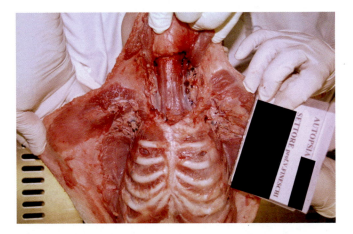

Figure 3.32 Inspection of the big and small pectoral muscles.

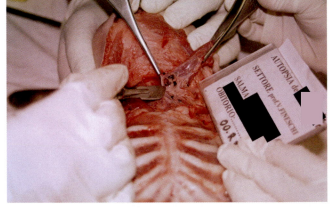

Figure 3.35 Isolation of the sternocleidomastoid muscle and the thymus edge.

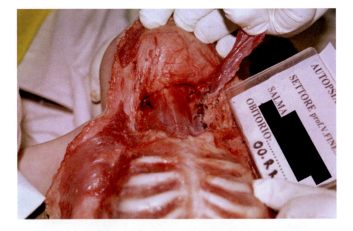

Figure 3.33 Isolation of the left sternocleidomastoid muscle and visualization of the vascular–nervous tract.

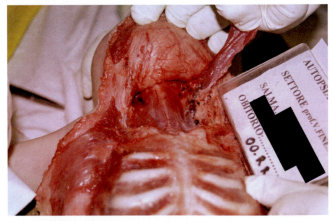

Figure 3.36 Left sternocleidomastoid muscle.

off the pericardium, and the pericardium should be opened *in situ* (Figures 3.46 and 3.47).

By retracting the apex of the heart toward the right, the connections of the pulmonary veins to the left lung and the left atria are visualized, with the heart in an anatomical position. When the heart is retracted to the left, the right pulmonary veins can be observed in the opening between the superior vena cava and the heart. The great vessels should be inspected, including all the vessels arising from the aortic arch (Figure 3.48 through Figure 3.50).

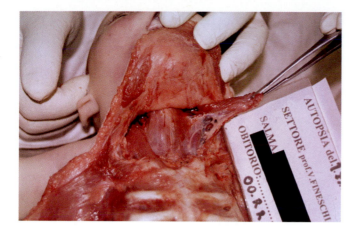

Figure 3.37 Left sternocleidomastoid muscle.

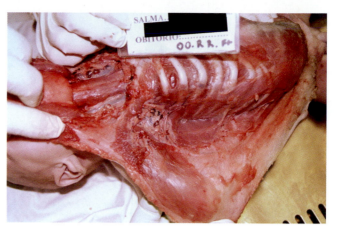

Figure 3.40 Inspection of the thoracic cavity at the back armpit level.

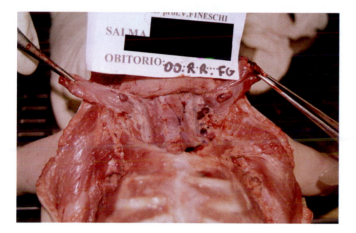

Figure 3.38 Sternocleidomastoid muscles.

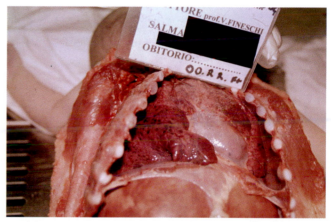

Figure 3.41 Removal of the chondrosternal layer and inspection of the thoracic cavities.

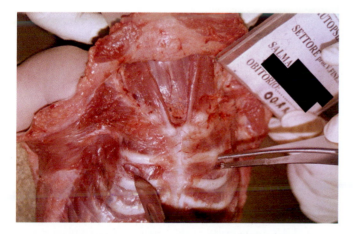

Figure 3.39 Incision of the intercostal muscles and of the parietal pleura at the second intercostal space level.

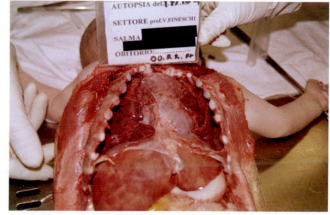

Figure 3.42 Inspection of the diaphragm.

3.4   Evisceration Methods

All evisceration techniques allow adequate visualization of malformations such as an anomalous pulmonary venous anastomosis, but removal of all the organs

en masse (the Letulle Technique) seems to be the most suitable method (Figure 3.51 through Figure 3.58). To allow for detailed examination of the heart, the heart and the great vessels should be removed *en bloc*, along with the entire aorta down to the iliac bifurcation. Then the inferior vena cava, esophagus, and aorta are divided

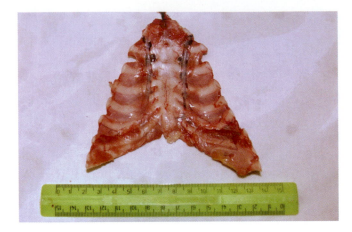

Figure 3.43 Inspection of the chondrosternal layer.

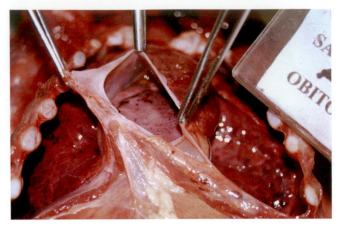

Figure 3.46 Upside-down, Y-shaped opening of the pericardium.

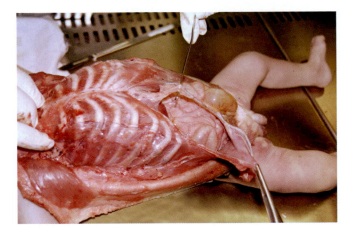

Figure 3.44 Inspection of the umbilical vein.

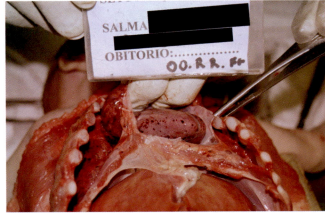

Figure 3.47 Inspection of the pericardium.

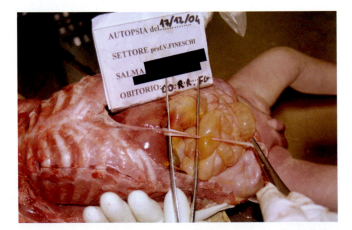

Figure 3.45 Inspection of the umbilical artery.

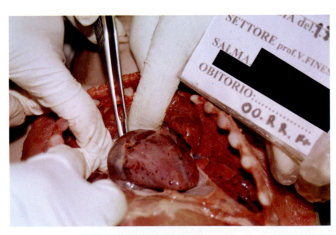

Figure 3.48 Inspection of the upper side of the heart.

at the level of the diaphragm, effectively isolating the heart–lung block (Figure 3.59 through Figure 3.67).

The gross examination of the heart should be performed only after it has been fixed *en bloc* along with the lungs and aorta. At this point, the shape, dimensions, weight, consistency, color, regular coronary arteries,

any abnormalities of the aortic arch, and neck vessels distribution should all be described. Last, find Botallo's duct (a fetal vessel that connects the left pulmonary artery with the descending aorta and normally becomes the arterial ligament after birth; also referred to as the arterial duct) by opening the aorta beginning in the

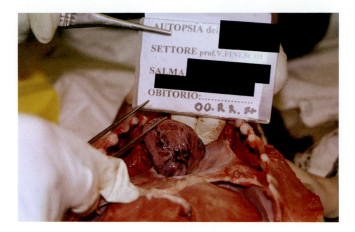

Figure 3.49 Inspection of the mediastinal side of the heart.

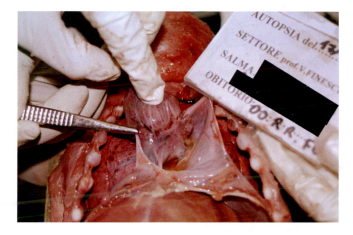

Figure 3.50 Inspection of the vascular root of the heart.

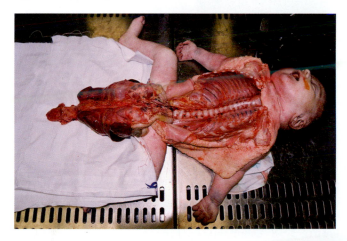

Figure 3.51 The Letulle Technique.

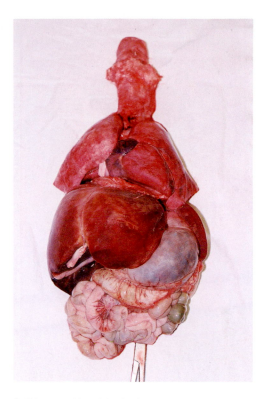

Figure 3.52 Letulle's block, front side.

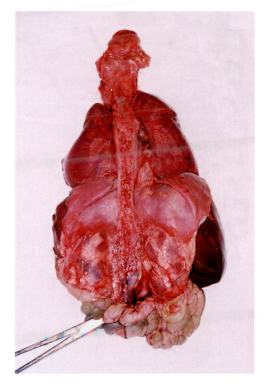

Figure 3.53 Letulle's block, posterior side.

abdomen and progressing upward to the ascending aortic arch (Figure 3.68 through Figure 3.70). There are two ways to section the heart: (1) along the short axis of the heart with coronal (transverse) sections from the apex to the atrioventricular plane (Figure 3.71), or (2) the older, more traditional approach "along the lines of normal blood flow." No matter what the approach, collect both

a blood spot (blood allowed to dry on a card that is later used for metabolic or DNA testing) and a tube of anticoagulated blood for DNA testing, and still another tube containing a sodium fluoride preservative. The concentrations of most drugs tend to increase after death,

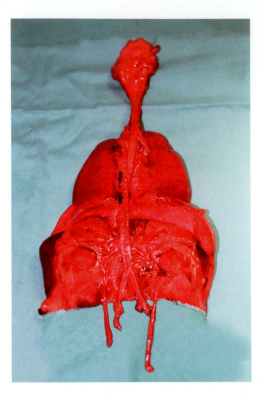

Figure 3.54 Letulle's block, posterior side.

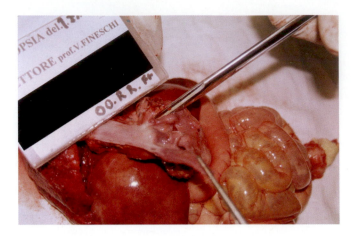

Figure 3.56 Larynx auditus (detail).

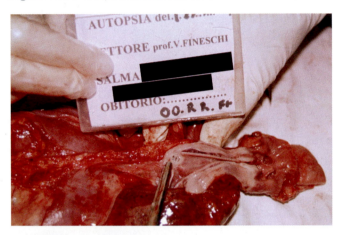

Figure 3.57 Trachea opening.

Figure 3.55 Inspection of the fauces, laryngotracheal aditus.

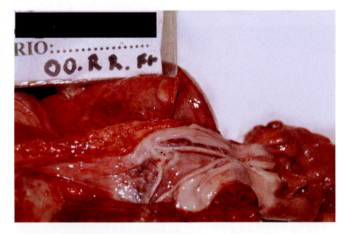

Figure 3.58 Esophagus opening.

especially in the heart. While this tendency makes interpretation difficult, it also makes heart blood an excellent matrix for drug screening; if any drug is present in the body it is likely to be detected in the heart.

The United States and many European countries require the collection of a *blood spot* that can be used to screen for the presence of metabolic diseases. No special care of the spot is required once it is collected. The tube of blood is for DNA extraction should that prove necessary at some later date.

The evisceration of other organs and procedures to be followed are exactly the same as in adults (Figure 3.72 through Figure 3.84).

During the autopsy, several organ samples and fluids should be collected and stored appropriately:

1. Postmortem toxicology: blood, vitreous humor, urine, bile, gastric contents, cerebrospinal fluid (CSF), liver, brain, kidney, muscle tissue
2. Postmortem microbiology: fluids, tissues, or purulent material collected using aseptic

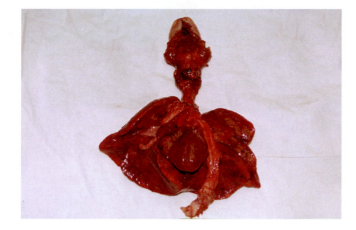

Figure 3.59 Visualization and isolation of the aorta.

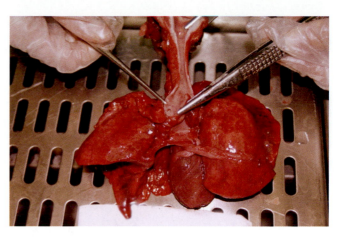

Figure 3.62 Right bronchus.

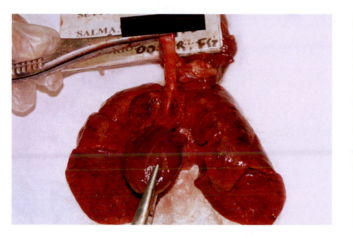

Figure 3.60 Visualization of the heart vessels.

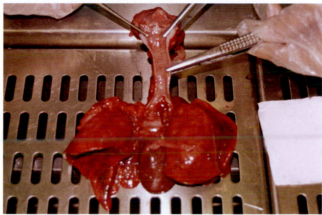
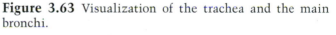

Figure 3.63 Visualization of the trachea and the main bronchi.

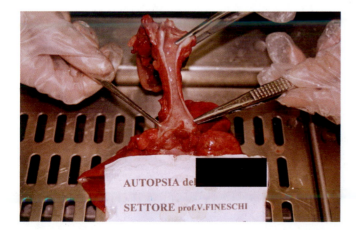

Figure 3.61 Visualization of the trachea up to the bronchi branch point.

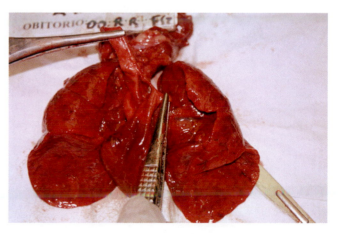

Figure 3.64 The great vasal trunks must be observed with extreme care so that a congenital heart condition may be detected.

technique (sterile syringe or sterile cotton-tipped applicator, sterile scalpel, and forceps) and stored in sterile plastic cups.

3. Molecular analysis: samples and fluids should be collected as soon as possible after death, then frozen and stored at −80°C.

4. Metabolic analysis: samples and fluids (blood, urine, vitreous, pericardial fluid, CSF) should be collected using aseptic technique, then frozen and stored.

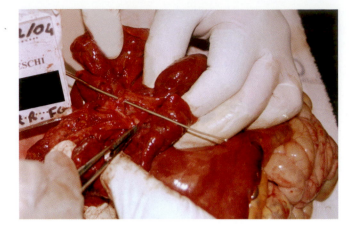

Figure 3.65 Isolation of the heart vascular components.

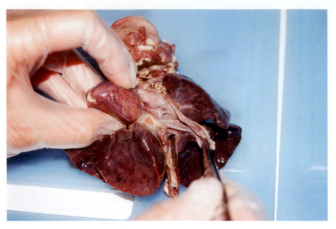

Figure 3.68 Visualization of the heart vascular components after fixation.

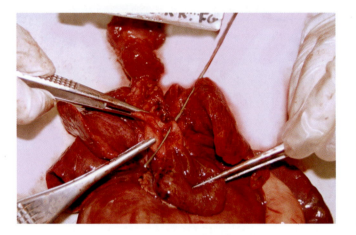

Figure 3.66 Specification and isolation of the vasal trunks.

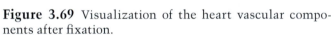

Figure 3.69 Visualization of the heart vascular components after fixation.

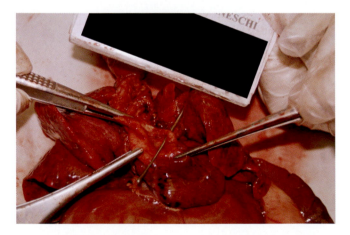

Figure 3.67 Isolation of the aorta with separation from the pulmonary trunk.

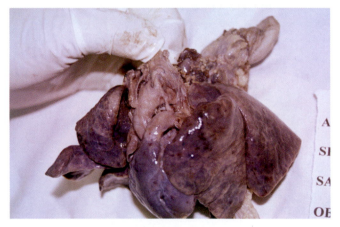

Figure 3.70 Visualization of the great vasal trunk after fixation to find the Botallo's duct.

Sections of all organs collected (for example, at least one sample of each pulmonary lobe, multiple samples of the heart, including the conduction system if possible, as well as skin, subcutaneous tissue, and diaphragm) should all be collected and submitted to the histology laboratory for preparation. The size of the sample need not be massive—generally a specimen measuring less than 2 centimeters across and 1 centimeter deep will suffice. Pathologists must resist the urge to economize by placing small slices of each organ in one cassette for mounting. Though the technique certainly saves money, it makes accurate examination almost impossible.

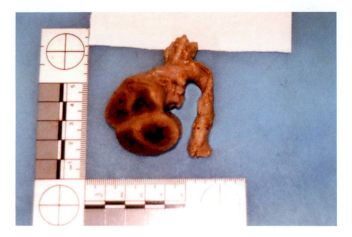

Figure 3.71 Short axis of the heart with transverse sections from the apex to the atrioventricular plane.

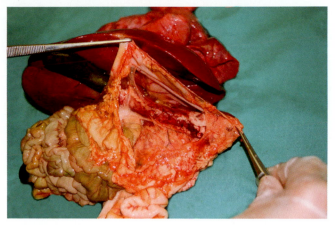

Figure 3.74 Letulle's block: examination of the pancreas and duodenum.

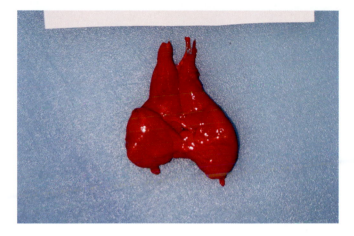

Figure 3.72 Gross examination of the thymus.

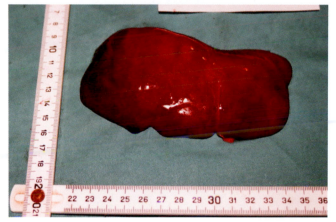

Figure 3.75 Liver inspection and measurements.

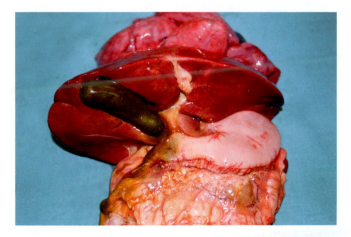

Figure 3.73 Letulle's block: visualization of the bile collection.

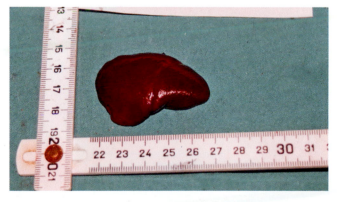

Figure 3.76 Spleen inspection and measurements.

3.5 Examination of the Placenta

The placenta, the fetal membranes, and the umbilical cord must always be studied (Figure 3.85). It is the autopsy physician's responsibility to make sure none of these are discarded before the autopsy begins. If the placenta is fresh it should be cultured both for bacteria and viruses. Additional material should also be collected for cytogenetic studies, electron microscopy, or simply frozen to allow for the later study of metabolic disorders (Figure 3.86).

Details describing the macroscopic examination of the placenta and the correct sampling procedures have been reviewed several times and will not be detailed (e.g., Langston et al. 1997). Gross and microscopic

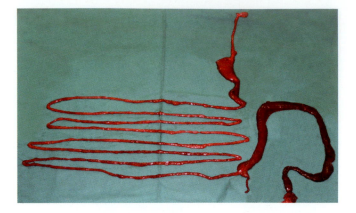

Figure 3.77 Examination of the esophagus, stomach, duodenum, and small and large intestines.

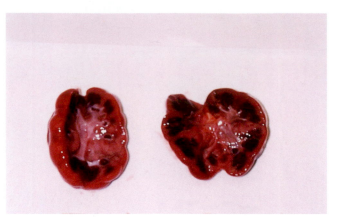

Figure 3.80 Kidneys: transverse incision through the convex border.

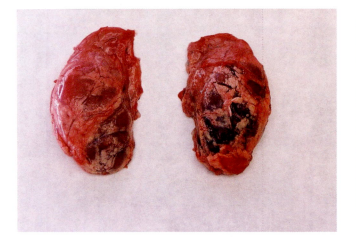

Figure 3.78 Kidneys with capsules.

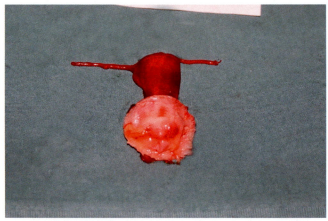

Figure 3.81 Gross examination of the uterus.

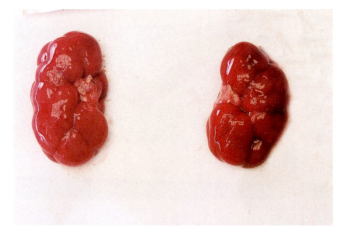

Figure 3.79 Gross examination of the kidneys without capsules.

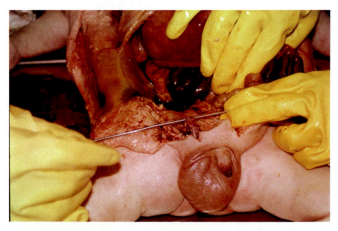

Figure 3.82 Isolation and removal of the testes.

examination of the placenta are mandatory when certain maternal, neonatal, and placental conditions are known to be present.

If none of these conditions have been identified, the placenta should be labeled, placed in an appropriate container, and refrigerated at 4°C for at least 3 to 7 days. A large container will be needed to transport the placenta

itself. If the container used is too small, the shape of the placenta will become deformed. The placenta should be fixed in at least 3 liters of 10% formalin (a volume of fixative fluid 5 to 6 times the size of the placenta's). Prior to fixation, drain the blood from the placenta, as its presence can cause difficulties during the fixation process.

The placenta may be weighed fresh or fixed, as long as the modality is specified in the report. What really

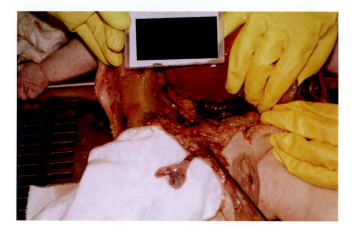

Figure 3.83 Isolation and removal of the testes.

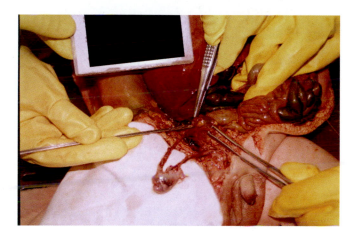

Figure 3.84 Isolation and removal of the testes.

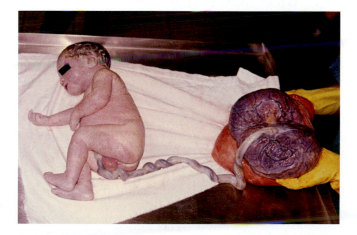

Figure 3.85 Inspection of the fetus, placenta, fetal membranes, and umbilical cord.

matters is the ratio of placenta weight to the weight of the fetus at the time of birth, and many feel it is sufficient just to indicate that a placenta appears "small," or of "average" size. Others suggest the placenta itself should be measured on both its main and perpendicular axes (Figure 3.87).

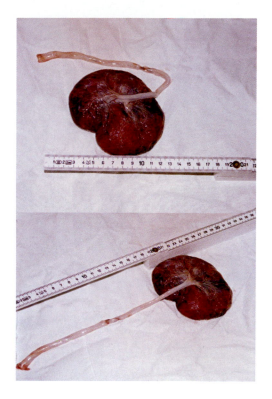

Figure 3.86 Gross examination of a fresh placenta and measurements.

The umbilical cord should be removed at a point 3 centimeters from its insertion. It is important to mark the point of amputation, showing the exact point at which the cord has been cut. Umbilical cord blood should be obtained in every case, even if it is not subsequently analyzed. When the report is finally generated, always specify the shape, consistency, number of cotyledons, the insertion point of the umbilical cord, and the type of attachment of membranes to the placenta.

The external inspection of the placenta should begin with the fetal surface (Figure 3.88). Its color should be noted, and then it should be inspected for the presence of subchorionic fibrin. Then inspect for opacities, hematomas, or abnormal vascular distribution, and look for evidence of squamous metaplasia or amnion nodosum (a nodular condition of the fetal surface of the amnion, observed in oligohydramnios associated with absence of the kidneys of the fetus).

The gross examination of the maternal surface focuses on the morphology and number of cotyledons, their distribution, and the presence of depressions, tears, calcifications, evidence of recent infarction, and the presence of hematomas (Figure 3.89). All significant changes and lesions should be described, measured, and localized (i.e., whether the cotyledons are intact, retroplacental hemorrhage, abnormal adhesions). Small lesions should be separately measured and described. When an abnormal process is seen to be extensive or

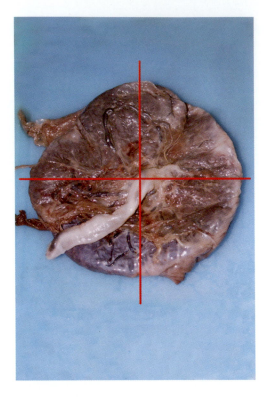

Figure 3.87 Fixed placenta: measurement of both diameters.

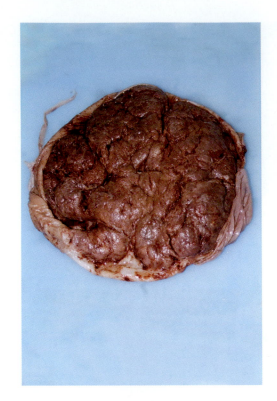

Figure 3.89 Gross examination of the maternal surface.

and extending to the fetal surface. One section must cross through the point of umbilical cord insertion (Figure 3.90). Variations of thickness within the section should be noted (Figure 3.91).

3.5.1 Gross Examination of the Umbilical Cord

First, record the length of the umbilical cord while it is still attached. The most reliable measurement of total cord length is obtained when measurement is performed in the delivery room. After recording the length, measure the diameter of the cord. The largest and the smallest diameter should be measured at a point 10 centimeters from cord insertion. Cord insertion in the placenta (centrally, eccentrically, at the margin, or in the membranes), numbers of vessels within the umbilical cord (this has to be assessed at least 5 centimeters from the placental insertion), the amount of Wharton's jelly, the presence of excessive twisting or strictures, true or false knots, edema, hemorrhages, and congestions or necrosis should all be noted, described, and, if possible, photographed.

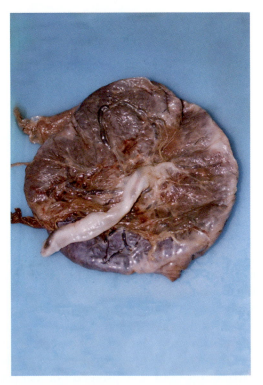

Figure 3.88 Gross examination of the fetal surface.

multifocal, always provide an estimate of the percentage of tissue involved.

The placenta should be sectioned with a long, sharp knife along its major axis, at intervals of approximately 1 to 1.5 centimeters, beginning at the maternal surface

3.5.2 Gross Examination of Placental Membranes

The fetal membranes should be placed in their usual anatomic position and then their mode of attachment

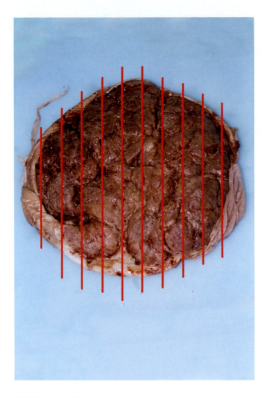

Figure 3.90 Fixed placenta: the intervals of 1 to 1.5 centimeters are in red for the section along its major axis.

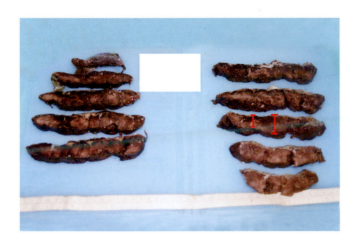

Figure 3.91 Serial section of the placenta. In red, major and minor thickness.

to the placenta (circumvallate, circumarginate, marginal) should be noted. Next, record the site and mode of rupture, the distance from the point of rupture to the edge of the placenta, the distribution of blood vessels, and the translucency and the color of membranes. The thickness of the membranes should be measured and opacities noted (this is best done in front of a bright light).

3.6   Histological Sections

The samples can be obtained from fresh or fixed placenta. The following sections are generally recommended:

1. "Membrane roll": This method is used to increase the surface area examined. A strip of membrane from the point of rupture extending to the nearest placental edge is used. The membrane should be wrapped around a long, thin object such as a forceps, and then cut to obtain a spiral cross-section.
2. Samples of umbilical cord: One sample should be taken near the fetal surface, the other near the maternal surface, and one additional sample from the center. Any obvious pathological lesions must be sampled as well.
3. Samples of placenta: These samples are obtained from both the maternal and fetal surface (full thickness, including amnions and deciduas). These samples must be taken from the central region of the placenta. One of these must be taken from under the umbilical cord insertion and others from any focal lesions discovered.

To study infections of the placental membranes, samples can be randomly collected or taken from the point of rupture. If the purpose is to study infections of the villi, it is important to take several samples from different cotyledons.

References

Beckwith, JB. 1989. The value of the pediatric postmortem examination. *Pediatr Clin North Am* 36: 29–36.

Bove, KE. 1997. Practice guidelines for autopsy pathology: The perinatal and pediatric autopsy. Autopsy Committee of the College of American Pathologists. *Arch Pathol Lab Med* 121: 368–376.

Chambers, HM. 1992. The perinatal autopsy: a contemporary approach. *Pathology* 24: 45–55.

Faye-Petersen, OM, Heller, DS, and Jashi, VV. 2006. *Handbook of placental pathology*. 2nd ed. London: Taylor & Francis.

Finkbeiner, WE, Ursell, PC, and Davis, RL. 2004. *Autopsy pathology: A manual and atlas*. Philadelphia: Churchill Livingstone.

Fulcheri, E, Grillo, F, and Musizzano, Y. 2006. Il trattamento della placenta per l'esame istopatologico finalizzato allo studio ed alla diagnostica del danno neurologico feto-neonatale. *Riv. It. Ost. Gin* 9: 475–481.

Gilbert-Barness, E, and Debich-Spicer, DE. 2002 *Handbook of pediatric autopsy pathology*. Totowa, NJ: Humana Press.

Hargitai, B, Marton, T, and Cox, PM. 2004. Examination of the human placenta. *J Clin Pathol* 57: 785–792.

Isaacson, G. 1984. Postmortem examination of infant brains (techniques for removal, fixation and sectioning). *Arch Pathol Lab Med* 108: 80–81.

Langston, C, Kaplan, C, Macpherson, T, Manci, E, Peevy, K, Clark, B, Murtagh, C, Cox, S, and Glenn, G. 1997. Practice guideline for examination of the placenta: Developed by the Placental Pathology Practice Guideline Development Task Force of the College of American Pathologists. *Arch Pathol Lab Med* 121: 449–476.

Pomara, C and Fineschi, V. 2007. *Manuale—Atlante di tecnica autoptica forense*. Padova: Piccin.

Saller, DN, Lesser, KB, Harrel, U, Rogers, BB, and Oyer, CE. 1995. The clinical utility of the perinatal autopsy. *JAMA* 273: 663–665.

Valdes-Dapena, M, and Huff, DS. 1989. *Manuale delle autopsie perinatali*. Edizione Italiana a cura di Terribile Wiel Marin V. e Salmaso R. Padova: Piccin.

Wigglesworth, JS. 1984. *Perinatal pathology*. Philadelphia: WB Saunders.

Wigglesworth, JS and Singer, D. 2001. *Perinatal pathology*. Philadelphia: Blackwell Scientific.

Laboratory Technologies and Methodologies

4

F. BUCCHIERI
F. RAPPA
F. CAPPELLO

Contents

4.1 Introduction

The histological study of organs is a fundamental passage in an autoptic investigation. It allows the confirmation of observations made during macroscopic investigations as well as helping to obtain useful information and dissolving diagnostic and legal doubts. However, a histological investigation is a complex process that requires specific, accurately followed procedures in order to obtain a sample that can be observed and interpreted with a light microscope. Also, because histological and histochemical techniques are numerous and wide in variety, several structural components of the human body can be seen individually or, in some cases, simultaneously. Therefore, to choose the appropriate investigation procedure based on the kind of study, a good understanding of histopathological techniques is essential.

This chapter briefly sums up the main conventional histological techniques as well as the most commonly used histochemical procedures used for examining cells and tissues in histological preparations of human organs during autoptic investigations.

However, this chapter is not fully comprehensive; further information can be found in specialistic publications.

4.2 Specimen Collection Techniques

Autoptic investigation requires removal of internal organs. This removal phase is a fundamental passage that initiates the macroscopic and histological study of tissues. The first step in the procedure is a visual observation of the organ, followed by the evaluation of its anatomical position. All organs removed during an autopsy, in some cases after fixation, must be meticulously sectioned and sampled. The first process consists of sectioning the organ in strips between 5 and 10 mm thick, depending on the organ in question, that can subsequently be observed to detect eventual solid or cystic lesions, necrosis, and so forth. Instead, the sampling process consists of the removal of smaller but diagnostically significant biopsies, which will subsequently be dehydrated and paraffin embedded.

It is important that the specimens be accompanied with an accurate macroscopic description of the organ. This description must contain the following:

1. Macroscopic data of the organ, such as dimensions, weight, physical appearance, color of the tissue, and so forth.
2. Detailed description of the quantity and site of biopsies that need to be progressively numbered.

4.3   Fixation

Fixation is the foundation of the sequence of procedures required to prepare a sample of biological matter (tissues or cells) for microscopy or other analysis. It preserves cells and tissues from decay, deactivating proteolytic enzymes and common microorganisms (in particular, bacteria) that could damage the sample. Once tissues are removed from the body, they undergo a process of self-destruction or autolysis, initiated soon after cell death by action of intracellular enzymes that cause breakdown of protein and eventual liquefaction of the cell. Therefore, tissue samples should be fixed as soon as possible after death or, when this is not immediately possible, refrigerated.

Tissues should be cut to such thickness (no more than 1 cm) that fixing fluid readily penetrates throughout in a reasonably short period of time. This time varies with the fixative and inversely with the fixation temperature. Various classifications of fixatives are used. The primary fixatives are classed in coagulants and noncoagulants.

4.3.1   Primary Coagulant Fixatives

Ethanol has only a limited application as a fixing fluid because it can cause distortion of nuclear detail, shrinkage of cytoplasm, and denaturation of proteins. If fixation is prolonged, ethanol removes histones from the nuclei and later extracts RNA and DNA. Nevertheless, it is often used undiluted for preservation of glycogen, and for fixation of pigments and blood. At a 60% to 80% concentration and low temperature, ethanol can be used

as a fixative for preserving certain proteins and enzymes in a relatively undenatured state.

Mercuric chloride is highly toxic and corrosive. It is seldom used alone, but can be combined with acetic and other acids, formaldehyde, alcohol, and various mixtures. It hardens the cytoplasm, increasing its affinity for acid dyes, and decreases the affinity of cellular and bacterial components for basic aniline dyes.

Chromium dioxide is a strong oxidizer that is used with other ingredients. It penetrates slowly and may cause shrinkage of tissues during subsequent processing. This fixative decreases the affinity of proteins for basic dyes.

Picric acid leaves tissue soft and penetrates well, precipitating all proteins. It will continue to react with tissue structures and cause loss of basophilia.

4.3.2   Primary Noncoagulant Fixatives

Formaldehyde is the most widely employed universal fixative for pathologic histology. It is a gas with a very pungent odor, ordinarily available as an approximately saturated solution of the gas in water. Such solution contains 37% to 40% of formaldehyde gas and is commonly called *formalin*. In samples prepared for microscopy, 10% formalin is used. Formaldehyde is also obtainable in a stable, solid form, composed of high molecular weight polymers, known as paraformaldehyde.

Formalin requires a relatively short fixation time, but can also be used for long-term storage, as it produces no deleterious effects on tissue morphology, with nuclear and cytoplasmic details being adequately preserved. Formalin does not precipitate proteins and only slightly precipitates other components of the cell. It does not harden or render albumin insoluble, but subsequent hardening with alcohols is prevented. Formalin neither preserves nor destroys adipose tissue and is a good fixative for complex lipids, but has no effect on neutral fats. Although not the fixative of choice for carbohydrates, it preserves proteins so that they hold glycogen, which is otherwise readily leached from the cell.

Potassium bichromate is a strong oxidizing agent and does not coagulate proteins, but jellifies them. It does not fix carbohydrates. This fixative increases the affinity of tissues for basic and acid dyes.

Acetic acid is never used alone but often combined with other fixatives that cause shrinkage, such as ethanol and methanol. Acetic acid penetrates tissues thoroughly and rapidly, but lyses red blood cells. It also increases cytoplasm affinity for acid dyes.

Glutaraldehyde is an oily liquid at room temperature, miscible with water, alcohol, and benzene. It is used as a tissue fixative for electron microscopy. Glutaraldehyde has also been extensively used as an agent for protein–protein linkage. It has an inhibitory effect on catalase, allowing the selective demonstration of peroxidase activity of peroxisomes and on other enzyme altering immunological property.

Fixative mixtures, composed of compatible fixatives, are also routinely used. These must meet specific requirements including the following: they must penetrate quickly, be compatible with the dyes used, and must not be too expensive. For example, a mixture of osmium tetroxide and glutaraldehyde has been shown to be effective for neutral fat and fine structural localization of acid phosphatase. Other mixtures, such as osmium tetroxide–zinc iodide, have been used postfixation for delineating synaptic vesicles and Langerhans cells.

After fixation, the specimen must be rinsed under running water and can be conserved in 70% ethanol or 5% to 10% formalin. Ethanol and formalin alter tissues, so it is advisable to embed the sample in paraffin as soon as possible after fixation.

Cryofixation is a conventional chemical fixation technique used, for instance, in postmortem structural alterations. Antigenicity of constituents of specimens can be deteriorated and soluble elements relocated in the process of chemical fixation. Cryofixation can overcome these drawbacks.

Another simple fixation method that is easy to apply and does not require expensive equipment is the *freeze-substitution fixation.* This technique produces excellent results and has many advantages. It ensures an adequate conservation of morphological details as well as that of certain tissue components that can deteriorate during the application of traditional fixation methods. Freeze-substitution is based on rapid freezing of tissues followed by solution ("substitution" by alcohol or other solvent) of ice at a very low temperature. This method can also be employed, at a low temperature, after dehydration in a polar solvent. Among the various procedures, the Peyrot technique is particularly recommended for studies on glycogen, whereas the Feder and Sidman technique has more of a general application. After fixation, the tissue samples must be embedded, sectioned, and stained.

4.4   Inclusion Technique

The freezing process is used to prepare specimen sections for rapid diagnosis and study of fatty and lipoid substances, which would be lost if paraffin or nitrocellulose methods were employed. These specimens are sectioned with a cryostat.

Other commonly used sectioning methods require infiltration with embedding medium. These include paraffin, gelatin, agar, soaps, nitrocellulose, and carbowax. Of these, carbowax, agar, and soap masses are water soluble, and tissue may be infiltrated directly. Paraffin is soluble in various fat solvents, whereas nitrocellulose is soluble in a mixture of 100% alcohol and ether. In these cases tissue must first be dehydrated, and subsequently the dehydration agent must be replaced with a solvent before infiltration with the embedding medium. The specimen is sectioned with a microtome (see "The Microtome" at the end of this chapter).

4.5   Frozen Sections

The frozen section procedure is used for a rapid microscopic analysis of a specimen. The instrument used for cryosection is the cryostat, which is essentially a microtome in a freezer. The specimen is rapidly frozen to about –20°C. At this temperature, most tissues become rock hard. Subsequently, the specimen is cut with the cryostat in sections of 10 to 15 μ. These sections are transferred on a glass slide and stained. For a quick diagnosis, the frozen sections can be stained in toluidine blue or thionin. The good slice success depends on the correct piece and knife cooling. If the specimen is hard the sections crumple.

Before cutting a frozen section, from any fresh tissue, it is essential to obtain as much information as possible on the source of the sample. Where this is not possible, all the precautionary measures used when handling infected material should be adopted.

4.6   Embedding Methods: Paraffin

Paraffin is a common name for a group of alkane hydrocarbons. These are in a solid form and insoluble in water, but soluble in various solvents (ether, benzene, and certain esters).

Before infiltrating tissue with paraffin, it is necessary to dehydrate the tissue. The traditional dehydrating agent is ethyl alcohol. Tissues are usually transferred from water into 70% alcohol, and subsequently into 80%, 95%, and finally into 100% alcohol. Some omit the first step and start directly with 80% alcohol. Afterward, it is necessary to remove the water or alcohol from the tissue by replacing them with paraffin solvents. The best paraffin solvents are xylene, benzene, toluene, chloroform, and cedar oil. All of these are miscible with paraffin at 56°C. Xylene is a clarifier that allows easy detection of complete dehydration of the sample (Table 4.1).

Table 4.1 Paraffin Inclusion Method

Passage	Note
1. Dehydrate in 30%, 50%, 70%, 95%, and 100% alcohol	1 h in each alcohol
2. Diaphanize in xylene (paraffin solvent)	1 h at 60°C
3. Embed in paraffin	Overnight at 60°C
4. Paraffin block	

Benzene is cheap and can be removed from the paraffin more quickly than xylene, as well as producing the softest and most friable sections. Toluene hardens tissues less than xylene. Chloroform hardens tissues, while cedar oil is an excellent dealcoholization or clearing agent.

Subsequently, the specimens are embedded in paraffin. During the embedding process, the tissue must be positioned so that sections will be cut in the desired plane. Paraffin is solidified in specific metal moulds containing the specimen. This block can then be sectioned with a microtome.

4.7 Other Embedding Media

The specimens can be embedded in other media, such as celloidin and polyester wax. In particular, celloidin is a mixture of mono- and dinitrocellulose. It is used for larger samples. In pathology, this method is utilized principally for studies on eyes and bones.

4.7.1 Adhering Sections to Slides and Preliminary Treatment for Staining

The sections must be well attached to the slides before undergoing the following treatments. It is paramount for the slides to be perfectly clean to avoid losing sections during treatment. It is possible to purchase precleaned slides or to clean them with a 5% solution of acetic acid or sulphochromic solution followed by a water rinse.

Many operators prefer to spread a minimal quantity of various adhesive liquids, such as Mayer's albumen glycerol, Masson's gelatin, and Ruyter's liquid, on the surface of the slide before floating the section onto it. Mayer's albumen glycerol is made by mixing one volume of fresh eggs with an equal volume of pure glycerol. The mixture is then filtered through absorbent cotton or filter paper at 55°C to 58°C. Masson's gelatin is constituted by 0.1% to 0.2% of gelatin solution in distilled water. Ruyter's liquid is constituted by acetone, benzoate of methyl, and glycerinate albumin.

Before proceeding to the staining of the sections, some fundamental preliminary treatments are necessary.

Ordinarily, paraffin sections are dried overnight before deparaffinizing and staining. Subsequently the sections are deparaffinized by immersing them in xylene to dissolve the paraffin. A second change of xylene is necessary to prevent carrying paraffin into succeeding reagents. Xylene is then removed from the sections in two successive changes of 100% alcohol. Finally, the sections are hydrated in one change each of 95%, 80%, and 50% alcohol, followed by water. After these treatments, staining can be performed.

4.8 General Staining Procedures

According to the type of the sample, there are different staining procedures. For nonpermanent samples, a single dye is used, which is generally enough to detect any malignant cells; for permanent samples, the employment of two dyes allows an easier reading (see "Classification of Dyes" at the end of this chapter). Blue toluidine stain is used for nonpermanent samples, whereas for permanent ones, hematoxylin–eosin stain is used (Table 4.2 and Figure 4.1).

For morphological study of the tissue, various staining procedures are used according to the type of tissue and study.

4.8.1 Epithelial Tissue

For the staining of epithelial tissue, hematoxylin–eosin is commonly used (Table 4.2). Hematoxylin is a basic dye that specifically stains the nuclei of cells that contain acid residues (DNA). When using hematoxylin, basophilic structures in the tissue appear blue. Eosin is an acid dye that stains the cytoplasm of cells by binding itself to the basic residues of proteins. With eosin, acidophilic structures appear various shades of pink.

Table 4.2 Hematoxylin–Eosin Method

Passage	Note
1. Remove paraffin	Through xylene, 10 min
2. Rehydrate sections	Descending scale of alcohol from 100% to 30%, 5 min in each alcohol, and then water for 5 min
3. Stain in hematoxylin	8 min
4. Rinse in running water	2–3 min
5. Stain in eosin	2 min
6. Rinse in running water	1–2 min
7. Dehydrate in 30%, 50%, 70%, 95%, and 100% alcohol	5 min each in alcohol
8. Mount with Canada balsam	

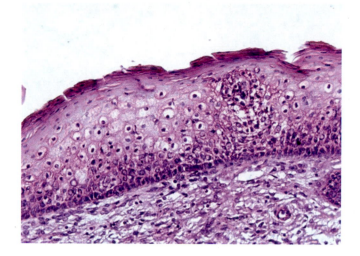

Figure 4.1 Hematoxylin–eosin stain. Uterine esocervix: hematoxylin stains nuclei violet and eosin stains cytoplasm pink.

4.8.2 Nervous Tissue

Toluidine blue stains chromophilic substances (Table 4.3). Cresyl violet stains Nissl substances purple (Table 4.4). Thionin stains chromophilic substances brilliant blue (Table 4.5). Gallocyanin stains the nuclei (Table 4.6).

4.8.3 Connective Tissue

There are a variety of staining agents for collagen fibers, elastic tissue, fundamental substance, fibrin and

Table 4.3 Toluidine Blue Method

Passage	Note
1. Remove paraffin and rehydrate sections	Thickness sections <10 μ
2. Stain in 0.5% Toluidine blue in water solution	5 min
3. Pass through one change of 95% alcohol, two changes of 100% alcohol, and one change of xylene	1–2 min each in alcohol
4. Mount with Canada balsam	

Table 4.4 Cresyl Violet Method

Passage	Note
1. Remove paraffin and rehydrate sections	<10 μ thick sections
2. Stain in 0.5% water solution of cresyl violet in 1% acetic acid	3–5 min
3. Rinse in distilled water	1–2 min
4. Dehydrate with one change each of 95%, 100% alcohol and xylene	1 min each in alcohol
5. Mount with Canada balsam	

Table 4.5 Thionin Method

Passage	Note
1. Remove paraffin and rehydrate sections	<10 μ thick sections
2. Treat with 0.55% lithium carbonate in water solution	5 min
3. Stain in 0.05% lithium carbonate in 0.25% thionin solution	5–10 min
4. Rinse in distilled water	2 min
5. Pass through one change of 70% alcohol	1 min
5. Pass through two changes of butilic alcohol	Each 2–3 min
6. Mount with Canada balsam	

Table 4.6 Gallocyanin Method

Passage	Note
1. Remove paraffin and rehydrate sections	<10 μ thick sections
2. Treat with 0.4% to 0.5% floxin B solution	5 min
3. Rinse in distilled water	6–8 min
4. Pass through 95% alcohol	5 min
5. Rinse in distilled water	1–2 min
6. Stain in gallocyanin solution	Overnight at room temperature or 3 h at 56°C
7. Rinse in running water	2–3 min
8. Stain in eosin	1 min
9. Dehydrate and mount with Canada balsam	

collagen, elastic and reticular fibers, and blood components. Staining of collagen fibers can be classified in methods based on the competition between two acid staining agents and methods that use phosphomolybdic or phosphowolframic acids.

Methods falling in the first category use a mixture of two acid dyes. The more diffusible dye penetrates the more compact structures, whereas the less diffusible dye is restricted to more permeable structures. In particular, these methods use picric acid in water solution, acid fuchsin, methylene blue, and aniline blue. They have the advantage of being quick and simple to execute, but generally have weak contrast levels, weakly staining the cytoplasm as well as the secretion granules.

Among these methods, the trichromic Cajal-Gallego method stains the nuclei, cartilage, granulations of cells, and mucin red purple; stains the cytoplasm light green or yellowish; stains collagen fibers blue; and stains muscular fibers yellow green (Table 4.7).

Methods of the second type, using phosphomolybdic or phosphowolframic acid, require a suitable fixation and perfect sections with a thickness not greater than 10 μm. Among these methods, are the trichromic

Table 4.7   Cajal-Gallego's Trichromic Method

Passage	Note
1. Remove paraffin and rehydrate sections	<10 μ thick sections
2. Stain 5 min in fuchsin solution	10 ml of distilled water, 5 drops of Ziehl's fuchsin, 1 drop of glacial acetic acid
3. Rinse in distilled water	1–2 min
4. Fix 5 min in acetic formol	10 ml of distilled water, 2 drops of formalin, 2 drops of acetic acid
5. Rinse in distilled water	1–2 min
6. Stain 1 min in picro-indigo carmine	10 ml of picric acid solution and 0.25 g of indigo carmine
7. Rinse in distilled water	1–2 min
8. Dehydrate in 30%, 50%, 70%, 95%, and 100% alcohol	Rapid rinsing in 95% and 100% alcohol
9. Mount with Canada balsam	

Table 4.8   Mallory Method

Passage	Note
1. Remove paraffin and rehydrate sections	<10 μ thick sections
2. Stain in 1% acid fuchsin in water solution	1 min
3. Rinse in 1% phosphomolybdic acid in water solution	15 min
4. Stain 25 min in the mixture of Mallory	0.5 g of aniline blue or methylene blue, 2 g of orange G, 2 g of ossalic acid, and 100 ml distilled water
5. Rinse in distilled water	1–2 min
6. Dehydrate in 80%, 95%, and 100% alcohol	Rapid rinsing of 95% and 100% alcohol
7. Mount with Canada balsam	

Mallory method that stains the nuclei red, cytoplasm bright orange, and connective tissue blue (Table 4.8). Masson's trichromic method (Figure 4.2) stains the nuclei blue; the cytoplasm red green; and collagen fibers green (Table 4.9). Gomori's trichromic method stains the reticular fibers black (Table 4.10 and Figure 4.3).

Another staining method specific for collagen is the Sirius red method that stains the connective tissue red and collagen fibers yellow (Table 4.11).

Methods that are specific for elastic fibers employ orcein and basic fuchsin. The Unna–Tanzer–Livini method (Table 4.12) and the orcein method stain elastic fibers red (Table 4.13 and Figure 4.4). Basic fuchsin, in particular Ziehl's fuchsin, stains elastic fibers and nuclei purple. It is used in the Gallego method (Table 4.14).

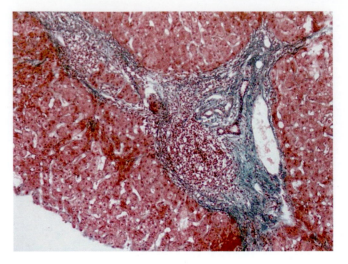

Figure 4.2 Masson method. Hepatic biopsy. Nuclei in blue, cytoplasm in red, collagen fibers in green.

Table 4.9   Masson's Trichromic Method

Passage	Note
1. Remove paraffin and rehydrate sections	<10 μ thick sections
2. Stain in Carazzi hematoxylin	5 min
3. Rinse in water	1–2 min
4. Stain in solution A (Table 4.9A)	5 min
5. Rinse in 1% acetic acid in water solution	5 min
6. Stain in solution B (Table 4.9B)	5 min
7. Rinse in 1% acetic acid in water solution	5 min
8. Stain in solution C (Table 4.9C)	5 min
9. Rinse in 1% acetic acid in water solution	5 min
10. Pass through one change of 100% alcohol	Rapid rinsing
11. Mount with Canada balsam	

Table 4.9A   Solution A

0.2 g of Ponceau 2 R
0.1 g of fuchsin acid
300 ml of distilled water
0.6 ml of acetic acid

Table 4.9B   Solution B

3 to 5 g of phosphomolybdic acid
100 ml of distilled water
0.2 ml of acetic acid

Table 4.9C   Solution C

0.1 to 0.2 g of green lux
100 ml of distilled water
0.2 ml of acetic acid

The Weigert staining method is specific for fibrin, staining the nuclei red, fibrin purple, and the cytoplasm gray purple (Table 4.15).

There is a wide range of staining methods used for collagen, and elastic and reticular fibers. The Humason and Lushbaugh method stains collagen blue, reticular fibers black, and elastic fibers red (Table 4.16).

Table 4.10   Gomori's Trichromic Method

Passage	Note
1. Remove paraffin and rehydrate sections	<10 μ thick sections
2. Treat with 0.75% potassium permanganate	5 min
3. Rinse in water	1–2 min
4. Treat with 2% potassium meta-sulfite	3–5 min
5. Rinse in distilled water	1–2 min
6. Treat with 2% ferric alum	3–10 min
7. Rinse in distilled water	1–2 min
8. Stain in solution A (Table 4.10A)	30 sec
9. Rinse two times in distilled water	3–5 min each time
10. Treat with 15% formalin	1 min
11. Treat with 0.1% gold chloride	5 min
12. Rinse in distilled water	1–2 min
13. Dehydrate in 80%, 95%, and 100% alcohol	Rapid rinsing
14. Mount with Canada balsam	

Table 4.10A   Solution A

5 cc of AgNO$_3$ 10%
0.5 cc of KOH 10%
Distilled water to double the volume

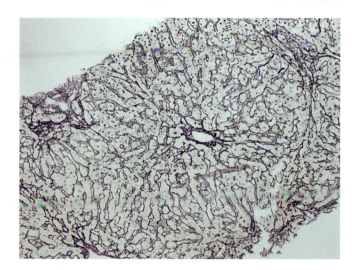

Figure 4.3 Gomori's trichromic. Hepatic biopsy. Reticular fibers are stained black.

The Giemsa staining method is used for studying the morphology of blood cells. It stains eosinophils bright orange and other cellular types in purple (Table 4.17 and Figure 4.5).

4.8.4   Muscle Tissue

Muscle tissue should be cut in small sections and fixed in Carnoy's liquid. Morphologic studies of muscle tissue use various staining and histochemical reaction procedures. In particular, the Welsch method permits a fine bands differentiation in skeletal and cardiac muscle (Table 4.18).

Table 4.11   Sirius Red Method

Passage	Note
1. Cut sections with the cryostat	<8 μ thick sections
2. Stain with Sirius red	1 h
3. Rinse in distilled water	1–2 min
4. Treat with 0.01 M HCl	2 min
5. Rinse in distilled water	1–2 min
6. Dehydrate in 80%, 95%, and 100% alcohol	Rapid rinsing
7. Mount with Canada balsam	

Table 4.12   Unna–Tanzer–Livini Method

Passage	Note
1. Remove paraffin and rehydrate sections	15–30 μ thick sections
2. Stain in a mixture of solutions A and B (Tables 4.12A and 4.12B)	12 h, solution A should be prepared 2 months before use
3. Dehydrate in 90% alcohol and then in 95% and 100% alcohol	3–5 min in 90% alcohol for three times, and rapid rinsing in 95% and 100% alcohol
4. Mount with Canada balsam	

Table 4.12A   Solution A

1 g of orcein
100 ml of 100% alcohol
1 ml of chloride acid

Table 4.12B   Solution B

20 ml of 95% alcohol
2 ml of distilled water
0.10 ml of chloride acid

Table 4.13   Orcein Method

Passage	Note
1. Remove paraffin and rehydrate sections	<10 μ thick sections
2. Treat with solution A (Table 4.13A)	15 min
3. Rinse in distilled water	2–3 min
4. Treat with 2% ossalic	10 min
5. Rinse in distilled water	2–3 min
6. Treat with solution B (Table 4.13B)	10 min
7. Treat with "acid alcohol"	1 cc HCl in 100 cc of 70% alcohol
8. Dehydrate in 95% and 100% alcohol	Rapid rinsing
9. Mount with Canada balsam	

Table 4.13A   Solution A

0.5 g of potassium permanganate
100 cc of distilled water
0.015 cc of H$_2$PO$_4$ concentrate

Table 4.13B   Solution B

1 g of orcein
100 cc of 100% alcohol
2 cc of chloride acid

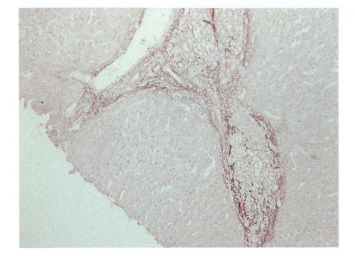

Figure 4.4 Orcein method. Elastic fibers in red.

Table 4.14   Gallego Method

Passage	Note
1. Remove paraffin and rehydrate sections	<10 μ thick sections
2. Treat sections for 10 min with ferric–nitric formalin	10 ml of distilled water, 2 drops of formalin, 1 drop of 10% water solution ferric perchloride, 1 drop of nitric acid
3. Stain for 5 min in Ziehl's fuchsin	10 ml of distilled water, 15 drops of Ziehl's fuchsin, 1 drop of acetic acid
4. Rinse in distilled water	1–2 min
5. Fix in ferric–nitric formalin	5 min
5. Stain in 0.5% orange	5 min
6. Dehydrate in 95% and 100% alcohol	Rapid rinsing
7. Mount with Canada balsam	

Table 4.15   Weigert's Method

Passage	Note
1. Remove paraffin and rehydrate sections	<10 μ thick sections
2. Stain in carmallume or nuclear red	15 sec
3. Rinse in water	1 min
4. Stain in crystal violet	15 sec
4. Treat with a Burke's solution iodo-iodurate	15 sec
5. Pass in xylene	1 min
6. Mount with Canada balsam	

4.9   Histochemical Stainings

The staining procedures described until now cannot provide precise information on the chemical nature of the substances present in the tissues. For this purpose, the sections are subjected to chemical reactions that,

Table 4.16   Humason and Lushbaugh Method

Passage	Note
1. Remove paraffin and rehydrate sections	<10 μ thick sections
2. Treat with 2% silver nitrate in water solution	30 min
3. Rinse in distilled water	2–3 times, each for 2–3 min
4. Treat 15 min with ammoniacal silver solution	20 ml of silver nitrate solution, 20 drops of 10% caustic soda in water solution, some drops of ammonium hydrate and distilled water
5. Rinse once in distilled water	2–3 min
6. Treat in 30% formalin	3 min
7. Rinse once in distilled water	2-3 min
8. Treat with gold chloride	1 min
9. Fix in 5% $Na_2S_2O_3$ solution	1 min
10. Pass in 70% alcohol	1 min
11. Stain 15 min in a orecin solution at 37°C	0.5 g of orcein, 100 ml of 70% alcohol, 0.6–1 ml of chloride acid
12. Pass through one change of 70% alcohol	1 min
13. Rinse in distilled water	5 min
14. Treat with 1% phosphomolybdic acid in water solution	5 min
15. Rinse in distilled water	2–3 min
16. Stain 5 sec in Sirius supra blue solution	2 g of Sirius supra blue, 100 ml distilled water, and 2 ml of glacial acetic acid
17. Rinse in distilled water	2–3 min
18. Dehydrate in 80%, 95%, and 100% alcohol	Rapid rinsing
19. Pass in xylene and mount with Canada balsam	

without damaging the cellular structure, produce colored substances that allow locating chemical components in the tissue. Ideally, histochemical studies aim to cause as little damage as possible to the tissue, as well as maintaining the researched components in their natural positions. To achieve these goals, it is essential to use fixatives that do not alter the chemical nature of the researched factors and secure them in locations corresponding to those *in vivo*.

Histochemical reactions can be classified in direct and indirect reactions. In direct reactions, the researched substance forms, with a reagent, a product that can be identified according to its physical properties. In indirect reactions, the researched substance is first modified by a fixative and subsequently forms, with a reagent, a colored product.

Some of the most common techniques are described next.

Table 4.17   Giemsa's Stain

Passage	Note
1. Remove paraffin and rehydrate sections	<10 μ thick sections
2. Stain in Giemsa's solution (Table 4.17A)	5 min
3. Rinse in running water	1–2 min
4. Decolorize in 90% alcohol	1 min
5. Stain in hematoxylin	1 min
6. Stain in Giemsa's solution (Table 4.17A)	10 min
7. Rinse in running water	1 min
8. Dehydrate in 30%, 50%, 80%, 95%, and 100% alcohol	Rapid rinsing
9. Pass in xylene and mount with Canada balsam	

Table 4.17A   Giemsa's Solution

1. 0.8–0.1 g of Giemsa
2. 50 ml of methylic alcohol
3. 50 ml of glycerin
4. Dilute 1:20 with distilled water before use

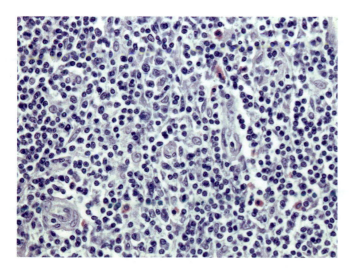

Figure 4.5 Giemsa staining method. Eosinophils are stained bright orange and other cellular types in purple.

Table 4.18   Welsch's Method

Passage	Note
1. Remove paraffin and rehydrate sections	5–6 μ thick sections
2. Stain in 0.1% thionin solution in 20% alcohol	1 min
3. Rinse in distilled water	1–2 min
4. Dehydrate in 80%, 95%, and 100% alcohol	Rapid rinsing in 95% and 100% alcohol
5. Pass in xylene and mount with Canada balsam	

Table 4.19   PAS Reaction

Passage	Note
1. Bring sections to water	10 μ thick sections
2. Treat with 0.5% periodic acid solution	5–10 min
3. Rinse in distilled water	5 min
4. Treat with Schiff's reactive (Table 4.19A)	15 min
5. Rinse 5 min in sulfurous solution	10 cc HCl N/1 and 10 cc of 10% Na bisulfate
6. Rinse in running water	5 min
7. Stain in Harris's hematoxylin	1 min
8. Dehydrate and mount	

Note: Usually, the commercially available Schiff's reactive already contains the sulfurous solution.

Table 4.19A   Schiff's Reactive

1. Melt 1 g of basic fuchsin in 200 cc of boiling distilled water
2. Make cold at 50°C, filter, and add 20 cc of HCl N/1
3. Make cold at 25°C and add 1 g of potassium metabisulfate or sodium dust
4. Leave the solution 12 h in fridge
5. Add 4 g of activated carbon, shake, and filter
6. Leave in fridge
7. Use at room temperature

4.9.1   Periodic Acid-Schiff Staining (PAS)

Periodic acid-Schiff staining (PAS) is used for staining structures containing carbohydrate macromolecules (glycogen, glycoprotein, proteoglycans) in connective tissues, mucus, and basal laminae. The reaction of periodic acid selectively oxidizes glucose residues, creates aldehydes that react with the Schiff reagent, and stains in a purple magenta color. A basic stain is often used as a counterstain. In particular, this method is used for detection of glycogen in tissues such as liver, as well as cardiac and skeletal muscle; in formalin-fixed, paraffin-embedded tissue sections; and for frozen sections. Glycogen, mucin, and fungi will stain purple, whereas nuclei will stain blue (Table 4.19).

4.9.2   Specific Methods for Sialic Acid

Sialic acids are the neuraminic N-acetylate acids and form some glycoproteins and glycolipids. The only reliable method for their identification is using the Bial reagent following the Ravetto method (Table 4.20)

4.9.3   Specific Methods for Glycogen

There are various methods to detect glycogen. In particular, it is possible to detect glycogen by combining a preliminary digestion procedure by applying diastase or

Table 4.20   Ravetto's Method

Passage	Note
1. Treat with Bial N reactive and take at volume with distilled water	200 mg of orcinol, 0.25 ml of copper sulfate 0.1 M, 80 ml of chloride acid 12
2. Put 5–10 min at 70°C in a box containing HCl	
3. Pass through one change of xylene	
4. Mount	

Table 4.21   PAS Reaction of Glycogen

Passage	Note
1. Bring sections to water	5 μ thick sections
2. Treat 30 min at 37°C with 0.1% diastase solution in phosphate tampon 0.02 M, a PH 6, and containing sodium chloride	It eliminates the endogen glycogen
3. Make the PAS reaction	Table 4.19

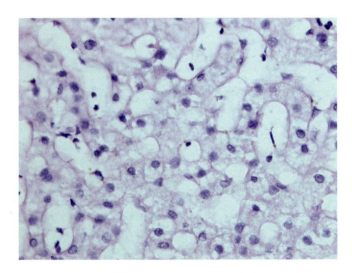

Figure 4.6 Specific methods for glycogen: PAS diastase. This method stains glycogen red purple.

amylase to a PAS staining. This method stains glycogen red purple (Table 4.21 and Figure 4.6).

4.9.4   Specific Methods for Amyloid

Amyloid is deposited in human or animal connective tissues in a variety of pathologic circumstances. It consists mainly of protein, with up to 5% of carbohydrates, largely in the form of mucopolysaccharides. Using iodine reaction techniques, amyloid will stain in red (Table 4.22).

Table 4.22   Reaction of Iodine

Passage	Note
1. Rinse 1–10 min in Lugol's solution	2 g of potassium iodide in 300 ml of distilled water and add 1 g of iodine
2. Rinse in running water	
3. Mount in Apathy's rubber	

4.9.5   Specific Methods for Inorganic Components

There are histochemical methods for detecting some anions (for example, phosphates) and some cations (for example, iron). In particular, it is possible to detect ferric iron with the Perl method. This method uses potassium ferrocyanide that interacts with ferric ions, forming ferric ferrocyanide that appears green (Table 4.23 and Figure 4.7).

Table 4.23   Perl's Method

Passage	Note
1. Bring sections to water	
2. Treat with methylic alcohol	10 min
3. Rinse in distilled water	5 min
4. Treat with a mixture of potassium ferric–cianure and chloride acid	2% of potassium ferric–cianure and chloride acid in water solution
5. Rinse in distilled water	
6. Stain in 1% neutral red in water solution	10 min

4.9.6   Specific Methods for Acid Mucopolysaccharides

The method of the easiest application that also gives an assured result is PAS reaction accompanied by staining with alcian blue to evidence mucopolysaccharides (Table 4.24 and Figure 4.8).

Table 4.24   Alcian–PAS Method

Passage	Note
1. Bring sections to water	5 μ thick sections
2. Treat with Alcian	1 min
3. Rinse in distilled water	5 min
4. PAS reaction	Table 4.19

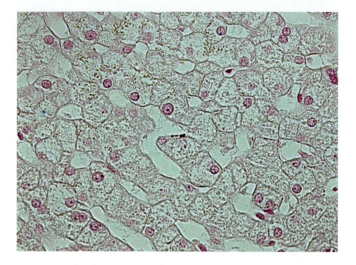

Figure 4.7 Specific methods for inorganic components: the Perl method. Ferrocyanide interacts with ferric ions, forming ferric ferrocyanide that appears green.

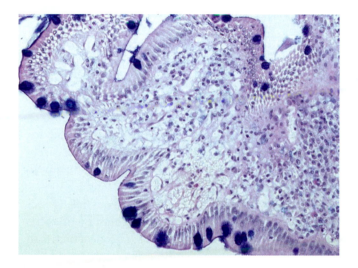

Figure 4.8 Specific methods for acid mucopolysaccharides: PAS Alcian. Mucopolysaccharides are blue.

4.10 Mounting Procedures

After sections stained by ordinary methods have been cleared in xylene, they are mounted in some resinous or aqueous medium.

After staining, paraffin sections are dehydrated with one change each of 50%, 80%, 95%, and 100% alcohol, followed by one change of xylene. Cover glasses of the appropriate size to cover the section are selected and one drop of resinous medium is deposited in the center of a square cover. The cover glass adheres by capillary attraction. Opaque areas in stained, mounted sections are often due to incomplete dehydration. Microscopic

examination reveals numerous small droplets of water in and above the section. The remedy is simple: remove the cover slip, wash off the resin, dehydrate, and remount.

Resinous mounting media are composed of a solid natural or synthetic resin dissolved in a suitable solvent. Xylene or chloroform solutions of Canada balsam (naturally resinous) are usually preferred as a mounting media. As an alternative, synthetic resins can be used such as polystyrene media, which is usually employed in aromatic hydrocarbon solvents. There are also aqueous mounting media, for example, a colloidal solution of polyvinylpyrrolidone.

4.11 Immunohistochemistry

Immunohistochemistry is the process of localizing proteins in cells of a tissue section, exploiting the principle of antibodies binding to antigens (Tables 4.25 and 4.26). To perform the standard staining procedure, tissue sections must first be deparaffinized and then rehydrated

Table 4.25 Immunohistochemistry on Paraffin Sections

Passage	Note
1. Pass through one change of xylene	30 min
2. Hydrate in one change each of 100%, 96%, 80%, 50% alcohol and water	Each 5 min
3. Rinse in PBS 1x	5 min
4. Treat with hydrogen peroxide	10 min
5. Rinse in PBS 1x	5 min
6. Incubate with protein block	10 min
7. Remove excess of protein block	
8. Incubate with primary antibody	1 h
9. Rinse in PBS 1x	5 min
10. Incubate with secondary antibody	10 min
11. Rinse in PBS 1x	5 min
12. Incubate with streptavidin–peroxidase	10 min
13. Rinse in PBS 1x	5 min
14. Incubate with cromogen	10 min
15. Rinse in PBS 1x	5 min
16. Stain in hematoxylin	2–5 min
17. Rinse in running water	1–2 min
18. Mount	

Table 4.26 Freezer Section Immunohistochemistry

Passage	Note
1. Fix in 4% acetone or in 4% paraformaldehyde	10 min
2. Dry at room temperature	10 min
3. Continue as in Table 4.25	

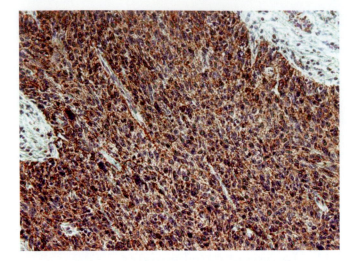

Figure 4.9 Immunohistochemistry.

with one change each of 100%, 95%, 80%, and 50% alcohol, followed by two changes of water. Subsequently, endogenous peroxidase activity is inhibited by pretreating the section with hydrogen peroxide prior to incubation with a primary antibody. The section is then incubated with biotinylated secondary antibody and enzyme–streptavidin conjugates (HRP–streptavidin or AP–streptavidin) in order to replace the complex of avidin–biotin peroxidase. The enzyme is then revealed by application of substrate chromogen solutions to produce different colorimetric products.

Occasionally, when weak or no staining is observed, an antigen "unmasking" by enzyme digestion may be required. Finally, the sections are mounted in an aqueous medium and observed with a light microscope (Figure 4.9).

Recently, immunohistochemical techniques have acquired great diagnostic importance for the characterization of tissues and differential diagnosis among various pathologies.

Like all the other techniques, immunohistochemistry can be deceptive. It is necessary for the pathologist to interpret the reaction recognizing possible artificial effects triggered by the technique and repeating the reaction when necessary. To avoid technical errors, it is essential not only to meticulously follow the protocol recommended in the instructions of the kit used, but also to periodically check the validity of antibodies, as well as using appropriate positive and negative controls for the reactions.

I. The Microtome

The microtome is a mechanical instrument used to section paraffin-embedded specimens. There are different types of microtomes:

- Sledge microtome, where the specimen is immobilized and the blade moves to produce the cut; secure clamps allow the blade to be offset to the direction of the cut, a major advantage when sectioning large, hard blocks.
- Rotary microtome, where the specimen moves and the blade is blocked. The microtome operation is based on the rotary action of a handwheel activating the progression of the block toward a rigidly held blade. The block moves up and down in a vertical plane in relation to the blade and therefore flat sections are cut.
- Rocking microtome, where the blade is blocked and the specimen moves through an arc as it advances toward the blade producing curved sections. The rocking microtome has largely been replaced by the more precise rotary microtome.

Modern microtomes are precision instruments designed to cut uniform, thin sections of a variety of materials for detailed microscopic examination. For light microscopy, the thickness of a section can vary between 1 and 10 μ. In particular, the standard thickness of a section is 2 to 5 μ for immunocytological studies and 8 to 10 μ for histological research. In exceptional cases, the thickness can be up to 20 to 30 μ.

With most microtomes, a section is cut by advancing the material holder toward the blade while it is held rigidly in place. The cutting action, which can be either vertical or horizontal, is coupled with the advance mechanism that moves the material holder after each cut.

The angle between the surface being cut and the back of the microtome knife is called the clearance angle. A correct clearance angle is necessary to prevent compression in cut sections. It is also important for reducing friction as the blade passes through the sample. Various angles ranging between 2 and 4 degrees have been recommended for paraffin-embedded samples. If the cutting angle is too great, it can cause compression in the cut section, and if it is too small, the blade can vibrate causing chatter in the section. A balance between these extremes will provide the best results. Generally, a sharper knife will have a smaller cutting angle.

The sections obtained are subsequently mounted on slides, stained, and observed with a light microscope.

II. Classification of Dyes

Dyes used for staining can be classified in different categories according to their origin, in natural or synthetic.

Natural dyes are of an animal or vegetable origin, and they are limited in number. The most common are carmine (animal origin), hematoxylin (vegetable origin), and orcein (vegetable origin).

Synthetic dyes are aromatic organic compounds, and their color is invariably due to the presence of chromophore. In order for the chromophore to have coloring properties, the dye must contain an auxochrome. Auxochrome is a group of atoms attached to a chromophore, which modifies the ability of that chromophore to absorb light.

Dyes can also be divided into acids and basics.

Dyes that are negatively charged and used for binding to positively charged tissue components are known as *acid dyes*. Their primary mechanism of staining is by ionic bonding. The groups responsible for ionizing capability are the auxochromes. Acid dyes have hydroxyl, carboxyl, or sulfonic groups as their auxochrome, and consequently have an overall negative charge. An example of a dye with hydroxyl groups as their auxochrome is martius yellow; with carboxyl groups, eosin Y; and with sulfonic groups, Biebrich scarlet.

Dyes that are positively charged and used for binding to negatively charged tissue components are known as *basic dyes*. Their primary mechanism of staining is also by ionic bonding. Basic dyes have amino groups or alkylamino groups as their auxochromes, and consequently have an overall positive charge. An example of a dye with amino groups as their auxochromes is pararosanilin; and with alkylamino groups, methylene blue.

Dyes are used in water or alcohol solutions and conserved in glass bottles that can be tightly closed. Some dyes can be used right after preparation, whereas others, such as hematoxylin, can only be used after a maturation period.

References

Bancroft J and Gamble M. 2002. *Theory and practice of histological techniques*, 5th edition. Edinburgh: Churchill Livingstone.

Bancroft JD and Cook HC. 1994. *Manual of histological technique and their diagnostic applications*. Edinburgh: Churchill Livingstone

Bancroft JD and Hand NM. 1987. *Enzyme histochemistry*. Royal Microscopical Society Handbook 14. Oxford: Oxford Science Press.

Horobin RW and Bancroft JD. 1998. *Troubleshooting histology stains*. New York: Churchill Livingstone.

Kiernan JA. 1999. *Histological and histochemical methods: Theory and practice*, 3rd edition. Oxford: Butterworth Heinemann.

Pearse AGE. 1980. *Histochemistry, theoretical and applied*, 4th edition, vol 1. Edinburgh: Churchill Livingstone.

Pomara C and Fineschi V. 2007. *Manuale atlante di tecniche autoptiche*. Padova: Piccin.

Beyond and Together with Autopsy Techniques
Confocal Laser Scanning Microscopy in Forensic Medicine

5

M. NERI

Contents

Forensic pathology has long been permeated by the need to increase objectivity and certainty in the desire for an evidence-based forensic medicine not only in research but also in routine forensic practice. The laboratory technologies and methodologies used in forensic pathology are now very advanced and sophisticated. They have been utilized in research but rarely in daily cases. One of the most obvious ways to improve the quality of forensic investigations is by utilizing the most recent innovations in the field of microscopy.

The light microscope, so called because it employs visible light to detect small objects, is probably the most well-known and well-used research tool in forensic pathology. The bright field microscope is best known, but frequently it may have dark field or phase contrast optics.

In a conventional bright field microscope, light from an incandescent source is aimed toward a lens beneath the stage called the condenser, through the specimen, through an objective lens, and to the eye through a second magnifying lens, the ocular, or eyepiece. We see objects in the light path because natural pigmentation or stains absorb light differentially or because they are thick enough to absorb a significant amount of light despite being colorless. A good quality microscope has a built-in illuminator, adjustable condenser with aperture diaphragm (contrast) control, mechanical stage, and binocular eyepiece tube. The condenser is used to focus light on the specimen through an opening in the stage. After passing through the specimen, the light is displayed to the eye with an apparent field that is much larger than the area illuminated. The magnification of the image is simply the objective lens magnification (usually stamped on the lens body) times the ocular magnification. A phase contrast microscope can be used for unstained and living biological specimens, like spermatozoa, that have little contrast with their surrounding medium, even though small differences of refractive index exist in their structures. The specimen retards some light rays with respect to those that pass through the surrounding medium.

The use of polarized light microscopy has many useful and diagnostic applications. Numerous crystals, fibrous material, both natural and artificial, pigments, lipids, proteins, bone, and amyloid deposits exhibit birefringence.

As Ying and Monticello stated, other bioimaging technologies with (forensic) applications have been developed over the past decades mainly due to the innovation of computed tomography. Meanwhile, light microscopy imaging techniques with biological applications continue to develop due to innovations of novel fluorescence probes, confocal microscopy, automated microscopy, and digital imaging.

Beyond classical microscopes, the autopsy and the related histological examination need to use innovative methods of study. One such method is a new technique for microscopic imaging: confocal laser scanning microscopy (CLSM).

Confocal laser scanning microscopy is a relatively new imaging technique, introduced in 1980 by M. Petran and A. Boyde. It has found wide applications in the biological sciences. At no other time have so many technologies and methodologies been available to forensic scientists, but, unfortunately, they are rarely applied in daily judicial practice. One of the most obvious ways to improve the quality of forensic investigations is by utilizing the most recent innovations in the field of microscopy. The existence of CLSM has radically transformed the field of biology in general and forensic pathology in particular. While most new techniques with forensic applications are still undergoing development and testing, the value of CLSM has already been demonstrated, although this technique is not yet available to most forensic scientists. High-speed and high-resolution confocal and multiphoton microscopes allow researchers to obtain three-dimensional (3D) and four-dimensional

(4D) information. This development has prompted us to study and evaluate their possible applications in the specific field of forensic sciences.

CLSM has been widely applied in the general sphere of biological sciences, and it has completely changed the study of cells and tissues. It allows greater resolution, optical sectioning of the sample, and 3D reconstruction of the same sample. Objects may now be viewed in a four-dimensional space (4D microscopy, xyzt) via a spatial analysis, repeated in time, and then combined with the spectral characterization of luminous signals coming from samples under examination (five-dimensional [5D] microscopy, xyzt). By combining additional technologies such as fluorescent lifetime imaging (FLIM)-based analysis, the capabilities of CLSM have been further extended so that now, in some cases, it is possible to speak of six-dimensional (6D) microscopy. The great possibilities provided by CLSM stem basically from two peculiar characteristics:

1. The sample is illuminated by the projection of a punctiform light source on the focal plane of the objective.
2. The collection of the emitted signal is limited by the introduction of a pinhole disk of variable aperture placed before the detector. Therefore the light coming from a region's external to the focal plane is blocked, thus eliminating the contribution of the image coming from the overhanging and beneath planes.

The unquestionable value of confocal microscopy exists in the creation of optical sections: the laser beam sections the sample so that it is no longer necessary to prepare sections.

The noninvasive nature of optical sectioning, which may be realized on both living and fixed cells, allows scientists to obtain images with an optimal spatial resolution but without any dramatic alteration of their "architecture," in an environment that is as close as possible to the biological reality.

CLSM provides precious information regarding the distribution of a substance in the entire volume of the sample (e.g., fragment of tissue or cultured cells) and of structural and nonstructural components that can emit a luminous signal, either by themselves or by means of specific stain, which will emit light when they are hit by a laser beam.

CLSM also provides information regarding the various focal planes of the sample (information about depth).

Confocal microscopy can be utilized in forensic medicine when the investigation presents particular diagnostic difficulties or the macroscopic examination cannot explain the cause of death, for example, sudden cardiac death (myocytes morphology, role of calcium, channelopathies), neonatal hypoxic–ischemic lesions (timing), infection (tetanus infection), amniotic fluid embolism, fat embolism, air embolism, or fatal anaphylactic shock.

Forensic investigation in cases of sudden cardiac death represents one of the most promising fields of application for confocal microscopy. The ability to detect the fine structures of myocytes both in normal conditions (distribution of structural proteins, Z disks, etc.) and especially in the presence of pathological alterations (e.g., contraction band necrosis) provides the forensic pathologist with imaging possibilities that were unthinkable until a few years ago. In recent years, clinical and medicolegal attention has focused on the genetic causes of sudden death. Our knowledge about these disorders has deepened and widened thanks to the incessant progresses in the field of cardiovascular genomics. CLSM is a sophisticated research tool that may be diagnostic in some types of channelopathies, particularly those where a causal role of calcium-channel alterations has been implicated. It is well established that intracellular sodium homeostasis has a relevant role in myocellular function; sodium channels and transporters, which couple sodium influx to either co- or countertransport of other ions and solutes, may influence the regulation of intracellular pH and calcium homeostasis, thus impairing excitation–contraction coupling and energy production mechanisms. In these cases, the absence of histological signs of either ischemia or inflammation and the exclusion of systemic hypercalcemia suggest that the presence of intracellular calcium deposits might be specifically related to the underlying molecular defect. The ability to visualize intracellular Ca^{2+} deposits with confocal microscopy provides the forensic pathologist with a set of diagnostic tools capable of screening for molecular abnormalities (Figure 5.1).

CLSM support is necessary in case of Brugada syndrome (BrS), which is an ion channelopathy inherited in an autosomal dominant trait. BrS is characterized by a specific electrocardiographic pattern of right bundle branch block and ST segment elevation in leads V_{1-3} with a normal QT interval, and no structural heart disease.

BrS is associated with life-threatening ventricular arrhythmias and with high incidence of sudden death, but no morphologic changes are usually observed in subjects with structurally normal hearts. Even when the genetic abnormality is present, the electrocardiographic pattern may be normal, but it can be unmasked by fever, vagotonic agents, sodium channel blockers, other medications, and even external factors may act as trigger for ventricular arrhythmias in patients with this disorder. The SC5NA has been identified as the gene involved in

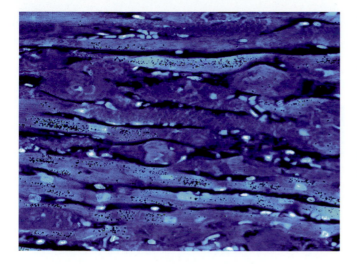

Figure 5.1 CLSM micrograph of contraction band necrosis in the heart with a myocyte showing calcium deposits composed of needle-like crystals.

heritable forms of BrS; this channel produces a depolarizing inward sodium current I_{na} and then inactivates within milliseconds. Mutations in SC5NA leading to the BrS phenotype are associated with a loss of channel function and a reduction of the Na^+ current.

Immunohistochemistry and CLSM on sections collected from heart formalin-fixed, paraffin-embedded tissues led us to confirm the cellular localization of the Na^+CP type Vα (C-20) at the intercalated disks of ventricular myocytes and nearly 50% reduction in Na^+ channels expression in ventricular myocytes when compared to control cases (Figure 5.2).

The correct forensic approach to cases of neonatal cerebral palsy is complex and requires detailed study (clinical file examination, x-ray, computed tomography,

and magnetic resonance imaging studies before autopsy, accurate postmortem examination), in addition to an exhaustive histological examination by means of advanced laboratory techniques.

The timing of hypoxic–ischemic damage is the central element in any medicolegal evaluation of obstetric professional liability for cerebral palsy.

In particular, the histopathological timing of the hypoxic–ischemic damage using qualified immunohistochemical and microscopic investigations becomes the central moment of the forensic practice in cases of fetal hypoxic–ischemic sufferance. The pattern of hypoxic–ischemic damage in neonates varies with gestational age, and in premature infants the cerebral white matter is particularly susceptible.

Manifestations of injury range from relatively selective apoptotic loss of oligodendrocytes in telencephalic leukomalacia to focal or multifocal coagulative necrosis in periventricular leukomalacia. Ischemic degeneration of neurons may also occur, mainly in the basal ganglia, thalamus, cerebellar granule cell layer, and brain stem, and apoptosis is usually prominent. In full-term infants, hypoxic–ischemic damage is most prominent in the gray matter and manifests itself with various combinations of neuronal apoptosis, selective neuronal necrosis, and clear infarction that can involve the cerebral cortex, basal ganglia, thalamus, cerebellar cortex, cerebellar dentate nucleus, and brain stem. The application of confocal microscopy to these investigations allows the acquisition of images with an exceptional definition and resolution (Figure 5.3).

Another neuropathological application of confocal microscopy is the study of a case of tetanus infection.

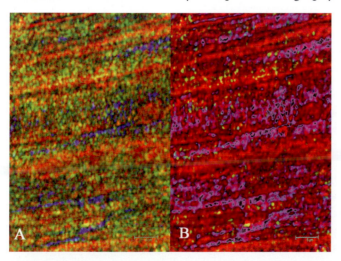

Figure 5.2 CLSM micrographs of cellular localization of the Na^+CP type Vα (C-20) at the intercalated disks of ventricular myocytes (A) with a 50% reduction in Na^+ channel expression in ventricular myocytes of a BrS case (B) compared to a control case.

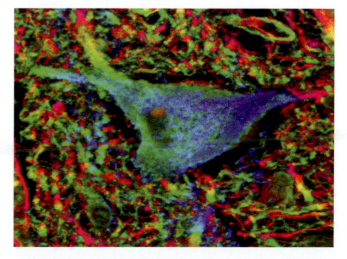

Figure 5.3 3D view of neurons: microvacuolar degeneration and typical morphological features of apoptosis associated with marked condensation of chromatin and its fragmentation into discrete bodies.

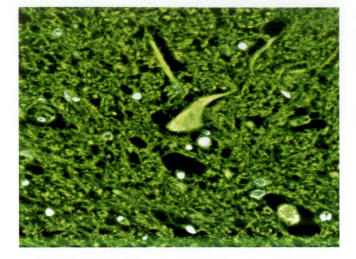

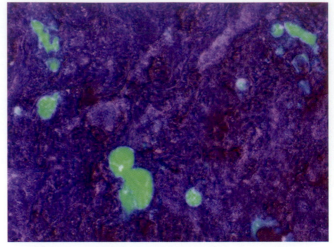

Figure 5.4 High-power magnification of the ventral horn of spinal cord gray matter samples show tetanus toxin fragment C (TTC) immunoreactivity in motor neuron axons and cell bodies using CLSM.

Figure 5.5 Large intravascular air globules surrounded by fibrinogen and platelet layers laid on the interface in pulmonary samples with CLSM.

An immunohistochemical study was conducted with an antibody directed against tetanus toxin fragment C (TTC), for the evaluation of alteration in large motor neurons in the ventral horn. Using a confocal laser scanning microscope, high-power magnification of ventral horn of spinal cord gray matter samples showed TTC immunoreactivity in motor neuron axons and cell bodies, as well as presynaptic fibers synapsing on the motor neuron cell bodies. Confocal laser scanning microscope 3D reconstruction, obtained from the z-line cut surface along the x-line (right insert) and y-line (bottom insert) demonstrated the immunopositive reaction for TTC (Figure 5.4).

A confocal microscope is useful in case of air embolism, fat embolism, and amniotic fluid embolism. The lung samples examined under a confocal laser scanning microscope and a three-dimensional reconstruction can show, in the case of air embolism, large intravascular globules surrounded by fibrinogen and platelet layers to the interface.

The single components (large intravascular globules of air, erythrocytes, platelets) may be studied using the imaging spectroscopy of a confocal laser scanning microscope (Figure 5.5).

For the fat embolism is possible a 3D reconstruction of fat globules contained in capillaries lumen obtained from the z-lines cut surface along the x-line and y-line respectively (Figure 5.6).

Pathologic features of amniotic fluid embolism estimated using immunohistochemical investigation (antibodies anti-fibrinogen, anti-tryptase, anti-C_{3a}, and anti-cytokeratin) are better estimated with confocal laser microscopy; so mucin and lanugo hairs appeared clearly fluorescent, and the evidence of mast cell degranulation

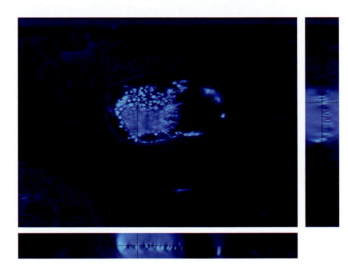

Figure 5.6 Intravascular fat globules with 3D reconstruction of globules (lateral and inferior inserts) obtained from the z-line cut surface along the x-line (right insert) and y-line (bottom insert), respectively.

and a great number of degranulating mast cells with tryptase-positive material outside the cells was documented (Figure 5.7).

The clinical diagnosis of pulmonary thromboembolism is notoriously inaccurate, with many cases either wrongly diagnosed (overdiagnosed) or missed (underdiagnosed), and autopsy is still regarded as the diagnostic gold standard. Deep venous thrombosis and pulmonary thromboembolism are very often undiagnosed in life, thus representing one of the most frequently missed antemortem diagnoses in sudden, unexpected death.

The histological age determination of thromboses and embolisms is an important task of forensic medicine and requires thorough knowledge of the general and

Figure 5.7 Confocal laser microscopy: the mucin, lanugo hairs, degranulating mast cells appear clearly fluorescent.

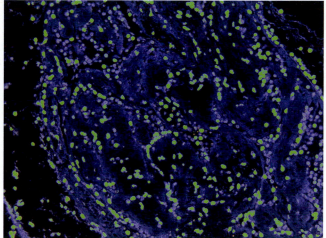

Figure 5.8 Examination under a confocal laser scanning microscope of a clamp showing the distribution of blood components in the entire fragment of tissue and of the structural components of the red cells (purple), fibrins (blue), neutrophils (green), and platelets.

specific pathology of pulmonary thromboembolism. The features must be estimated using histologic sections stained by hematoxylin–eosin (H&E) and trichromic stains (Masson, Azan, Mallory, PTAH, Van Gieson). Perl's stain for hemosiderin must be used to confirm the presence of iron.

In addition, immunohistochemical investigation of thrombi and emboli samples must be performed utilizing antibodies anti-fibrinogen, CD 61, CD 45, CD 15, and CD 68.

The examination under a confocal laser scanning microscope permits obtaining images with an optimal spatial resolution, providing precious information regarding the distribution of blood components in the entire fragment of tissue and of structural components that can emit a luminous signal, either by themselves or by means of specific stain, which will emit light when they are hit by a laser beam. CLSM also provides information regarding the various focal planes of the sample (information about depth) (Figure 5.8).

The autopsy of fatal anaphylactic shock presents immediate medicolegal problems; indeed in such fatal anaphylactic cases, it is necessary to underline the relevance for pathologists of a complete methodological approach, because macroscopic autopsy features are poor and need an integration with clinical data. So a careful microscopic study is essential using the routine histological stain like H&E and immunohistochemical dye with an antibody anti-β-tryptase. The examination with confocal laser microscopy confirmed the presence of mast cells in the trachea, bronchial walls, and pulmonary capillary septa with a great number of degranulating mast cells and allowed visualization of tryptase-positive material outside the cells (Figure 5.9).

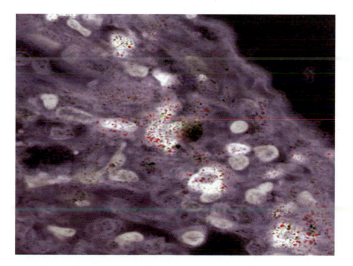

Figure 5.9 Confocal laser microscopy shows the presence of mast cells in the pulmonary capillary septa with a great number of degranulating mast cells (tryptase-positive material outside the cells appears in green).

In conclusion, the primary value of CLSM to the forensic scientist is its ability to produce optical sections through a 3D specimen, for example, an entire cell or a piece of tissue that, to a good approximation, contains information from only one focal plane. By moving the focal plane of the instrument step by step through the depth of the specimen, a series of optical sections can be recorded. This property of CLSM is fundamental for solving 3D biological problems where information from regions distant from the plane of focus can obscure the image (thick objects). As a valuable by-product, the computer-controlled confocal laser scanning microscope produces digital images amenable to image analysis and processing that can also be used to compute surface or volume-rendered 3D reconstructions of the specimen. Thick and opaque specimens that can barely be observed under a conventional light microscope are easily visible with a confocal laser scanning microscope. For example, 20- to 25-mm thick sections of bone, skin, or muscle are ideally suited for 3D imaging in the confocal laser scanning microscope. Independent of the thickness and surface quality of such tissue sections, individual confocal planes readily reveal a lateral resolution of 0.3 mm.

The ability to acquire, keep, and work with images such as those obtained with confocal microscopy, perform 3D reconstruction (and even more with some particular applications of confocal microscopy), produce optical sections of the same sample, and the excellent definition of the image all provide knowledge and ideas for further research, which surely can allow for additional forensic innovations.

References

Amos, W.B., White, J.G. 2003. How the confocal laser scanning microscope entered biological research. *Biol Cell* 95:335–342.

Bancroft, J.D., Gamble, M. 2002. *Theory and practice of histological techniques*. London: Churchill Livingstone.

Blair, E., Watson L. 2006. Epidemiology of cerebral palsy. *Semin Fetal Neonatal Med* 11:117–125.

Borg, T.K., Stewart, J.A. Jr., Sutton M.A. 2005. Imaging the cardiovascular system: Seeing is believing. *Microsc Microanal* 11:189–199.

Boyde, A. 1994. Bibliography on confocal microscopy and its applications. *Scanning* 16:33–56.

Bracci, R., Perrone. S., Buonocore, G. 2006. The timing of neonatal brain damage. *Biol Neonate* 90:145–155.

Braet, F., Ratinac K. 2007. Creating next generation microscopists: Structural and molecular biology at the crossroads. *J Cell Mol Med* 11:759–763.

Di Paolo, N. 2005. Microscopy and art (genius and art). *Int J Artif Organs* 28:660–662.

Diaspro, A. 2001. *Confocal and two-photon microscopy: foundations, applications, and advances*. New York: Wiley-Liss.

Fineschi, V., Riezzo, I., Cantatore. S., Pomara, C., Turillazzi, E., Neri, M. 2009. Complement C3a expression and tryptase degranulation as promising histopathological tests for diagnosing fatal amniotic fluid embolism. *Virchows Arch* 454(3):283–290.

Fineschi, V., Turillazzi, E., Neri, M., Pomara, C., Riezzo, I. 2009. Histological age determination of venous thrombosis: A neglected forensic task in fatal pulmonary thromboembolism. *Forensic Sci Int* 186(1–3):22–28.

Frustaci, A., Priori, S.G., Pieroni, M., Cimenti, C., Napoletano, C., Rivolta, I., Sanna, T., Bellocci, F., Russo, M.A. 2005. Cardiac histological substrate in patients with clinical phenotype of Brugada syndrome. *Circulation* 112:3680–3687.

Greenwood, C., Newman, S., Impey, L., Johnson, A. 2003. Cerebral palsy and clinical negligence litigation: A cohort study. *BJOG* 110:6–11.

Hausmann, R., Seidl, S., Betz, P. 2007. Hypoxic changes in Purkinje cells of the human cerebellum. *Int J Legal Med* 121:175–183.

Lichtman, J.W. 1984. Confocal microscopy. *Sci Am* 271:40–45.

Love, S. 2004. Acute haemorrhagic and hypoxic–ischaemic brain damage in the neonate. *Curr Diagn Pathol* 10:106–115.

Lucitti, J.L., Dickinson, M.E. 2006. Moving toward the light: Using new technology to answer old questions. *Pediatr Res* 60:1–5

Madea, B. 2007. Case histories in forensic medicine. *Forensic Sci Int* 165:111–114.

Minsky, M. 1988. Memoir on inventing the confocal scanning microscope. *Scanning* 10:128–138.

Neri, M., Cerretani. D., Fiaschi, A.I., Laghi, P.F., Lazzerini, P.E., Maffione, A.B., Micheli, L., Bruni, G., Nencini, C., Giorni, G., D'Errico, S., Fiore, C., Pomara, C., Riezzo, I., Turillazzi, E., Fineschi, V. 2007. Correlation between cardiac oxidative stress and myocardial pathology due to acute and chronic norepinephrine administration in rats. *J Cell Mol Med* 11:156–170.

Oehmichen, M. 2006. *Forensic neuropathology and neurology*. Berlin: Springer Verlag.

Pawley, J.B. 2006. *The handbook of biological confocal microscopy*, 3rd ed. New York: Plenum.

Pieske, B., Houser, S.R., Hasenfuss, G., Bers, D.M. 2003. Sodium and the heart: A hidden key factor in cardiac regulation. *Cardiovasc Res* 57:871–872.

Riezzo, I., Bello, S., Neri, M., Pomara, C., Turillazzi, E., Fineschi, V. β Tryptase and specific IgE post-mortem determination, TNF-α, IL-1β and IL15 immunohistochemical expression in a fatal anaphylactic shock after intradermal testing with betalactam antibiotic. *Allergy*. DOI: 10.1111/j.1398.9995.2009.02088.x.

Turillazzi, E., Glatter, K.A., Neri, M. 2006. Sudden cardiac death and channelopathies. In: *Pathology of the heart and sudden death in forensic medicine,* eds. Fineschi, V., Baroldi, G., Silver, M.D., 255–270. Boca Raton, FL: CRC Press.

Turillazzi, E., Karch, S.B., Neri, M., Pomara, C., Riezzo, I., Fineschi, V. 2008. Confocal laser scanning microscopy: using new technology to answer old questions in forensic investigation. *Int J Legal Med* 122:173–177.

Turillazzi, E., La Rocca, G., Anzalone, R., Corrao, S., Neri. M., Pomara, C., Riezzo, I., Karch, S.B., Fineschi, V. 2008. Heterozygous nonsense SCN5A mutation W822X explains a simultaneous sudden infant death syndrome. *Virchows Arch* 453(2):209–216.

Turillazzi, E., Neri, M., Pomara, C., Riezzo, I., Cecchi, R., Fineschi, V. 2008. A quantitative analysis of pulmonary fat embolism for the agreement between post-mortem and clinical findings. *Pathol Res Pract* 204(4):259–266.

Turillazzi, E., Neri, M., Pomara, C., Riezzo, I., Fineschi, V. 2009. An immunohistochemical study on a tetanus fatal case using toxin fragment C (TTC). Should it be a useful diagnostic tool? *Neuropathology* 29(1):68–71.

Turillazzi, E., Pomara, C., Bisceglia, R., Neri, M., Riezzo, I., Pomara, G., Francesca, F., Fineschi, V. 2009. Vascular air embolism complicating percutaneous nephrolithotomy: Medical malpractice or fatal unforeseeable complication? *Urology* 73(3):681.e1-4.

Turillazzi, E., Pomara, C., La Rocca, G., Neri, M., Riezzo, I., Karch, S.B., Anzalone, R., Lo Iacono, M., Fineschi, V. 2009. Immunohistochemical marker for Na+ CP type valpha (C-20) and heterozygous nonsense SCN5A mutation W822X in a sudden cardiac death induced by mild anaphylactic reaction. *Appl Immunohistochem Mol Morphol* 17(4):357–362.

Wedekind, H., Schulze-Bahr, E., Debus, V., Breithardt, G., Brinkmann, B., Bajanowski, T. 2007. Cardiac arrhythmias and sudden death in infancy: Implication for the medicolegal investigation. *Int J Legal Med* 121:245–257.

Wheeler, B.P., Wilson L.J. 2008. *Practical forensic microscopy.* West Sussex: Wiley-Blackwell.

White, J.G., Amos, W.B., Fordham, M. 1987. An evaluation of confocal versus conventional imaging of biological structures by fluorescence light microscopy. *J Cell Biol* 105:41–48.

Wilson, T., Sheppard, C.J.R. 1984. *Theory and practice of scanning optical microscopy.* London: Academic Press.

Ying, X., Monticello T.M. 2006. Modern imaging technologies in toxicologic pathology: An overview. *Toxicol Pathol* 34:815–826.

Postmortem Radiology and Digital Imaging

6

S. D'ERRICO
V.G. GUGLIELMI
C. POMARA

Contents

The relevance for dealing with "modern" postmortem techniques in the medicine "system" is supported by the need of a modern and shared reflection on the contribution of eidologic science in necroscopic practice for forensic purposes.

The improvement and evolution of radiological sciences toward a broader definition of the technical parameters meant to study the details of the human body and its components, both in an anatomical–structural and physiological–physiopathological sense, brought the two disciplines closer together.

In fact, both disciplines—radiology and forensic medicine—are based on the study and interpretation of anatomical reports.

The methodological and operational approach between the two disciplines has roots dating to the first uses of traditional radiology for the study and report of foreign bodies retained in the corpse. Back in the 1970s in the United States, the American College of Pathologists signaled the importance of the correct use of a preventive radiographic inquiry in some deaths and, concurrent with its introduction, studied the use of echoguided techniques of anatomical sampling. In 1982 in Italy, Pierucci edited a handbook for the correct use of radiography in the study of deaths by firearms, which immediately gained credibility for the discipline.

The prior identification of bullets held undamaged or in fragments was considered essential for a correct cross-sectional experiment. It was as essential as their consequential removal and report.

In the 20 years and more since and especially in the last few years, the increasing availability—practically and economically—of eidologic exams has allowed radiology and forensic medicine to work in close collaboration, refining methods and gaining experience.

6.1   Radiography

Postmortem radiography is an important part of a complete forensic examination. A radiology table or a portable x-ray machine should be always present in a modern autopsy service.

Wide availability makes radiography a useful application in forensic pathology. A complete x-ray examination (total body) is extremely useful for locating bullets or other metallic foreign objects, and its use is well known in forensic pathology for firearm-related fatalities or in cases of unknown or burned cadavers. A routine anteroposterior and laterolateral radiograph is an acceptable approach to fetus autopsies for the diagnosis of skeletal abnormalities. Lytic, inflammatory, degenerative, and developmental lesions of bones and joints are particularly best revealed by radiographs.

6.2   Computed Tomography and "Virtopsy"

Computed tomography (CT) uses x-rays to obtain transverse (axial) images of body sections. The tube rotates around the longitudinal (z) axis of the cadaver lying on the CT table, transmitting radiation through the body from many angles. X-rays are absorbed according to the different radiographic density of tissues; those not absorbed reach the detector system beyond the cadaver, contributing to the absorption profile of one specific tube angle. The many profiles measured during one rotation are used by the computer to calculate a density map of the body section with discrete absolute density values of all image elements (voxels).

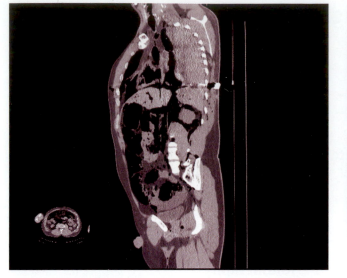

Figure 6.1 CT scan application in a case of a firearm fatality. Imaging allowed a complete *in situ* study of the intrathoracic trajectory of bullets before the autopsy.

Modern multidetector row scanners (multislice computed tomography [MSCT] scanner) are able to acquire information for several slices during one rotation, which can be used to improve z-axis, volume coverage, or speed.

Images of the slice thickness requested will then be calculated from those data at any selected z-axis position within the volume, according to the reconstruction interval chosen. This gives a resolution that is equivalent to isotropic imaging; voxels have similar dimensions in all three axes, for example, 1 mm. Isotropic voxels are ideal for image postprocessing using multiplanar reformation to obtain images in sagittal, frontal, or oblique planes, or even three-dimensional presentation methods (Figures 6.1 and 6.2).

CT application on the postmortem examination allows forensic pathologists an excellent *in situ* reconstruction of injuries (i.e., traffic fatalities, mass disaster, falls) or a complete *in situ* study of a trajectory of bullets (firearm fatalities) (Figures 6.3 and 6.4). It has also been stated that CT study of the cadaver in gunshot-related deaths can be useful in determining firearm distance by detecting gunshot residues deep in the entrance wound.

An unusual application of CT in forensic pathology is in the anthropologic study of body remains (Figure 6.5). In its original meaning, the word *virtopsy* (*virtual* + *autopsy*) was meant to refer to a futuristic approach to the cross-sectional experiment based on the use of MSCT equipment and magnetic resonance (1.5 Tesla GE scanner with spectroscopy software). Today, we could associate virtopsy with digital autopsy. Indeed, going through the contents of the scientific work produced until today,

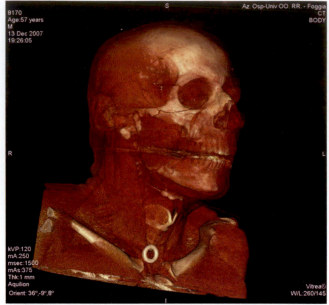

Figure 6.2 Postprocessing image using multiplanar reformation to obtain images in sagittal, frontal, or oblique planes, or even three-dimensional presentation methods.

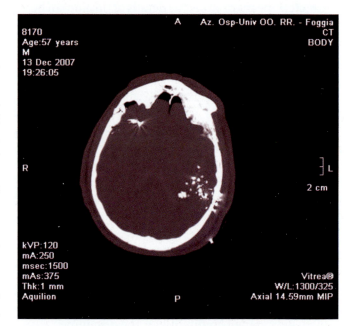

Figure 6.3 CT application on the postmortem examination of a firearm homicide case. Multiple fractures of the cranial vault and intracranial bullet fragments. A wide area of frontal pneumoencephalus is well documented.

it is easy to understand how, in view of the outstanding work performed, digital autopsy hinges well on a basic notion of forensic medicine, that is, the investigation of scientific evidence as means of proof.

The necroscopic technique aided by the digital investigation typical of a CT and magnetic resonance (MR) exam appears to be really improved in terms of report

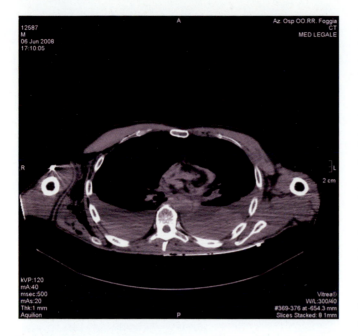

Figure 6.4 CT application of a firearm homicide case. Reconstruction of the intrathoracic trajectory of the bullet (retained in the left arm).

investigation and inexpensiveness, first for the choice of the cross-sectional technique and, subsequently, for the explanatory capability of the iconography.

It is easy to understand the reasons why some pathologists seek a CT study of the corpse with firearm deaths. A virtopsy can be configured as an observer-independent instrument, which does not alter the reality of the corpse and, since it is digitized and archived, is always repeatable and objectified, even if time has passed.

Undoubtedly, the three-dimensional study of the human body (nowadays it is possible to provide up to 64 slices) allows for the finding of metallic foreign bodies (e.g., bullets, shrapnel, and nails) and offers an excellent contribution to the exact recognition of intracorporeal internal trajectory (entrance wound) with a precision achieving levels that can be superimposed to the cross-sectional observation (Figures 6.6 and 6.7).

Actually, before stepping toward the future of the autopsy, it seems appropriate to wonder about its present: Do we still need the autopsy? The most recent national and international literature clearly finds that the autopsy is not only necessary, but it must be considered indefeasible. Indeed, as noted earlier, the judicial autopsy is far from exhausting the investigations on the corpse.

Autopsy, as an external exam of the corpse and a cross-sectional experiment, is just one (inescapable) approach to the corpse. Perhaps it is not the most important, but it is absolutely preliminary to the correct sampling, collection, and histological study of each organ or

part of it. Toxicological, genetic–forensic investigation, and so on to the most specialized exams of metabolomics or proteomics constitute today the right corollaries to a modern postmortem investigation.

In the range of such auxiliary grafts to the main investigation (autopsy), the eidologic–forensic investigation rises to a new dimension, which can be counted with full rights among the means of research for scientific evidence (as such, legitimate and repeatable).

The awareness of the need for a great guarantee of validity (the best in a technical sense) and the capability to refer to more objective technical–scientific backups, have influenced coroners' sensitivity in the last few years. In forensic medicine the need for a description as objective, straight, controllable as possible has grown so the eventual laboratorial controls must be reported within the whole results, the images must be enclosed, the clinical objectification must be complete and detailed, and still more the recording of the morphological surveys (postmortem, histological and so on)."

The autopsy can be improved upon but not replaced. Autopsy remains irreplaceable when it comes to the value of macroscopic features like margins, edges, and auras, even in the parenchyma intracorporeal and it is indispensable for a correct framing of the death (not just as the causative moment, but the information pertinent to the modus and time of the death).

Nevertheless, the ultimate impetus to the implementation of radiology application in forensic medicine came surely from the evolution of the imaging instruments typical of the CT means, that is, from the introduction of a new multilayer CT apparatus in which the procedure to capture the images is not restricted to single slices of predetermined thickness but to the evaluation of an entire "volume," which can even coincide with the whole human body.

Digital processing of images through last-generation software reproduces the composite image in its tridimensionality and therefore is more useful to the unaccustomed eyes of those not specialized in radiology, such as coroners, judges, and lawyers.

The application of radiology in the practice of forensic medicine on the occasion of a necroscopic examination is an extraordinary benefit, including the possibility to proceed to new evaluations, to verify at a later time, and to have multidisciplinary consults for complex investigations, even after the classic postmortem procedures are closed. The possibility also exists to use this instrument when religious or general cultural contexts do not allow traditional postmortem procedures.

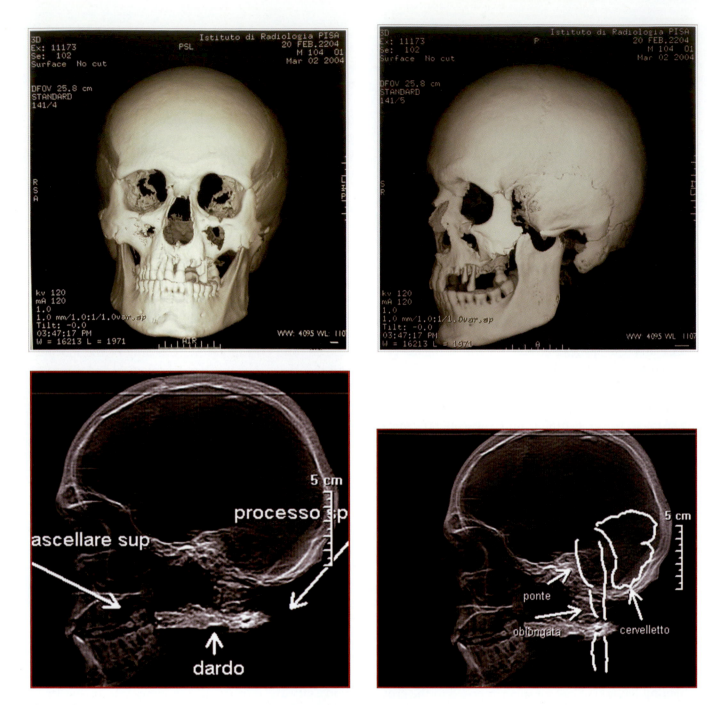

Figure 6.5 An unusual application of CT in forensic pathology is also represented from the anthropologic study of body remains. Translation: Bottom left: Mascellare superiore → Maxilla; Dardo → Dart; Processo spinoso → Spinous process. Bottom right: Ponte → Pons; Oblongata → Medulla oblongata; Cervelletto → Cerebellum.

Digital autopsy can provide surveys that could escape even the most careful and tried observation (a minuscule bony splinter, for instance, can easily avoid direct observation). Though accurate the digital autopsy is not an aseptic database that will return this piece of information for follow-up evaluation, allowing, for instance, further confirmation of the differential diagnosis between the entry and the exit wounds. However, the digital autopsy is, and will be, just a backup to the forensic medicine practice; it is not always available and it cannot be considered as an alternative to the usual postmortem procedures.

An undoubtedly unusual application of multilevel CT is the evaluation of skeletonized human remains, which pertains to archaeology and anthropology. This methodology could seem totally superfluous for the study of bones, since the visual ascertainment made by the coroner or by the anthropologist is, obviously, quite

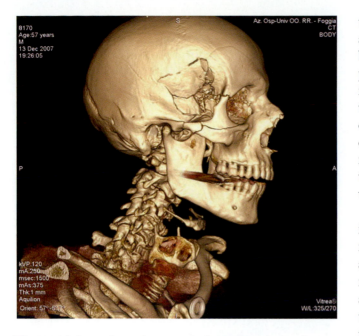

Figure 6.6 A three-dimensional study of the human body in a firearm fatality. An excellent contribution to the exact recognition of an intracorporeal internal trajectory (entrance wound).

Figure 6.7 A three-dimensional study of the human body in a firearm fatality. Characteristics of an exit wound.

appropriate. And yet there could be some even unperceivable fundamental elements such as the destruction of reports inadmissible for inquiry purposes.

There has been a large-scale employment of CT scans during the last few years because they are useful for various postmortem surveys (traumatic injuries in traffic accidents, drowning, hanging, infanticides, etc.) and even for studies on the living (abuse, assault with blunt instruments, etc.). However, in this particular phase of the debate, all the foresaid must lead to a correct interpretation and methodological–operational collocation of digital autopsy as an asset to two interdependent disciplines for the purposes of specific diagnostic conclusions. A radiographer cannot validate a postmortem result in a courtroom without necroscopic corroborations; similarly a coroner cannot validate a digital result without the assistance of a postmortem confirmation.

This warning is certainly more binding for the medical examiner. The drive toward an objective and documentary direction of the forensic inquiry in the area of autopsy and histopathology aspires today to rise from a moment of convergence of standards to a guarantee of a correct survey of pathogenetic courses—starting with the immediate and direct injury, proceeding through the possible intermediate pathologies to the final event.

The forensic autopsy must, therefore, account for the preliminary and subsequent phases of the reporters' survey and of their objective ascription to scientific (biologic), and be adaptable to present needs. The surveys must allow positive or likely statements open to confrontation and not be based just on personal experiences, even though strengthened by authoritativeness. Thus it is necessary, as scientific methodology obliges, to research and standardize the operativeness the two disciplines share, define spaces and borders for each of them, and pursue objectiveness empowered by investigation and study. By applying a logical postmortem intervention, we shall not forget that any modular control cannot, by itself, give an absolute guarantee.

Form is not a substitute of essence. Operative protocols are no more than a collection of information, unable to ensure *ex nunc* that a physician using it will increase his or her skills, since these protocols are not an alternative to scientific knowledge, being procedures whose application can grant a complete exploitation of science's potential. Actually, beyond the apparent sternness of standards and protocols, the only real limit to the use of the cross-sectional experiment as an effective means to "discover the truth" is the lack of experience, training, and imagination of cross-sectional experts; in a single word: mastery. It is easy to realize, subscribing to these principles, that it is impossible to esteem the virtual autopsy as a technical moment based on imaging methods, which grants qualitative and quantitative assessments of pathological entities, which had been viewed, until now, as information based just on "more or less subjective, depending on the inquirer's interpretation" elements, as Jannsen warns.

6.3 Magnetic Nuclear Resonance (MNR) Imaging

Magnetic nuclear resonance (MNR) application in forensic pathology might represent the future. A more detailed imaging of the human body mixed with the possibility of histochemical study of cells by means of spectroscopy could help in a better definition of timing in postmortem modifications. MNR contributions to forensic pathology should be considered as a work in progress.

Acknowledgments

A warm thank you to Dr. Gianpaolo Grilli, Director of the Radiology Department, Ospedali Riuniti, Foggia, Italy, for his kind support and for digitizing and elaborating the radiological images in this chapter.

References

Aghayev E, Yen K, Sonnenschein M, Jackowski C, Thali M, Vock P, and Dirnhofer R. (2005). Pneumomediastinum and soft tissue emphysema of the neck in postmortem CT and MRI: A new vital sign in hanging? *Forensic Sci Int* 153:181–188.

Andenmatten MA, Thali MJ, Kneubuehl BP, Oesterhelweg L, Ross S, Spendlove D, and Bolliger SA. (2008). Gunshot injuries detected by post-mortem multislice computed tomography (MSCT): A feasibility study. *Legal Medicine* 10:287–292.

Brüschweiler W, Braun M, Dirnhofer R, and Thali MJ. (2003). Analysis of patterned injuries and injury-causing instruments with forensic 3D/CAD supported photogrammetry (FPHG): An instruction manual for the documentation process. *Forensic Sci Int* 132:130–138.

Di Maio VJ. (1984). Basic principles in the investigation of homicides. *Pathol Annu* 19(2):149–164.

Dirnhofer R, Jackowski C, Vock P, Potter K, and Thali MJ. (2006). VIRTOPSY: Minimally invasive, imaging-guided virtual autopsy. *Radiographics* 26:1305–1333.

Dolinak D, Evan M, and Lew E. (2005). *Forensic pathology: Principles and practice.* Burlington, MA: Elsevier Academic Press.

Donchin Y, Rivkind AI, Bar-Ziv J, Hiss J, Almog J, and Drescher M. (1994). Utility of postmortem computed tomography in trauma victims. *J Trauma* 37:552–556.

Finkbeiner WE, Ursell PC, and Davis RL. (2004). *Autopsy pathology: A manual and atlas.* Philadelphia: Churchill Livingstone.

Harke HT, Levy AD, Abbott RM, Mallak CT, Getz MJ, Champion HR, and Pearse L. (2207). Autopsy radiography: digital radiographs (DR) vs. multidetector computed tomography (MDCT) in high velocity gunshot wound victims. *Am J Forensic Med Pathol* 29:13–19.

Hayakawa M, Yamamoto S, Motani H, Yajima D, Sato Y, and Iwase H. (2006). Does imaging technology overcome problems of conventional postmortem examination? A trial of computed tomography imaging for postmortem examination. *Int J Legal Med* 120(1):24–26.

Ith M, Bigler P, Scheurer E, Kreis R, Hoffman L, Dirnhofer R, and Boesch C. (2002). Observation and identification of metabolites emerging during postmortem decomposition of brain tissue by means of *in situ* 1H-magnetic resonance spectroscopy. *Magn Reson Med* 48:915–920.

Jackowski C, Aghayev E, Sonnenschein M, Dirnhofer R, and Thali MJ. (2006). Maximum intensity projection of cranial computed tomography data for dental identification. *Int J Legal Med* 120(3):165–167.

Jackowski C, Lussi A, Classens M, Kilchoer T, Bolliger S, Aghayev E, Criste A, Dirnhofer R, and Thali M J. (2006). Extended CT scale overcomes restoration caused streak artifacts-3D color encoded automatic discrimination of dental restorations for identification. *J Comput Assist Tomogr* 30(3):510–513.

Jackowski C, Schweitzer W, Thali M, Yen K, Aghayev E, Sonnenschein M, Vock P, and Dirnhofer R. (2005). Virtopsy: Postmortem imaging of the human heart *in situ* using MSCT and MRI. *Forensic Sci Int* 149(1):11–23.

Jackowski C, Sonnenschein M, Thali MJ, Aghayev E, Allmen G, Yen K, Dirnhofer R, and Vock P. (2005). Virtopsy: Postmortem minimally invasive angiography using cross section techniques—Implementation and preliminary results. *J Forensic Sci* 50:1175–1186.

Jauhiainen T, Jarvinen VM, and Hekali PE. (2002). Evaluation of methods for MR imaging of human right ventricular heart volumes and mass. *Acta Radiol* 43(6):587–592.

Ljung P, Winskog C, Persson A, Lundstrom C, and Ynnerman A. (2006). Full-body virtual autopsies using a state-of-the-art volume rendering pipeline. *IEEE Trans Vis Comput Graph* 12(5):869–876.

Madea B, Henssge C, and Lockhoven HB. (1986). Priority of multiple gunshot injuries of the skull. *Z Rechtsmed* 97:213–218.

Magid D, Bryan BM, Drebin RA, Ney D, and Fishman EK. (1989). Three-dimensional imaging of an Egyptian mummy. Clin Imaging 13:239–240.

Notman DN, Tashjian J, Aufderheide AC, Cass OW, Shane OC 3rd, Berquist TH, Gray JE, and Gedgaudas E. (1986). Modern imaging and endoscopic biopsy techniques in Egyptian mummies. *AJR Am J Roentgenol* 146:93–96.

Oliver WR, Chancellor AS, Soitys J, Symon J, Cullip T, Rosenman J, Hellman R, Boxwala A, and Gormley W. (1995). Three-dimensional reconstruction of a bullet path: Validation by computed radiography. *J Forensic Sci* 40(2):321–324.

Patriquin L, Kassarjian A, O'Brien M, Andry C, and Eustace S. (2001). Postmortem whole-body magnetic resonance imaging as an adjunct to autopsy: Preliminary clinical experience. *J Magn Reson Imaging* 13:277–287.

Pomara C, Fineschi V, Scalzo G, Guglielmi G. (in press). Virtopsy versus digital autopsy: Virtuous autopsy. *Radiol Med* (E-pub: August 7, 2009).

Pomara C, Karch SB, Mallegni F et al. (2008). A medieval murder. *Am J Forensic Med Pathol* 29:72–74.

Pomara C, Fineschi V. (2007). *Manuale atlante di tecniche autoptiche*. Padova: Piccin.

Poulsen K and Simonsen J. (2007). Computed tomography as routine connection with medico-legal autopsies. *For Sci Int* 171:190–197.

Randall BB, Fierro MF, and Froede RC. (1998). Practice guideline for forensic pathology. Members of the Forensic Pathology Committee, College of American Pathologists. *Arch Pathol Lab Med* 122:1056–1064.

Ros PR, Li KC, Vo P, Baer H, and Staab EV. (1990). Preautopsy magnetic resonance imaging: Initial experience. *Magn Reson Imaging* 8:303–308.

Ross S, Spendlove D, Bolliger S, Christe A, Oesterhelweg L, Grabherr S, Thali MJ, and Gygax E. (2008). Postmortem whole-body CT angiography: Evaluation of two contrast media solutions. *AJR Am J Roentgenol* 190:1380–1389.

Sidler M, Jackowski C, Dirnhofer R, Vock P, and Thali M. (2007). Use of multislice computed tomography in disaster victim identification: Advantages and limitations. *Forensic Sci Int* 169:118–128.

Thali MJ and Vock P. (2003). Role of and techniques in forensic imaging. In *Forensic medicine: clinical and pathological aspects*, eds. James JP, Busuttil A, and Smock W, 731–745. San Francisco: GMM.

Thali MJ, Braun M, Markwalder TH, Brueschweiler W, Zollinger U, Malik NJ, Yen K, and Dirnhofer R. (2003). Bite mark documentation and analysis: The forensic 3D/CAD supported photogrammetry approach. *Forensic Sci Int* 135:115–121.

Thali MJ, Braun M, Wirth J, Vock P, and Dirnhofer R. (2003). 3D surface and body documentation in forensic medicine: 3-D/CAD photogrammetry merged with 3D radiological scanning. *J Forensic Sci* 48:1356–1365.

Thali MJ, Dirnhofer R, Becker R, Oliver W, and Potter K. (2004). Is "virtual histology" the next step after the "virtual autopsy"? Magnetic resonance microscopy in forensic medicine. *Magn Reson Imaging* 22:1131–1138.

Thali MJ, Jackowski C, Oesterhelweg L, Ross SG, and Dirnhofer R. (2007). Virtopsy: The Swiss virtual autopsy approach. Leg Med 9:100–104.

Thali MJ, Markwalder T, Jackowski C, Sonnenschein M, and Dirnhofer R. (2006). Dental CT imaging as a screening tool for dental profiling: Advantages and limitations. *J Forensic Sci* 51:113–119.

Thali MJ, Schweitzer W, Yen K et al. (2003). New horizons in forensic radiology: The 60-second digital autopsy-full-body examination of a gunshot victim by multislice computed tomography. *Am J Forensic Med Pathol* 24:22-27

Thali MJ, Schweitzer W, Yen K, Vock P, Ozdoba C, Spielvogel E, and Dirnhorfer R. (2003). New horizons in forensic radiology: The 60-second digital autopsy–full-body examination of a gunshot victim by multislice computed tomography. *Am J Forensic Med Pathol* 24:22–27.

Thali MJ, Yen K, Plattner T, Schweitzer W, Vock P, Ozdoba C, and Dirnhofer R. (2002). Charred body: Virtual autopsy with multi-slice computed tomography and magnetic resonance imaging. *J Forensic Sci* 47:1326–1331.

Thali MJ, Yen K, Schweitzer W, Vock P, Boesch C, Ozdoba C, Schroth G, Ith M, Sonnenschein M, Doernhoefer T, Scheurer E, Plattner T, and Dirnhofer R. (2003). Virtopsy, a new imaging horizon in forensic pathology: Virtual autopsy by postmortem multislice computed tomography (MSCT) and magnetic resonance imaging (MRI)—A feasibility study. *J Forensic Sci* 48:386–403.

Thali MJ, Yen K, Schweitzer W, Vock P, Ozdoba C, and Dirnhofer R. (2003). Into the decomposed body-forensic digital autopsy using multislice-computed tomography. *Forensic Sci Int* 134:109–114.

Thali MJ, Yen K, Vock P, Ozdoba C, Kneubue WBP, Sonneschein M, and Dirnhorfer R. (2003). Image-guided virtual autopsy findings of gunshot victims performed with multislice computed tomography (MSCT) and magnetic resonance imaging (MRI) and subsequent correlation between radiology and autopsy findings. *For Sci Int* 138:8–16.

Wallace SK, Cohen WA, Stern EJ, and Reay DT. (1994). Judicial hanging: Postmortem radiographic CT, and MR imaging features with autopsy confirmation. *Radiology* 193(1):263–267.

Yen K, Lövblad KO, Scheurer E, Ozdoba C, Thali M, Aghayev E, Jackowski C, Anon J, Frickey N, and Zwygart K. (2007). Post-mortem forensic neuroimaging: Correlation of MSCT and MRI findings with autopsy results. *For Sci Int* 173:21–35.

Yen K, Thali M, Aghayev E, Jackowski C, Schweitzer W, Boesch C, Vock P, Dirnhofer R, and Sonnenschein M. (2005). Strangulation signs: Initial correlation of MRI, MSCT and forensic neck findings. *J Magn Reson Imaging* 22:501–510.

Yen K, Thali MJ, Aghayev E, Jackowski C, Schweitzer W, Boesch C, Vock P, Dirnhofer R, and Sonnenschein M. (2005). Strangulation signs: Initial correlation of MRI, MSCT, and forensic neck findings. *J Magn Reson Imaging* 22(4):501–510.

Yen K, Vock P, Tiefenthaler B, Ranner G, Scheurer E, Thali MJ, Zwygart K, Sonnenschein, M, Wiltgen M, and Dirnhofer R. (2004). Virtopsy: Forensic traumatology of the subcutaneous fatty tissue. Multislice computed tomography (MSCT) and magnetic resonance imaging (MRI) as diagnostic tools. *J Forensic Sci* 49(4):799–806.

zur Nedden D, Knapp R, Wicke K, Judmaier W, Murphy WA, Seidler H, and Platzer W. (1994). Skull of a 5,300-year-old mummy: Reproduction and investigation with CT-guided stereolithography. *Radiology* 193:269–272.

Genetic Disease and DNA Diagnosis

7

C. POMARA
S.B. KARCH
V. FINESCHI

Contents

7.1 Introduction

Most cases of sudden death are a consequence of atherosclerotic heart disease and only occasionally the consequence of some recognizable malformation or infection. Even so, the etiology of sudden death goes undetermined 5% to 10% of the time. Many common diseases result from either genetic modification leading to increased disease susceptibility (such as the channelopathies) or unsuspected viral infection (such as myocarditis). This chapter contains an overview of the genetic disorders that forensic pathologists are likely to encounter in their daily practice and an equally brief review of what actual resources are available that would allow the diagnosis of these disorders.

Many, if not most, of the cases that medical examiners rule "undetermined" are actually a consequence of genetic polymorphisms that most medical examiners are ill equipped to diagnose, either because of a lack of training or lack of funds or both. However, all centers are able to prepare paraffin slides, and it has become feasible to isolate both DNA and RNA from embedded tissue. To be sure, formalin and DNA do not mix well together, but much of the damage caused by DNA fixation can be overcome (Jackson, 1990 #6287).

Several DNA extraction techniques capable of providing enough DNA and RNA for the polymerase chain reaction (PCR) are possible. One of the earliest to be introduced is still effective. For paraffin wax-embedded tissues, 5 days of incubation with proteinase K are required to produce enough DNA. None of the other known techniques (incubation with sodium dodecyl sulfate or boiling) produce truly acceptable results. However, DNA extracted by these methods is suitable for the PCR amplification of a single copy gene. Proteinase K digestion also yields large amounts of RNA, which is also suitable for PCR analysis. It matters very little if there has been some delay before extraction—DNA can still be recovered, but fixation in Carnoy's reagent results in a much better preservation of DNA than formalin fixation, and should greatly improve analytical results (Jackson, 1990 #6287).

7.2 Sudden Cardiac Death and Genetic Disease

Many "nearly normal hearts" are, in fact, genetically abnormal, but it is difficult to estimate just how many. The most widely recognized genetic abnormality associated with sudden death is hypertrophic cardiomyopathy (HCM), which, in some series, is estimated to have an incidence of 1:500. It is an autosomal-dominant inherited disease of the heart muscle manifested usually, but not always, as unexplained hypertrophy of the left and/or the right ventricle. However, there are other forms carrying a much more benign prognosis that do not jeopardize a patient's health or life. The clinical symptoms of HCM are partly dependent on mutations in affected sarcomeric genes. Different mutations in the same gene can present with a high risk of sudden cardiac death, while other mutations can be benign. In today's working environment, forensic pathologists confronted with the sudden and unexpected death of a young person have two problems: first, they must explain the cause of sudden death, and second, they must screen close family members to see if they are also at risk. Given the technology available today this can be a daunting problem (Fokstuen, 2008 #6288).

More than 450 pathogenic mutations in at least 16 HCM genes have been identified. Traditional techniques simply are inadequate for screening large allelic and heterogeneous HCM genes. High-throughput, rapid, and affordable mutation detection technologies are needed. Currently, reagent makers are experimenting with lower cost methods to screen DNA. The most promising of these is the high-throughput HCM resequencing array. It seems to be the most rapid and cost-effective tool for molecular testing of HCM. Just how soon an affordable version will come to market is not clear, but the solution is feasible, should be affordable, and should be available in the not too distant future.

Besides HCM there exist a wide variety of heritable heart diseases, all capable of causing sudden cardiac death: dilated cardiomyopathy (DCM), arrhythmogenic right ventricular dysplasia (ARVD), and channelopathies (long QT syndrome [LQTS] and others). In fact, the number of heritable channelopathies has increased from 2 to 3 just 5 years ago to more than a dozen today, and that number does not include the rapidly proliferating number of channelopathies involving muscle (Meola, 2009 #6289), epithelial transport and tumor growth (Zhang, 2009 #6290), and possibly even sudden death during epilepsy (SUDEP) (Aurlien, 2009 #6291).

Channelopathies are perhaps the best known of the noninfectious genetic diseases, and they are not that uncommon a cause of sudden cardiac death in young people. Those afflicted with this disorder have delayed repolarization following depolarization (excitation) of the heart, and this delay is associated with syncope as a consequence of ventricular arrhythmias. Fatal arrhythmias in individuals with LQTS are often associated with exercise or excitement. Individuals with LQTS have a prolonged QT interval on the ECG. The QT interval is measured from the Q point to the end of the T wave. Whereas many individuals with LQTS have persistent prolongation of the QT interval, some individuals do not always show the QT prolongation. In these individuals, the QT interval may be prolonged with the administration of certain medications; the phenomenon is known as unmasking. Young adults who may well have had normal previous physical examinations, may succumb to an arrhythmia simply because they develop a fever from a respiratory infection or use a stimulant drug (administration of stimulant drugs can be used to provoke LQTS in the laboratory).

LQT syndrome was first described by Jervell and Lange-Nielsen in 1957, followed by another described by Romano in 1963 and another by Ward in 1964. Each researcher described the consequences of a different polymorphism. Today more than 10 LQTS syndromes have been described. Each is due to a polymorphism in a different gene. No doubt, by the time of this book's publication, half a dozen more will be added to the list. The first syndrome described involved actual structural

defects in the pores that control the passage of sodium and potassium currents into and out of cardiomyocytes. Today it is understood that similar mutations can affect the flow of calcium into and out of the endoplasmic reticulum, and even the proteins that bind receptors to the surface of cells. A list of clinically significant LQTS symptoms that have been identified is in Table 7.1.

7.3 Diagnostic Techniques

The PCR is fundamental to the diagnosis of genetic polymorphism. It is used to amplify millions of times a single or, at most, a few copies of a portion of DNA. Thermal cycling (repeated cycles of heating and cooling) and enzymatic replication of the DNA are combined to produce these new copies. A short DNA fragment, called a primer, is composed of nucleic acid sequences complementary to the region being investigated are combined with the enzyme DNA polymerase. As PCR progresses, the newly generated DNA is also used as a template for further replication and the rate of production increases in an exponential fashion.

Almost all PCR systems use a heat-stable DNA polymerase, most often the one named Taq polymerase, which was originally isolated from bacteria. It assembles new DNA strands by using DNA nucleotide building blocks. Single-stranded DNA is used as a template and DNA primer. These thermal cycling steps are needed to physically separate the strands of DNA that are to be used as the template for DNA synthesis. Different primers are used that are complementary to the targeted region of DNA that is to be amplified.

PCR is especially useful for detecting infectious agents, because it produces so much DNA that immunohistochemical testing and *in situ* hybridization become much simpler. Until very recently, the PCR process required fresh or frozen tissue be used as the source of RNA or DNA. Recently, DNA extraction methods of formalin-fixed, paraffin-embedded (FFPE) tissues and PCR analysis have become available.

RNA is much more difficult to work with than DNA extracted from paraffin because the fixation and paraffin-embedding procedures destroy the RNA. Still, it is possible, but the process requires days and utilizes complex extraction methods. The extraction process reduces the RNA to severely degraded fragments, each averaging 100 to 300 nucleotides long. The formalin fixation process further modifies RNA by adding methylol groups ($-CH2OH$) to nucleotides—this addition can interfere with reverse transcription of RNA, reducing PCR efficiency.

Table 7.1   Genes Associated with LQTS

Type	Online Mendelian Inheritance in Man (OMIM)	Mutation	Notes
LQT1	192500	Alpha subunit of the slow-delayed rectifier potassium channel (KvLQT1 or KCNQ1)	The current through the heteromeric channel (KvLQT1 + minK) is known as I_{Ks}. These mutations often cause LQT by reducing the amount of repolarizing current. This repolarizing current is required to terminate the action potential, leading to an increase in the action potential duration (APD). These mutations tend to be the most common yet least severe.
LQT2	152427	Alpha subunit of the rapid-delayed rectifier potassium channel (HERG + MiRP1)	Current through this channel is known as I_{Kr}. This phenotype is also probably caused by a reduction in repolarizing current.
LQT3	603B30	Alpha subunit of the sodium channel (SCN5A)	Current through this channel is commonly referred to as I_{Na}. Depolarizing current through the channel late in the action potential is thought to prolong APD. The late current is due to failure of the channel to remain inactivated and hence enter a bursting mode in which significant current can enter when it should not. These mutations are more lethal but less common.
LQT4	600919	Anchor protein Ankyhn B	LQT4 is very rare. Ankyrin B anchors the ion channels in the cell.
LQT5	176261	Beta subunit MinK (or KCNE1), which coassembles with KvLQT1	
LQT6	603796	Beta subunit MiRP1 (or KCNE2), which coassembles with HERG	
LQT7	170390	Potassium channel KCNJ2 (or $K_{ir}2.1$)	The current through this channel and KCNJ22 ($K_{ir}2.2$) is called I_{K1}. LQT7 leads to Andersen–Tawil syndrome.
LQT8	601005	Alpha subunit of the calcium channel Cav1.2 encoded by the gene CACNA1c	Leads to Timothy's syndrome.
LQT9	611818	Caveolin 3	
LQT10	611819	SCN4B	
LQT11	611820	AKAP9	
LOX12	601017	SNTA1	

Source: Reproduced with permission from Wikipedia.

Note: Genetic LQTS can arise from mutation to one of several genes. These mutations tend to prolong the duration of the ventricular action potential (APD), thus lengthening the QT interval. LQTS can be inherited in an autosomal-dominant or an autosomal-recessive fashion. The autosomal-recessive forms of LQTS tend to have a more severe phenotype, with some variants having associated syndactyly (LQT8) or congenital neural deafness (LQT1). A number of specific genes loci have been identified that are associated with LQTS. Genetic testing for LQTS is clinically available and may help to direct appropriate therapies. The most common causes of LQTS are mutations in the genes KCNQ1 (LQT1), KCNH2 (LQT2), and SCN5A (LQT3).

A commercial assay called TaqMan® (based on the Taq enzyme discussed earlier) allows real-time quantitative reverse transcriptase–polymerase chain reaction (RT-PCR) testing by detecting increases in fluorescent emission. The technique is ideal for analyzing RNA from formalin-fixed tissue. The United States Army Medical Research Institute of Infectious Diseases (USAMRIID) has developed a standard operating method for safely dealing with infected tissues. It accomplished this by slightly modifying a readily available commercial testing kit. The possibility of extracting amplifiable RNA and detecting West Nile virus (WNV)-, Marburg virus (MARV)-, and Ebola virus (EBOV)-infected tissues using TaqMan assays has already been demonstrated (McKinney, 2009 #6286).

Although not many medical examiners will be called on to work with such dangerous pathogens, just about everyone in practice will be called upon to make the diagnosis of myocarditis. The worldwide incidence of this disorder is thought to be well over 5%, and over the last few years it has become increasingly obvious that pure histological criteria for myocarditis are not very accurate (Baughman, 2006 #1135). Some decedents with normal appearing hearts may still have died as a consequence of an occult viral infection.

A very important study was published in 2003 when researchers studied 24 consecutive patients who had been admitted to the hospital within 24 hours after the onset of chest pain. Each patient manifested all the classical symptoms of acute coronary syndrome and, accordingly, underwent angiography. When the angiography was negative, biopsies were obtained, divided in half, and then analyzed both histologically and with DNA testing. DNA from each biopsy sample was analyzed (nested polymerase chain reaction/reverse transcriptase–polymerase chain reaction) for all of the viruses most commonly associated with myocarditis (EV, ADV, PVB19, human cytomegalovirus, Epstein–Barr virus, Chlamydia pneumoniae, influenza virus A and B, and Borrelia burgdorferi genomes). In addition, both acute and convalescent serum samples were collected for later measurement of viral titers.

Only one patient met the standard histological criteria (Dallas) for myocarditis. In sum, viral genomes were found in 71% of patients with symptoms of acute myocardial infarction (AMI); but with normal coronary anatomy, presumably a result of coronary artery spasm, Parvo B-19 is the agent most frequently responsible (Kyto, 2007 #5773; Kyto, 2005 #5772). In another study three experienced cardiac pathologists reexamined the heart in 142 cases where death had previously been attributed to myocarditis and compared the results to those obtained by DNA analysis (Kyto, 2005 #5772). Traditional light microscopy was only able to identify one-third of those who were actually infected.

The diagnosis of myocarditis has always been a conundrum. As medical examiners well know, obvious cases of asymptomatic myocarditis may be detected in trauma victims, and patients with symptoms and laboratory testing suggesting the presence of myocarditis may often display no abnormalities. The necessity for DNA testing in such cases is obvious and, fortunately, as the technology becomes less expensive, it should become possible for medical examiners to implement this technology.

7.4 The Future of Large-Scale Screening Techniques

Much of what we know today is an outgrowth of the Sager technique. The key principle of this method involves the use of dideoxynucleotide triphosphates (ddNTPs) as DNA chain terminators. As the techniques were first developed, a single-stranded DNA template (also known as DNA primer), a DNA polymerase, and labeled nucleotides were mixed together along with modified nucleotides that terminate DNA strand elongation.

The DNA sample is divided into four separate sequencing reactions, containing all four of the standard deoxynucleotides (dATP, dGTP, dCTP, and dTTP) along with DNA polymerase. To each reaction is added only one of the four dideoxynucleotides (ddATP, ddGTP, ddCTP, or ddTTP), which are the chain-terminating nucleotides, but they lack the 3′-OH group that is need to form the phosphodiester bond between two nucleotides, thus terminating DNA strand extension. The resulting brew consists of DNA fragments all of variable length.

The labeled DNA fragments are then heated to denature them, following which they are separated by size using gel electrophoresis. DNA bands are then visualized by UV light, and the DNA sequence can be directly read off the x-ray film or gel image. On the right side of the image the dark bands will correspond to DNA fragments of different lengths. A dark band in a lane indicates a DNA fragment that is the result of chain termination after incorporation of a dideoxynucleotide (ddATP, ddGTP, ddCTP, or ddTTP). The relative positions of the different bands among the four lanes are then used to read (from bottom to top) the DNA sequence. A number of sophisticated variations, most of which are proprietary, exist.

Chain termination is a new method that has greatly simplified DNA sequencing, and the devices required are not prohibitively expensive. Dye-terminator sequencing, which is also becoming more popular, requires the preparation of the four dideoxynucleotide chain terminators labeled with fluorescent dyes; each has a different wavelength. Owing to its greater expediency and speed, dye-terminator sequencing is now the mainstay in automated sequencing. Its limitations include dye effects due to differences in the incorporation of the dye-labeled chain terminators into the DNA fragment. This sometimes causes unequal peak heights and shapes in the electronic DNA sequence trace chromatogram after capillary electrophoresis. This problem has been addressed with the use of modified DNA polymerase enzyme systems and dyes that minimize incorporation variability, as well as methods for eliminating "dye blobs." The dye-terminator sequencing method, along with automated high-throughput DNA sequence analyzers, is now being used for the vast majority of sequencing projects.

Autopsy Protocol for the Examination of the V3–V4 Segments of the Vertebral Artery: The Introna-Corrado Method

8

F. INTRONA
S. CORRADO

Contents

8.1 Introduction

Whenever certain circumstances suggest the presence of a basal subarachnoid hemorrhage, the possibility of a vertebral artery lesion must be considered. It should be then either confirmed or ruled out. According to Whitwell and Milory (2005), "The demonstration of the site of rupture in a traumatic subarachnoid hemorrhage *could be one* of the most difficult *entities in a postmortem* examination. The frequency of demonstration of the rupture will depend on the diligence with which the research is carried out" (pp. 71–81).

There are a number of ways to identify the site of rupture, but none have ever been completely described in the literature. The traditional anterior approach does not allow for complete dissection of the vertebral arteries.

The authors have developed a technique using a posterior approach, which allows for the *in situ* examination of the intracranial tract of the vertebral arteries (V4), as well as the continuous removal of the V3 and V4 segments.

8.2 Autopsy Protocol

The cadaver is placed in the prone position using a thoracic support. This permits only the frontal region of the head to come into contact with the autopsy table. A classic bimastoid incision of the scalp is performed beginning at the crown of the head. The incision is then carried out posteriorly by way of a longitudinal incision following along the posterior midline, extending to the sixth cervical vertebra (Figure 8.1).

As a result, three flaps are created: one anterior, which is reflected forward to the point at which the eyebrow arches are exposed; and two posterior flaps, which are reflected laterally in order to completely expose the cervical posterior arches down to the parietal bones, both those of the squama and of the entire occipital bone (Figure 8.2).

The spinal processes and the posterior portions of the vertebral arches are then exposed by progressive

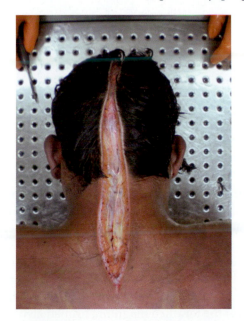

Figure 8.1 The longitudinal incision following along the posterior midline, extending from the crown of the head to sixth cervical vertebra.

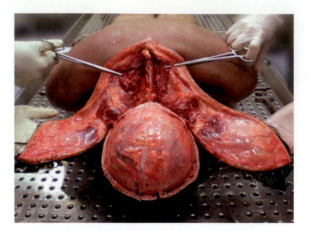

Figure 8.2 Two posterior flaps reflected laterally.

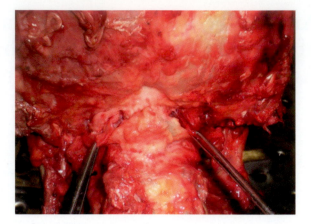

Figure 8.4 The V3 segment of the vertebral artery from the transverse process of the isolated atlas.

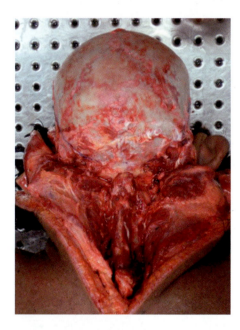

Figure 8.3 The spinal processes and the posterior portions of the exposed vertebral arches.

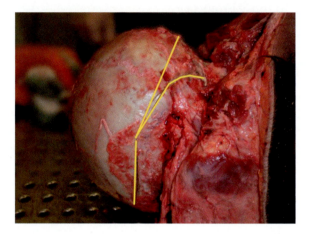

Figure 8.5 Lateral-view showing two oblique and symmetrical incisions from the lateral margins of the foramen magnum, immediately posterior to the occipital condyle, to the central part of the squama of the temporal bone, converging with the circular dissection of the skullcap.

dissection of the paravertebral muscles (Figure 8.3). Special care must be taken to isolate the V3 segment of the vertebral artery from the transverse process of the atlas allowing it to be dissected as distally as possible, and then the V3 segment can be reflected (Figure 8.4).

At this point, a classic circular dissection of the skullcap is performed with *a horizontal* incision extending through from the external occipital protuberance to the frontal bone above the superciliary arches. Following that, the cranial floor of the posterior cranial fossa is dissected bilaterally, thereby creating two oblique and symmetrical incisions. The incisions arise from the lateral margins of the foramen magnum, immediately posterior to the occipital condyle, and are extended up to the central part of the squama of the temporal bone, converging with the circular dissection of the skullcap that has just been performed (Figure 8.5). In this way, the dissector

has created two segments: one from the skullcap, and the other from the occipital bone, with its trapezoidal shape.

Subsequently, the laminae of the vertebral arches are dissected up to C5, followed by a transverse incision of the C5 spinous process in order to allow the caudocranial removal of all the posterior vertebral arches from C5 to C1, just as in other routine approaches for posteriorly accessing the spinal medulla. The previously isolated occipital segment is then removed (Figure 8.6), leaving the remaining anterior skullcap *in situ* to contain the encephalic mass.

At this point the dura mater, which continuously covers the cerebellum and the spinal medulla, appears. The dura mater is then dissected caudocranially up to the posterior confluence of the transverse sinuses (torcular Herophili). Then, proceeding laterally, a "T" incision is

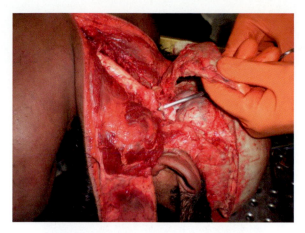

Figure 8.6 Removing the occipital segment.

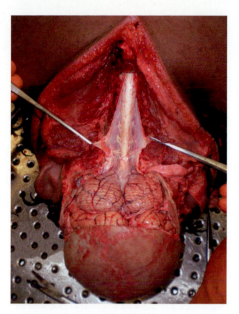

Figure 8.8 Exposure of the cerebellum, spinal medulla, and the spinal nerves.

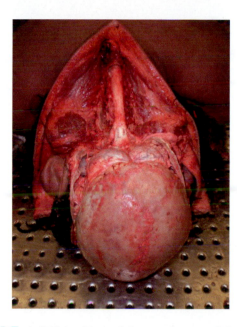

Figure 8.7 A "T" incision of the caudocranial dura mater up to the posterior confluence of the transverse sinuses and the posterior insertion of the tentorium cerebellum.

made to dissect the posterior insertion of the tentorium cerebellum (Figure 8.7). The dura mater is then laterally reflected to expose the cerebellum, spinal medulla, and the spinal nerves (Figure 8.8). The endocranial entrance of the vertebral arteries (V4) is now exposed laterally (Figure 8.9).

The longitudinal cut of the dura mater is then laterally extended up to the vertebral ostium of the atlanto-occipital membrane (Figure 8.10). In this way, the conditions for the successive extraction of the continuous V3–V4 segments are put into place (Figure 8.11). The skullcap is then removed; and the dura mater is dissected by circular incision, the tentorium and the base of the falx cerebelli are cut following the inferior sagittal sinus. And finally, the dissection of the spinal medulla is begun and reflected at the C4 level.

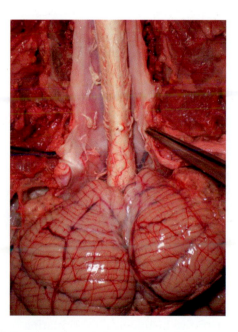

Figure 8.9 Exposure of the endocranial entrance of the vertebral arteries.

The spinal nerves, cranial nerves, carotid artery, and the optic chiasm are dissected. At this point, while paying close attention to segments V3 and V4 of the recently isolated vertebral arteries, it is possible to extract the continuous cervical spinal medulla, using caudocranial traction, along with the medulla oblongata, the pons, the cerebellum, and the entire encephalic mass, which may now be slipped off like a glove (Figure 8.12).

Done in this manner, the entire circle of Willis, the basilar artery, and the two vertebral arteries, including the V3 and V4 segments, respectively, will be visible (Figure 8.13).

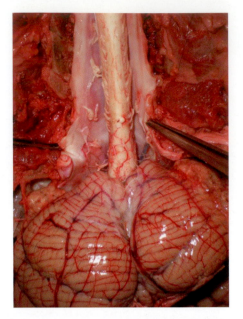

Figure 8.10 The cut up to vertebral ostium of the atlanto-occipital membrane.

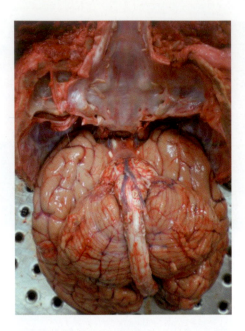

Figure 8.12 The continuous cervical spinal medulla, the medulla oblongata, the pons, the cerebellum, and the entire encephalic mass may now be slipped off like a glove.

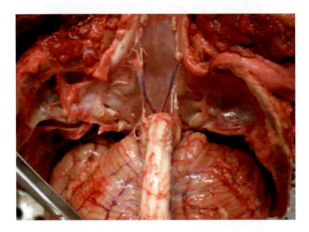

Figure 8.11 The continuous V3–V4 segments.

The brain is then fixed in a 20% formalin solution for subsequent macro- and microscopic examination. Comparative histological examination of both the intracranial vertebral vessels is carried out using special staining to identify the rupture site, which allows for the differentiation between a traumatic rupture and a spontaneous dissection. It also makes it possible to establish the time of the rupture, as well as to identify any possible preexisting pathology of the arterial walls.

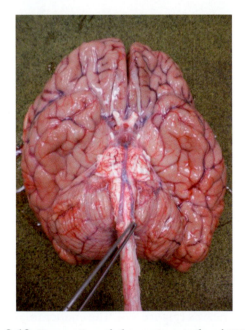

Figure 8.13 Extraction of the entire circle of Willis, the basilar artery, and the two vertebral arteries, including the V3 and V4 segments.

References

Bromilow A and Burns J. (1985). Technique for removal of the vertebral arteries, *J Clinical Pathol*, 38, 1400–1402.

Gross A. (1990). Traumatic basal subarachnoid haemorrhages: Post-mortem examination material analysis, *Forensic Sci Int*, 45, 53–61.

Hooper AD. (1979). A new approach to upper cervical injuries, *J Forensic Sci*, 24, 39–45.

Leadbeatter S. (1994). Extracranial vertebral artery injury— Evolution of a pathological illusion, *Forensic Sci Int*, 67, 35–40.

McCarthy JH, Sunter JP, and Cooper PN. (1999). A method for demonstrating the source of bleeding in cases of traumatic subarachnoid haemorrhage, *J Pathol*, 187, 30A.

Saukko P and Knight B. (2004). *Forensic pathology*, 3rd edition. Chapter 5, 202–204. Edward Arnold.

Vanezis P. (1979). Techniques used in the evaluation of vertebral artery trauma at postmortem, *Forensic Sci Int*, 13, 159–165.

Whitwell HL and Milory CM. (2005). *Subarachnoid haemorrhage and cerebro-vascular pathology, in forensic neuropathology*, (ed.) Whitwell, HL, 71–81. Edward Arnold.

Index

"f" indicates material in figures. "t" indicates material in tables. "n" indicates material in footnotes.